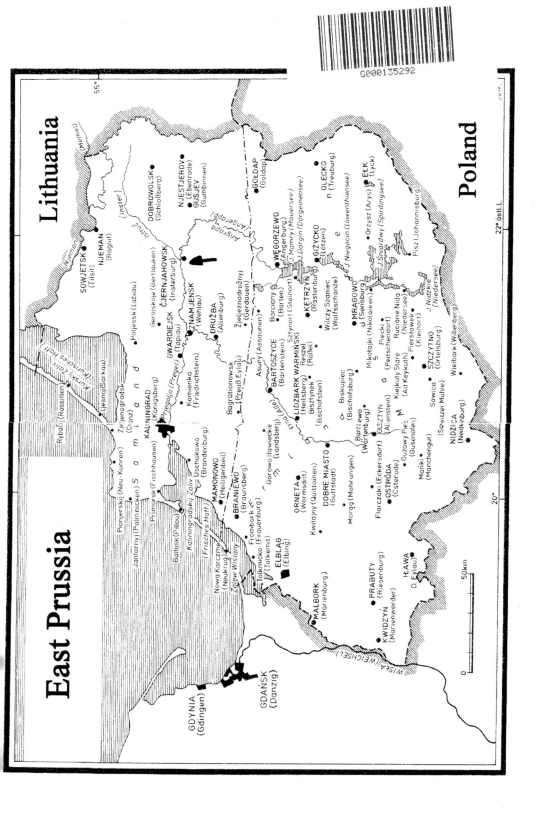

Refuge

from a **BROKEN Land**

(A Childhood in Central Europe after World War II)

Brigitte Ziegler

Published by Brigitte Ziegler

Printed in Great Britain by
Orbital Print Ltd.
Sittingbourne
Kent

Cover design: Kristin Zeller

ISBN 978-0-9932324-0-4

*This is for my daughter Annette and my grandchildren
Thea, Toby and Kitty
and to the memory of my younger daughter Kitty.*

Introduction

Ask most people what they know about Prussia and the majority will respond with a blank, puzzled expression.

"Prussia? I've heard of it but I couldn't tell you where it is exactly."Some older people and especially those with a background of higher education, will surprise you and say: "Oh yes, Koenigsberg or Kaliningrad, up by the Baltic; close to Poland." When this happens, I nod my head enthusiastically and reply:

"And next to Lithuania. How wonderful, that you actually know of it!"The more academic among them will also add: "Kant, Emanuel Kant!" Then I nod even more enthusiastically, brimming all over my face with pleasure and relief.

I am pleased that the land of my birth is not totally forgotten then. Not totally sunk in the annals of distant history like, say Atlantis. But very, very nearly forgotten, I fear. Yet it has had a most interesting history. Like its shifting dunes along the Baltic Sea, its borders, its people, even its language have undergone dramatic changes in the last 800 years. The last huge shift took place in 1945, with destructive consequences for millions of people. Without doubt, this was Prussia's swansong and its darkest hour.

In May of 1945 World War II ended with Germany's unconditional surrender to the Allied Forces. It was a catastrophic ending to a disastrous war for the whole of Germany, yet immensely more so for the eastern provinces of the Reich. East and West Prussia, German Pomerania and Silesia were annexed to Poland while the historic northern part of East Prussia was handed over to the Soviet Union. It spelt the end of Prussia as it had been known for approximately 700 years.

Nomadic pagans were the first human inhabitants in that Baltic part of Europe. They appeared between 10,000 and 8,000 years before our time. Jerzy Szynkowski writes in his book "Masuren:

"Polish and German historians agree that the "Pruzzen" already lived between the lower and middle river Vistula in the west and the town of Memel (now called Klaipeda in Lithuania) in the east 1000 years BC. They were a mixture of Lithuanians, Latvians and Courian tribes, neither related to the Germans nor the Slavs. They were a healthy and strong-built people, often reaching the age of one hundred or more. They remained a pagan people until the start of the 13th century when Polish bishops made two failed attempts to christianize and to incorporate them into Poland. Two more attempts were initiated by Pope Innocence III and the Duke of Masovia but the Pruzzen resisted and in turn invaded Masovia, laying waste to it.

In despair, Conrad of Masovia invited the Teutonic Knights (a military religious order from Germany) to conquer the warrior Pruzzen and to try once and for all to convert them to Christianity, denouncing all Polish rights to the region.

Thus the northern knights began their task in 1231, conquering Pomerania, formerly a Polish area, which included the city of Danzig (now Gdansk) as well as the more eastern regions. The German author/journalist Sebastian Haffner writes in his book PREUSSEN OHNE LEGENDE that :

The Teutonic Knights brought Christendom to the Pruzzen using the sword. To christen the Pruzzen was their first and foremost request. Those who did not agree to be christened met with their death.

This was the fate of many Pruzzen. The knights built castles as their strongholds and colonised the land with immigrants from the centre and the west of Germany.

Until the early sixteenth century the region was part of the monastic state of the Teutonic Knights although, for a period, the region shifted from German authority to Polish/Lithuanian rule, it being so close to the Polish/Lithuanian Empire. Swedish invaders also tried to lay claim to it. Even tartars tried to overrun it, but were beaten back.

Following the collapse of the Teutonic Order, Prussia fell to the German House of the Hohenzollern/Brandenburg ruling dynasty. In 1701 the Prince Elector of Brandenburg crowned himself *"King in Prussia"* and the Ducal

East Prussia became the Kingdom of Prussia. The Prussian kings introduced more settlers from France and Austria, who had been persecuted in their native lands by the Catholic Church for having converted to Protestantism. They also invited Calvinists, persecuted Scots and Jews. Those Poles, who became Prussians, were allowed to practice their religion, customs and language as were the immigrants from other nations. Prussia, at that time in its history, was one of the most tolerant of European kingdoms.

Under King Frederick II – Frederick the Great, as he was lovingly called by his subjects - Prussia grew steadily into a great power, adding more European territories to its realm of which East Prussia was a province with Koenigsberg as its capital. Prussia continued to flourish until the outbreak of World War I.

As part of the Treaty of Versailles during the aftermath of World War I, the western part of East Prussia as well as part of Pomerania were separated from its larger eastern province of East Prussia to form the so-called "*Polish Corridor*". This strip of land had once been under Polish rule. The majority of the population in 1919 was still of Polish stock. The Versailles Treaty returned this small area to Poland, giving that country its only access to the Baltic at the mouth of the river Vistula. However, Danzig was excluded from this territory and became a Free City. The creation of this corridor isolated the rest of German East Prussia from the main Reich although free access via the corridor had been guaranteed by the treaty. Yet, during the Nazi era, Adolf Hitler demanded extraterritorial rights across this Polish land, a demand which Poland refused. It is arguable that this refusal triggered the start of World War II.

Towards the end of this catastrophic war, the borders of East Prussia and Lithuania were the first to be overrun by the advancing Russian Army. A large part of the Prussian population of approximately two and a half million people managed to escape. More were forcibly evacuated to the centre of Germany after the war had ended in an attempt to cleanse Prussia and the other annexed areas of their German history and culture. Properties of Prussians were burnt to the ground and speaking the German language was forbidden.

In February of 1945, when the defeat of the German army was imminent, the allied leaders of the USA, Britain and the Soviet Union met at a Conference in Yalta to confer on the progress of the war and the shape of the world order thereafter. They agreed to meet again after the unconditional surrender of Germany to decide on the punitive measures to be taken in respect of Germany and its people. Thus in July 1945, at Cecilienhof, the home of Crown Prince Wilhelm Hohenzollern in Potsdam, it was agreed to sever all German land behind the Oder/Neisse rivers, assigning it to Poland. This was to be in exchange for lands on the Polish eastern frontiers which Stalin insisted on incorporating into Russia. In addition, a small northern section of East Prussia was to go to the Soviet Union in order that Koenigsberg could become a Soviet military bastion: important because of its harbour by the Baltic which did not often freeze over, unlike that of St. Petersburg. The town of my birth, Insterburg (now called Chernyakhovsk) was situated within this northern area.

Towards the end of the war in January 1945, the borders of East Prussia with Lithuania were the first to be overrun by the revengeful Russian Army.
A huge number of refugees fleeing from East Prussia and from the German part of Pomerania, Silesia and Bohemia were killed during the Soviet offensive. Many more died on their trek of approx. eight weeks, travelling on foot, on sleighs or by horse and cart, during which time the temperature often reached as low as minus 20 degrees Celsius. To add to the refugees' misery the Siberian winds blew unremittingly and there was seldom any food. Almost 8.5 million Germans from these Eastern provinces of the Reich fled west, most were old men, women and children as all the able bodied men had been forced to join the Wehrmacht.
Many thousands of civilians from East Prussia who tried to cross over the frozen, bomb-riddled Baltic Sea on foot, or by horse and carts to Sweden or Denmark, drowned as a result of Soviet bombs and low flying air attacks. The weight of so many refugees, together with their livestock often proved too much for the sea ice to withstand, giving way with great loss of life.
The authorities of the Third Reich had delayed a timely evacuation on the pain of death until January 20th 1945 when it was too late. Therefore many of the civilians, who had obeyed this inhuman government order found themselves in the middle of perilous combat, were shot at sight and many of the women raped, often several times over, then sometimes mutilated afterwards, while their children looked on. Some civilians, like my immediate family, disobeyed the Nazi orders and started fleeing westwards as early as

autumn 1944 despite the threat of losing their lives. The bombing of Koenigsberg by the British and several other East Prussian towns, including my home town, during the summer of 1944 convinced the early refugees of an impending collapse.

Fortunately, as a result of my mother's decision to leave, my mother, my brother and I were spared these atrocities. We were lucky to have left our homeland by the last train leaving the town of Marienburg in West Prussia, to which we had fled a few weeks earlier, just in front of the advancing and much dreaded Red Army whose vengeful terror swept over the country like a raging sea. Despite hunger, terror and extreme cold, we all survived, having eventually been deposited in a small village near the river Elbe in southern Mecklenburg.

The following story describes my early life and that of my mother, father and brother from December 1944 onwards as best as I remember it now, almost seventy years later. It starts with our flight and eventual refuge in Mecklenburg where we settled (though not by our own free choice) for more than eight years.

After Germany's capitulation in May 1945, Mecklenburg became part of the Soviet occupied zone and later the DDR (German Democratic Republic). Life there, under the yoke of communist controlled rule, was anything but democratic, resulting in a steadily increasing flow of its population taking enormous risks by fleeing their country, one way or another. In 1953 our family, too, succeeded in escaping once more, thus becoming refugees for the second time around in our own country!

This book is not intended as a lesson in history but rather to illustrate how the decisions of the victors of WWII affected my young life and that of my family among those of millions of others. My childhood experiences have proved to me that the human spirit can conquer great trials and hardships for the sake of personal development and freedom of speech, of love and simple happiness but above all for the sake of freedom and a peaceful, secure life in a truly democratic environment.

Chapter One

On that mid-June day the sun shone on the southern fringes of England, as only it can in a good year. Day by day, more and more colour had exploded from the profusion of roses in the garden. The village green, beyond the brick wall, gleamed like a luscious carpet, still interspersed as it was, with a few remaining dew drops, glistening like tiny sparklers wherever the early morning sun caressed the blades of grass.

This was the magic of an English summer's day that I had read about but never experienced before. Warm, balmy, mildly scented air drifted towards me as I opened the little window of my bedroom with its leaded diamond panes twinkling in the sunlight to draw in the wonder of this glorious summer morning. A mass of shrub roses, philadelphus, blue and white Canterbury bells, foxgloves and clusters of carnations were gently swaying against shades of silver which merged into yellow and white in the morning sunshine. A tall bay-leaf tree, which had been clipped with great skill into the shape of a balloon, stood majestically among this sea of sparkling colour. This panoply of colour all lay below me as I anticipated, with a mixture of joy, excitement and some trepidation, this day of all days: of homecoming, trust and magical fulfilment – the day of my wedding!

To tell you that I remember every detail of this day would be an exaggeration. Too much time has passed since that time, back in the early years of the nineteen sixties. However, there are certain images and emotions which are as fresh for me today as they were on the day itself. Remembering them now fills me with warm and happy feelings. Yet I admit at times these reflections make me wonder whether the whole thing had ever really happened. The passing of time can fool you, even if only momentarily, especially if, at the same time, you want to block out bad memories, disappointments or even tragedies. For a split second you may succeed in doubting your memories as you try to regain your equanimity and numb the pain and anguish. It is not so with your happy times. Never mind how long ago they may have been, their memory grows and strengthens with the passing of the years. Like a burst of sunshine, happy memories have a life force of their own, consistent and fundamental; more so than the material things you may sometimes wish for. Only love can measure up to them; love and, possibly, marriage?

My eyes flickered across the sumptuous green towards the spire of the beautiful village church where I would be walking down the aisle in a few hours' time. I would be walking into a new and mysterious future too, and one which held so much promise of happiness, contentment, security and growth for me. A life which would mean for the two of us a secure home; a home for my real self, for my love; what I had always wanted without knowing where it would actually be. At last I knew; the mysterious future lay in England, my new homeland. It would, I hoped, prove my final destination, where I would be loved and wanted and most importantly, where I would belong.

A new chapter was about to begin. Richard and I would make the commitment to share our lives with one another *'all that we are and all that we have; from this day forward, for better, for worse, for richer, for poorer, in sickness and in health, to love and to cherish till death us do part'*. What a wonderfully expressive vow! I had learned it by heart weeks earlier and loved the solemnity of the promise it contained. Words which were so familiar to young English people that by the time they got married might not touch them as profoundly as they had touched me when I first heard them spoken by the local vicar during our preparation discussions. Although a similar vow had been used for centuries in Germany, somehow it sounded more magnificent in what was still to me a foreign language, more powerfully meaningful and, yes, even slightly intimidating in case you failed, *'....to love and to cherish.....in sickness and in health....for richer for poorer....from this day forward .... till death us do part'*. These were mighty words indeed! They resonated hugely with me and I could not wait to say them in the church. If keeping these promises might prove to be somewhat challenging somewhere along the road, we would tackle them together. I was well used to much bigger challenges. None had ever managed to rob me of my inner glow nor destroy my zest for life. In those days marriage had not, oddly enough, ever been a particular aspiration of mine. It might happen or it might not; either way my life felt precious and full of the promise of a better, calmer future after the turmoil of a childhood in ravaged, war torn and divided Germany just after the Second World War. Nothing, I was convinced, would be as traumatic for me ever again.

So why was I still leaning out of that window, whiling away the minutes of the morning with these reflections when there was so much awaiting me and so very much to do and enjoy? I must have made some noise when I turned away from the window and prepared to go downstairs as 'Ma' started calling, "Bee-darling, are you awake?"

She was waiting for me at the bottom of the stairs, arms outstretched and with a broad, warm, welcoming smile on her distinguished face. Ma was not my real mother, of course, but my future mother-in-law, called 'Ros' by all the family. The fairy-tale cottage was not that of my real parents but the home of my fiancé. Richard's parents were both keen amateur gardeners and Ros an even keener flower arranger. In the sixties and seventies flower arranging was as popular for the middle-class housewife as fitness training and cooking are for the woman of today. Ros was extremely talented in many respects. She was the product of a privileged background. Her life consisted of shopping and cooking; a 'domestic' would clean the house. In the remainder of her time when not in her garden she would occupy herself with some intricate needlework or playing the piano or – most frequently of all – she would go to her flower club where the other ladies would spend their leisure time learning to arrange flowers in the style of Constance Spry. Ma was exceptionally good at this. She had been asked to decorate the marquees and churches for weddings on a regular basis and had even exhibited at St. Paul's Cathedral earlier that year. The only regret she had was the knowledge that she could never display her talent in her own stylish way for a wedding at her own home. Richard was their only child and, traditionally, weddings were always held at the homes of daughters, not sons.

When Richard announced he was going to marry a refugee girl from Germany Ros seized her chance and persuaded us both (and eventually my parents) that our wedding should be a magical affair based on Ros's own village home and at Richard's parents' expense. It was too good an offer to refuse and my dear parents accepted this arrangement with wonderful composure and loving resignation.

11

"Good morning, Ma! What a fabulous day! I can't believe we are so lucky. Middle of June and this is just how it should be," I was gabbling away, "Sorry, Ma, how are you?"

"I am fine thank you. How about you; excited?"

"And how! Couldn't go to sleep at first, but that's not surprising. Oh, look, you have set the table already. I should have helped you."

"No, don't worry, Bee. Pa did it. I've only just come down myself. It was quite a day yesterday."

"It was indeed, just wonderful. Thank you both so much yet again. My parents looked quite different at the end of the afternoon. Really relaxed, don't you think?"

"Well, yes, we both do so want them to feel happy and at ease here. This entire event must be rather overwhelming for them. If only we could speak more German."

"I don't think that really mattered much yesterday, since you had invited so many good German speakers for our lunch. I watched my parents and brother quite carefully and always saw them deep in conversation, so there's no need to worry on that score. I know they loved it. They told me so when I drove them back to the hotel. Didn't I tell you?"

"Yes, Bee, you did, but it is a relief to hear it from you again."

"Yes, it was really comforting seeing them surrounded by happy talkers and watching them respond; a real ice-breaker. My father looked quite jovial by the time puddings were served, did you notice? I was a bit nervous about him but you clearly have won him over, Ma. Thank you so much. You could not have done better!"

"I'm so glad about that, Bee-darling. It was important to Alan and me that they should feel as comfortable as possible under the circumstances. It can't be easy for them not speaking the language. Let's hope today will go just as well. Now," she paused, "what would you like for breakfast?" She turned to her husband, "Alan, have you made some toast?"

"I have, and coffee too."

Pa, who seemed to enjoy his little kitchen duties as a form of relaxation from his city office, stood by the Aga as I went into the kitchen to try to pretend to help him. He turned, put his arms around me and gently kissed me on the cheek. It had taken me a huge effort to overcome my formal attitude to my elders, which is the natural way for us Germans, especially to those in any form of authority. Future parents-in-law commanded the utmost respect and to call them anything other than Mr or Mrs was inconceivable. Richard had explained this to them and had asked them not to be offended by my inbred reluctance to address them by their Christian names He told them that I would come round to the new way of life and etiquette soon enough if only they gave me a little more time. In the end it took somewhat longer than they had expected, but not as long as I had feared. Yet when the moment arrived, it was a delicious experience, the most natural in the world. We had settled on "Ma and Pa" rather than on Ros and Alan. Such an address seemed more respectful to me while at the same time turning them into another set of parents.

"Good morning, Pa."

"Morning, Bee. Slept well?" he replied.

"Well enough. I was too excited to fall asleep for quite a while and I missed Richard. Have you spoken to him yet? Oh, I do hope he is managing without us."

"No, not yet, but he'll cope; don't you worry."

" I hope so. Can I help you with anything, Pa?"

"You could take in the toast and marmalade. I'll bring the coffee."

He had the loveliest and most gentle smile that I had ever noticed in a man, except, of course, his son who was very like him. Both father and son had a soft, gentle, almost shy smile which was the most striking feature of them both and the one that had beguiled me instantly. I had met Alan many months ago in Hamburg where Richard and I were living at the time and where my friend Inge had introduced us that summer.

Alan had flown over from England for the weekend, to check out the German girl his son had fallen in love with. I suspected that this was something that he and his wife had hoped would never happen. I didn't look forward to our meeting, especially since Richard had told me very little about his parents and had never even shown me a photo of them. Consequently I had no perception of the man awaiting me, and the prospect of this 'inspection' was rather unnerving as my confidence had already been knocked by some unkind comments that Richard had received from his distant relations about my unsuitability! I did not exactly relish the thought of yet more personal grilling at almost no time to prepare, and this time from his father!

How would the evening go? I did not dare to speculate, but I quietly prayed a little. Richard, it was obvious, did not share my unease. He looked happy and confident when he told me of his father's unexpected visit. It helped a little but I resolved to do my best to appear cheerful, even somewhat nonchalant outwardly, whereas inwardly, I was very nervous and apprehensive.

I need not have been worried at all. One look at the gentle man facing us across the large sumptuous hotel reception hall and my heart relaxed. His gentleness expressed itself immediately by the way he sat – his slim body leaning towards the back of the chair, his arms resting on his lap with his hands meeting in a position of prayer, fingers crossing into each other. He was a picture of complete self-possession and inner peace which relaxed both of us as we walked towards him.
He got up with an unhurried air, enough for me to control my nerves and relax in front of him, smiling in a shy but attractive way. Success was instant; his smile was as gentle as his physical demeanour, gentle, yet reassuring and I instinctively knew that I liked him and that the feeling was mutual. Even before I glanced at Richard, who was standing slightly behind and to the right of me I sensed his body relaxing and his face expressing gentle happiness just as his father's was. I turned towards Richard. His blue eyes were caressing mine in the way I loved so much and his hand softly squeezed my right elbow as I stretched out my arm to shake Alan's hand.

Slightly more than fifty years have passed since this encounter, yet the passing of the years has eradicated none of these wonderful memories. None of their subtleties are lost to me even now; none of the pleasure of meeting someone for the first time and instantly feeling you know them already. His hand grasped mine.

"I'm so pleased to meet you, Brigitte".

He really meant it. Putting his left hand over our clasped hands confirmed it and our smiles grew fonder as our hands rested together and this, our special moment, turned into a little bit of magic for all of us.

The breakfast on our wedding day was sparse and simple. It consisted of nothing more than a piece of toast and a steaming large cup of freshly made coffee.

"Have another piece of toast, Bee. There won't be much time for lunch. A little bite of something, no more. Actually, we haven't got much time for breakfast either. Alan, can you clear the table? Bee and I must be off to the hairdresser's in a moment."

We came down to earth to deal with the practicalities of the morning, hair, a facial, a manicure; very necessary things like that. I had to look my very best, groomed to perfection to match the magnificent dress hanging upstairs. I had first seen the design for it on the women's page of The Daily Telegraph. It had a simple line with a narrow skirt overlaid by a half skirt from hip to hip at the back and ending in a very long train. The three-quarter length bell shaped sleeves gave the dress a touch of the medieval and completed the understated elegance which so appealed and excited me. I could hardly wait to step into it, let alone walk down the aisle in it. I cast my eyes lovingly over my dress as I rushed into the bedroom. The joy which lay before me made my heart beat furiously. Richard had no inkling of the kind of dress I had chosen and I could hardly wait to see the look on his face as he turned around to see me walk towards him. Me, the wedding princess swathed in organza silk, wearing a dress made by a real life French princess (or at least that is what she claimed to be) when for most of my previous life the oldest and simplest of home-made clothes were treasured. Madame Maggie who, if she really had been a minor French princess, must have fallen on hard times since she was now dressmaking for the aristocratic set and even the Royal Family.

"My daaarling, I will make you such a wonderful dress. Your figure! So magnifique oh, la, la, so petite. It will be such a plaisir!" she burbled on as we did the first fitting.

And a " plaisir" it was – for her to create it and for me to wear it; just a few more hours now.

15

Chapter Two

I had not felt so exquisitely cherished since I was a little girl, a very little girl. In those days we lived far away, in a part of Germany called East Prussia. It did not have its name for nothing, for it was indeed situated in the far east of the German Reich, north of Poland, south of the Baltic Sea with its eastern borders touching Lithuania. Koenigsberg was its capital city. We lived in a much smaller town, called Insterburg, somewhat east of Koenigsberg. Our town did have something in common though with the capital city, both lay on or near the river Pregel. Only my little town could boast two more rivers, the Inster and the Angerapp, which flowed together at Insterburg, forming the largest river in Prussia, the Pregel.

 What else is significant about Insterburg? Well, it was the home town of my mother, my brother and me! Sometimes there was also my father who came to visit. I cannot remember him actually living with us permanently, except he must have done, having been married to my mother and founded a family. But that was almost before my time. I only knew him then as a visitor wearing a uniform and looking very smart and hardly ever staying longer than 2 or 3 days when he had to return to the war once more.

What other points of interest were there about our pretty little town? World famous horses! Near Insterburg were several well-known studs, the most famous and most important in the whole of Germany was in Trakehnen. This special horse breeding stable was founded in 1731 and bred the lightest and most refined of warm bloods, the world famous Trakehner. The breeding of horses continues there to this very day, although now Trakehnen is called "Yasnaya Polyana" and is part of the Soviet Union.

Another well known stud in the area was Georgenburg, situated even closer to the town. In 1828 this stud had been acquired by William Simpson, a member of a Scottish aristocratic family who had been persecuted in Scotland for their religion and had settled in Prussia. His son, William von Simpson, was a diplomat and writer who wrote a two volume family saga called "The Barrings" in the 1930s. Sadly now out of print, they were very successful books in Germany at that time, being very evocative of the noble junker families in East Prussia of the period. I still have these volumes on my bookshelves and treasure them beyond any others.

My father often talked of Ernst Wichert, a judge and author, who was born in Insterburg in 1831 and died in 1902. Father had read some of his books in his youth, something I should do, too, since Wichert was quite famous once upon the time.

Insterburg was also an important military base. It always swarmed with soldiers in attractive uniforms. Was this the reason my father became a soldier right from the beginning of World War II? I never asked him.

In 1939 my beautiful town had a population of 49,000 and thrived on a flourishing light metal industry, its busy harbour and merchant businesses. Apart from a lovely white church and the market square I have no clear memories of this town, except that it felt a very happy and lovely place, a place I wish I had never been forced to leave. Yet history made different demands and, sadly, I have never been back. Perhaps this is a good thing. Whenever I search for pictures of my lovely town on the internet, I sometimes find a few new photos of my birthplace as it is now. Nothing reminds me of the beautiful town it once was. It looks drab and poor; the sort of place we have come to expect of smaller Russian towns – bleak and of no charm to say the least. Looking at these photos makes my heart bleed – I may not have the courage ever to return for a visit. The old Insterburg was practically wiped off the map at the end of the war and rebuilt in a cheap and utilitarian manner.

However, I have found out that there IS still just something of my lovely town left which is doing its duty to this very day - and in Germany! One of the very old bells of the Lutheran church near the river Angerapp where our mother took us for walks along the embankment has been pealing for prayers in a beautiful church in Hannover-Bothfeld. This is probably the only East Prussian church bell on German soil since anno 1722. I must have heard its peal many times as a small child while at the church yard or walking along the river with my mother. I may even have been christened in this church since the only other Lutheran church was further away from where we lived in the Schlossstrasse. It comforts me enormously knowing that something so venerable and important of my beloved town is still doing what it has done for centuries, calling the town's people to prayer.

Chapter 3

Heiddorf is a village in Mecklenburg, Germany, six kilometres along the river Elde from Doemitz, where the Elde flows into the more majestic river Elbe.

We had arrived in Heiddorf from our homeland in Prussia in January 1945. The lorry transporting refugees had finally stopped in the centre of the village, on the forecourt of the large village alehouse. I remember the whole area being full of people and horse-drawn wagons with a lot of to-ing and fro-ing going on as well as shouting and shuffling around. The entire forecourt was heaving with bags, suitcases, bundles made up of sheets or blankets; potato sacks filled with goodness knows what badly needed items for their owner's survival. We all looked pretty dishevelled, were bewildered, dirty and hungry having left Marienburg in West Prussia more than two days earlier on the last train allowed to leave the town just ahead of the Red Army which was rapidly advancing on the area. My mother, my brother Werner and I had fled from Insterburg to Marienburg in West Prussia in the hope of staying there until we could return home at the end of the war. We had hoped that the leaving of our home would be only for a few short weeks until the Russian Army was beaten back again from the area. German propaganda was strong and constant, persuading the population that this development was only a minor setback, no more and no less. Placards with huge lettering saying: WE WILL NEVER SURRENDER were plastered everywhere.

Now we were further away from home still and our hearts were filled with confusion and dread for our future. I was nearly six years old and my brother almost seven. We were not old enough adequately to understand what and why all this was happening to us kids and our family. Was everyone alive living through war and upheaval? Did everyone's daddy fight at the front? And why were our fathers fighting there in the first place? We knew the front was in Russia but where was Russia? When we were smaller it seemed a very long way off; so far away in fact that we children could barely imagine it as being a real place. Yet as we grew older the grown-up people around us began to talk about Russia anxiously and with fear in their eyes and we began to realise that the front and Russia were not somewhere unimaginable at the end of the world but getting ever closer. Perhaps too close already and certainly threatening us and our lives.

Several times before we left Insterburg, our little town had suffered bomb attacks at night and Mutti had grabbed us out of our beds and pulled us, in our pyjamas and still half asleep, across the road into an underground air-raid shelter. Sirens were howling, aeroplanes approaching, people streaming out of all the neighbouring houses, pushing and shoving ruthlessly; everyone anxious to get down below ground and into protection as quickly as possible before any bombs fell on us. Sometimes Mutti managed to grab a blanket or a jacket and carry it under her arm to keep us warm, but usually we had to cling to each other for warmth and for comfort, our hearts beating to bursting point. Neither Werner nor I ever cried; we were much too frightened to. We froze still and silent in the arms of our dear mother and closed our eyes as tightly as possible to avoid having to see the petrified faces of the other people. Then, suddenly, it would be all over. The sirens signalled us that it was safe to clamber out of the cold, dank shelter into the pitch dark street. Everyone's house was still standing. Our neighbours disappeared inside their houses as rapidly as they had come out of them before the raid began and the night fell into an eerie silence once again. We, too, were shocked into silence. The fear clung with us for the rest of the night knowing that 'the front' was no longer an abstract aberration but instead was very real indeed. We thought of it as something tangible; perhaps it was looming out there threateningly somewhere in the darkness, perhaps only just around the corner.

The front drew closer and closer. Soon Insterburg was overrun by the Red Army. Fortunately for us we had reached the safety of Marienburg by then. Mutti told us many years later that no one expected the Russians to hold their conquered towns for more than a few days or weeks at most. They had broken through the border into Prussia during the First World War but had soon been beaten back by the German Army. Everyone was convinced this would happen again and everyone would be able to return to their homes, taking up their normal lives and waiting for German victory! This time though the Red Army fought their way menacingly towards the west and not long after Christmas we were on our way into an uncertain future somewhere in the Reich. For us this was in Heiddorf.

Luckily we were not alone. Our hosts from Marienburg, my aunt's parents-in-law, were still with us, sharing the same uncertainty. We had only stayed with them for a few weeks and I remember it being a rather happy time. My father came to stay with us for a few days' leave at Christmas. He had brought with him a beautiful big doll's pram which he had bought while his unit passed through Riga. I will never forget my thrill when he gave me this wonderful present. To me it seemed as large as a proper pram and I pushed it determinedly along the snow trodden pavement outside our house, up and down, up and down, along the short strip which had been cleared of most of the snow. The overnight snowfall was nearly a metre high, which made running away with my pram quite impossible. The snow acted as a prison wall and kept me safely confined on the short pavement. Up and down I pushed that pram, backwards and forwards. It was bitterly cold, but I did not feel it; my cheeks were red with excitement and pride. A young mother taking her first baby for a walk couldn't have been any happier. I wanted everyone in the other houses to watch me walking my very own baby doll in my very own wonderful pram. Alas, I fear my proud parents were probably the only observers of this enchanting scene amidst the trauma of that bleak Christmas. Bleak that is, except for me and my wonderful pram from Riga. At least I believed it came from there.

A year or two earlier my father had bought my mother a magnificent fox stole in Riga, this mysterious town in the neighbouring country of Latvia to the north of Lithuania. I thought then that anything beautiful and exciting had to come from that city. In my small child's mind this city had become synonymous with beautiful treats and exciting luxuries like my mother's fox stole and, of course, my magnificent pram. I can still see mother wearing her stole diagonally draped around her shoulders over her long black overcoat. The fox's head including sparkling glass eyes was still attached to it and the mouth with its sharp teeth somehow held the tail in its grasp and stopped the fox stole from falling off. You could be fooled to believe a real life fox was giving mother a hug around her shoulders. She wore a broad brimmed black hat with this coat. Worn on a slant, it almost covered her left eye.

Mutti's eyes were a lustrous dark brown and very beautiful. They were as soft as deeply piled velvet and when she looked at me I felt as if molten chocolate was being poured all over me. I loved the sensation of two delicious chocolaty eyes looking down at me with her gentle smile, or even boring into me with displeasure when I had been naughty. I'm ashamed to say that this did happen quite often as I was an inquisitive, independent child with a surfeit of high spirits. But when Mutti wore her elegant hat and coat and we went out on smart occasions or just for Sunday walks, I usually behaved well enough to get her softer look of approval and love.

It was an icy cold January the day we managed to catch the last train leaving Marienburg. We were dressed warmly but looked bedraggled, tired and lost. The train was filled to the roof with a mixture of desperate families, children, old men and women with their pitiful possessions, all wanting to flee the fury of the Russian Army. Every inch of space was taken up with people or luggage. Some were reduced to sitting on the roof of the carriages despite the freezing cold. Others were hanging on the railings and open steps outside the carriages, clinging on for dear life as the stronger refugees tried to push them off. Mutti and her relations had been lucky to find some seats, but my brother and I had to roll under those seats on the dirty floor as other panic-stricken passengers were crowding into the centre aisle for dear life. We children were small enough to squeeze into the space below the wooden seats, but it was very uncomfortable to be crammed there for two days and nights, possibly more, unable to move, lying there packed close to one another like sardines in a tin.

Two days and two nights can feel like an eternity under these conditions; people crying or moaning, complaining, shouting and stamping their feet to keep them from turning numb in the icy cold, the train carriages being unheated. Thump, thump, rattle, rattle, it went on endlessly. I have forgotten how mother fed us or how we went to the lavatory. But I do remember feeling immensely relieved when the train finally came to a halt. We were so stiff and cold, walking again after two days under those seats was nearly impossible. Mother had to rub us to warm us for some minutes to get our circulation flowing again. Gradually we came to life and were able to stand up and walk and follow our anxious relations.

What would happen to us now? Would we have a proper bed to sleep in – and where? What about food? Our stomachs were empty; we felt cold and near to fainting. Mutti looked close to collapse. None of us spoke, we were too exhausted. Eventually we were deposited into an open wooden cart, drawn by two horses. Mutti, Werner and I huddled together on the floor of the cart with our belongings packed in all around us. Heaven knows how Mutti had managed to get them off the train, so that nothing was lost. It meant we still had SOMETHING to call our own, some belongings to remind us of home. Two large potato sacks were filled with our feather duvets. Later they would keep us from freezing to death in the bitter winter of 1947 with nothing for heating in the small room we lived in at that time. My aunt's father-in-law had had the idea of stuffing the duvets into the sacks. He was the driver of this last train leaving Marienburg and it was thanks to him that his family and the three of us had a place on the train and room for our luggage. We were also among the first people to board the train and therefore old Mr. S., the driver was able to lock up one of the lavatories once the family luggage was safely stacked inside it. He had a key to its lock; too bad if the other passengers couldn't use the lavatory for its intended purpose. This was a time of survival of the fittest and Mr. S. was in command of the train! It was lucky the other passengers had no idea who had locked this vital door or they surely would have lynched us. I expect they relieved themselves whenever the train stopped, be it in a station lavatory or by the snowy roadside or out of sight somewhere on the station platform. This was no Orient Express trip, human needs had to be expressed, however, when and wherever possible. When one is fighting for survival one can't be squeamish. We all learned that very quickly indeed!

In Heiddorf, the horse-drawn open cart followed a wide Tarmac road, lined with large trees. The houses on either side were built of red brick, not dissimilar to those in the villages back home where my grandparents had lived and where my brother and I had spent our summer holidays. The driver of the cart never turned nor spoke to us. There was a quiet understanding between the horses and their master; they knew their route without any need by the driver to interfere with them. They would have arrived at their destination even if they had been blindfolded. Guided solely by habit we arrived at a small farm yard. I remember seeing cows being milked in one of the outbuildings surrounding the yard, chickens fluttering around, a cat strolling slyly across the yard towards a house on the right. The door to the house was open and as the cat reached the top step a woman appeared in the frame of the door. I can only remember that she looked kindly, that she was wearing an apron over a full skirt and that her hair was blond and curly. She walked towards us as we climbed down off the cart. I do not recall more than that of our arrival at our new home. Weariness, hunger and fear must have combined to rob me of further impressions but later on, when recalling our stay with the Rose family (who were our hosts), I had nothing but fond memories of them both. I still feel deep grief and sadness concerning the course of their future lives only a year or so later.

For now though, all seemed well and stable and centred on their small farm, a wholesome world of animals and fields beyond their stables. Our family lived and slept together in one room. It was furnished with just our beds, one large wooden wardrobe and a small table. There was no need for much else as we ate all our meals with our new family. My mother helped Frau Rose with the cleaning and cooking in the house in exchange for our food and shelter while we children were busy all day exploring the exciting world of farm life. There was so much to learn about and wonder over. I was particularly intrigued by the milking process of the cows. Just being in their stable, breathing in the scent of the straw and the smell of the warm milk was a wonderful experience. But even more than this I was captivated by the rhythmic squeeze and pull of the cow's teats by the strong and experienced hands of the milkmaids. Often it took a while before a good amount of milk would leave the teats and drop into the waiting bucket before it grew into a thin but steady stream splashing noisily against the inside of the bucket until enough milk had been gained to fill it around half full. Then the milkmaid would pour it into a large churn standing by the door close to where I was standing watching, mesmerized. Next morning a horse and cart would appear to take the churns to the dairy for distribution.

Sometimes the farm workmen would come and drink the still steaming milk from a large ladle which hung from the rim of the churn ready for use. As it had only just been milked there was still a lot of foam floating on the top of it and when the empty ladle was replaced I delighted in watching the last drinker's tongue greedily licking off the foam from their lips and moustaches while uttering a sigh of blissful satisfaction. I found this process endlessly fascinating. Each man had his own way of conducting this ritual; some serious as if in prayer; some smiling either to themselves or to the milkmaids while giving them a wink in thanks for their evening treat. I just loved watching these scenes of simple country life as time went by and never tired of the rituals the milking sessions involved. You never knew how long the cow's patience would last before a kicking hind leg might try to push the maids off their stool. Then the bucket, which had been held in position between the milk maids' thighs while their competent hands were directing the thin streams of milk carefully into it, was bound to fall down as well and all that precious liquid was lost for good, mingling in the straw with the cows' urine and mess. Usually, the maids won this battle. They seemed to expect the kick before it happened, slapped the cow on her buttocks to keep her in check, swore quite a bit and saved the day for both stool and bucket.

Another thing I loved about the milking was the sound of the hard streams of milk leaving the teats and swishing noisily into the bucket, swish, swash, swish, swash, slowly but steadily draining the udder and filling the bucket until the liquid treasure could be saved into the vessel by the door. Even at my tender age I realized soon enough that I was witnessing a special relationship between animal and human.

Some of this special love and understanding leapt over to me as well and filled me with warmth and comfort of a kind which is hard to describe; you really have to have felt it yourself, and I hated missing it. Somehow I felt there was not enough love around then in my young life. Mutti was busy all day long, helping Frau Rose in the house or later on Herr Rose in the fields. My brother disappeared for most of the day romping around the farm or playing football with new friends or at school. Being eighteen months older than I was, he had to start school very shortly after our arrival. Papa was still fighting somewhere in Russia. I was on my own a lot of the time, feeling the lack of my father and the lack of the love of my friends. The intimacy of the milking ceremony compensated for a lot of what was lacking in my small girl's psyche during the day and I went into the house for our evening meal with the farmer and his wife content and cheerful.

"Ah, Brigittchen, there you are", the farmer's wife used to greet me, "I can tell where YOU have been!"
"Why?"
"Because you are smiling, dear. Come, help me set the table. Your mother is still out with Herr Rose but they should be here any minute. Did the milking go alright?"
"Yes. Greta said there was more milk today than yesterday."
"That's good. We need it. Perhaps my husband will allow me to keep some back for churning some more butter," and she looked up from cutting a large loaf giving me a mysterious look as if we had a secret, which we didn't.

That evening we had the same sort of supper we usually had: bread with sausage, all home-made of course, and some milk for all of us. Mutti looked very tired. She had started to help Herr Rose with some farm work that day. Not too much for she was still rather weak and not used to hard physical labour. She never complained though and went to bed early with us children, for the next day would be another hard one for her.

Although having been brought up in a large village she had never had to labour hard and was not used to this type of work. She volunteered gladly though because she realised we had been extremely fortunate in being placed with this kind family. I appreciated their kindness to us much more later on when we heard stories of the other refugees and how harshly they were treated by some of the people they were forced to stay with. Of course this was a cruel time for everyone, not merely for us who had lost our homes and our land and livelihood but also for the local population. Everyone who owned a house had to give up one or two rooms for these bedraggled strangers and had to feed them and live alongside them. No one knew how long this would go on for at a time when food had been strictly rationed and was very scarce. Only the farmers had enough to eat, but not everyone in the village owned a farm. We were very lucky indeed to have been billeted on this smallholding where the chickens laid eggs and the cows gave us milk. If the food was simple it was enough to still our hunger and was more than we had before.

With every passing day we got more used to one another. Mutti looked less anxious, Frau Rose continued to remain calm and friendly and a few days after our arrival even Herr Rose began to smile at us over supper and join in a little conversation. He was clearly a man of few words, a typical farmer who was closer to his animals and the soil than he was to humans.

Thinking back now I have great sympathy with his situation. His had been a stable, quiet life where the peace of the house was never disturbed until our enforced arrival; not only a strange woman but also her two young children were noisily crowding around him. If ever he and his wife had once had children, they were by now grown up and long gone. Tranquillity had reigned in their home for many years until we arrived. Their domestic peace had suddenly and unexpectedly been thrown asunder by these strangers from another world. Victims of the war were turning them into victims of another kind. No one could know how and when this situation was going to end. Would we be able to return home soon? Would we be forced to give up all hope of ever returning? As we began to feel fortunate to have been assigned shelter with them, Herr and Frau Rose appeared satisfied that they had not fared too badly with us in their household either. Although my brother and I were still very young, our mother had brought us up well and we were polite and well mannered, fitting in with the life and routine of a farming environment; watching, exploring and always trying not to be a nuisance. Rather than resenting us, the Roses soon began to warm to us as we had warmed to them and their lovely farm. Although the broader reaches of Germany were still in the last throes of a bitter war with many still dying and struggling, in our small world at the farm, harmony and peace reigned.

The following morning Frau Rose was nowhere near the kitchen, which was unusual. After our simple breakfast of home made bread and jam Werner ran out to explore the stables despite the very cold weather. He loved the horses and was keen to learn as much as he could about harnessing them, as well as feeding and grooming them. I, too, liked watching the horses but from a safe distance. They looked beautiful and I loved their huge mysterious eyes. Their sheer physical size scared me and I preferred to watch them from inside the house rather than get anywhere near them. This time Werner returned very quickly.

"I have found Frau Rose. She is sitting next to the cowshed in the freezing cold and pushing something up and down. Come and have a look. I don't know what she is doing."

The door to the small shed next to the cow shed was ajar and we could catch a glimpse of Frau Rose sitting on one of the milking stools with a tall wooden churn between her legs and pushing a long stick with both arms up and down, up and down without stopping, not even when she saw us peeping in.

"Want to know what I am doing?" she asked without interrupting her work. We nodded. The top end of the stick had a lid attached to it and she put this down firmly onto the vessel, giving herself a short break. "I'm churning butter. Remember we had more milk last night then usual? Well, this means, butter for us!"
"Can we have a look?"
"Of course, you can."
She lifted the lid and we looked inside the churn to see it filled with more than half of milk which was starting to separate. Small, yellowy clots were floating in the watery milk and she told us that the thrashing action of the stick which also had a disc attached to its bottom would eventually cause the milk to separate completely and the more solid parts would then gradually form into butter. We watched her strong arms drumming down the milk for a long time until we got a little bored and rather cold. It seemed an endless and very tough job to do; made worse by the wintry conditions. She seemed weary but continued on relentlessly.

"Can I have a go, Frau Rose, please? This looks really interesting!"
"I thought you would ask me that, little madam. You always need to try out everything, don't you? But seeing it's your birthday, here we are then, have a try".
My skinny arms reached out excitedly to grab the lidded stick, but try as I would I could barely move it. How did she manage to do this job for hours on end?
"Oh, dear, Frau Rose, this is really much too hard, you must be very strong to do this. Can't you have a good long rest?" "Good God, no! The butter wouldn't set and that wouldn't do, would it? Now run along, you two before you freeze to death and tell your mother to come and see me."

"Mutti, Mutti, Frau Rose wants to see you. She's outside by the cowshed and she is making butter. You know, real, real BUTTER. Can you imagine, really yellow BUTTER!"

I hoped that we would be getting some of it tonight on our bread for supper, I couldn't wait. I closed my eyes and began to imagine my slice of bread laden with a really thick layer of glorious butter. Supper was going to be heaven!

"You'd better not think about what I think you are thinking about," said Werner. "She may have to send that butter to the dairy, too, just like the milk. So stop it!" He always had to spoil things, but he was probably right.

I cannot remember how we passed the remainder of the day. After all, it all happened nearly a life-time ago and much has gone forever from my memory. Yet certain events have such relevance and meaning that they remain as fresh and powerful forever in one's mind. If this had been a normal time what happened would have been long since forgotten but this was not a normal time nor was it a normal place for us to live, in a single room in a stranger's house on a farm. Out in the countryside everyone was fighting for themselves and their families; survival was on everyone's mind, kindness was not something we could take for granted.

It was afternoon and I remember Mutti fussing about me, combing my hair and tying it up with a wide, cream coloured ribbon she had managed to bring along from home. She always made me wear this when there was a special occasion like Christmas or going to have your photograph taken. I couldn't see why I had to wear it today even though it was my birthday. War had not sprung upon us all of a sudden. We had learned what it meant year by year. Food became less and less available. Papa came home on fewer and fewer leaves from the Russian front, people looked more anxious, bomb attacks began to hit our town and we had to rush into air raid shelters almost daily. No one had to tell us these were difficult and threatening times. Our expectations had diminished quite naturally over time. So I knew there wouldn't be any celebration of my birthday. I had no friends in the village as yet. After all, we had arrived in Heiddorf only two weeks earlier. So why did Mutti insist on making me look as clean and as smart as she could? Supper was not going to be for another two or three hours. I could not see the sense of it.

"Well," she said. "You'll see why when we go into the kitchen!"

A tantalizing smell of baking wafted towards us as we got closer to the kitchen and when we entered I could not believe my eyes! Werner, Herr and Frau Rose were sitting around the table, looking smart and smiling at me and in the centre of the decorated table lay a lovely crumble cake (Streuselkuchen), my favourite cake of all time! I spied at once that it had a lot of crumble on it; this was the part of the cake which was the sweetest and most delicious and we children always ate that part first. There had been no cake for us for a long time and I had almost forgotten what it tasted like, and now, there it was right in front of me, specially baked for me, the birthday girl; six years old that day. I can't remember whether I flung my arms around Frau Rose's neck or not but she certainly deserved it and I probably did, if my shyness did not stop me. I will never forget the smile of happiness on her face when she saw how happy I was. A Streuselkuchen to eat on the 2nd February 1945 in war-torn Germany with a family of strangers who did not owe us anything but to whom we owed everything! It was such a great joy that I will never forget it to the end of my days. There was a fire in the wood-burning stove and the black cat lay nearby, purring. The room was warmer than it usually was; a steaming pot of coffee stood on the table for the adults. There was more love in the room than I had felt for a very long time, or so it seemed to me, and the happiness on everyone's face has etched itself into my soul forever. Now I knew why Frau Rose had made the butter so early in the morning. She needed it for the cake she was going to bake later when we were messing around outside or in the stables. She had worked hard all day long to make me happy on my birthday and I was not even her granddaughter! I was so shocked with delight that I could barely move or speak.

"Come on", my brother shouted excitedly. "We have been waiting too long already. I want to eat it. Come on, sit down".

With that we began to celebrate the best birthday of my childhood, perhaps of my entire life. No other Streuselkuchen since has tasted quite the same, not even with a really thick layer of Streusel on top. Frau Rose's cake did not just taste of the lashings of freshly churned butter mixed with flour and sugar but also of her efforts and immense kindness. Kindness for me, the little stranger, a girl who jumped around her feet for most of the day, asking too many questions, helping far less than I should and talking, talking, talking, literally until the cows came home. To my surprise I had won a bit of her heart; perhaps one day I might win it all.

Chapter Four

I loved my mother very much. She was beautiful with dark curly hair and soft brown eyes and was warm and gentle. She came from a family of eleven and was born somewhere along the middle of the string of siblings, having had to help with the younger ones until she left home when she married father. She had only just turned eighteen a few weeks earlier. Still, mothering was inbred in her. When my father had to join the army almost from the first day of the war, she was left alone with us and we became the centre of her world.

Then my brother became very ill and I recall mother crying all day long. Later, after my father's return from capture in Russia, he told us over and over again how, by a sheer miracle, my brother's life was saved. Father had been granted an unexpected leave to go home for two days. This leave had been a sudden reward for some action of his and there had been no time to let my mother know he was coming home. When he entered our apartment he found my mother by my brother's bedside crying her heart out. Werner had developed a very severe sinus infection which had become so serious that our doctor had suggested an operation to release the pus inside his head. However, no one was prepared to undertake this operation at our local hospital. According to the surgeons, the operation had been left too late and no one wanted to take the responsibility for failure or for his death. My mother had reached such a state of despair she was screaming with fear by his bedside when father unexpectedly entered the room.

After a brief explanation from mother he grabbed Werner there and then and carried him back to the hospital, where the surgeons still refused to operate.

Papa went to every hospital in the nearby towns, but they all refused to operate as every surgeon feared that Werner was beyond saving. In despair Papa decided to take him to Koenigsberg, the capital of Prussia. My father was a very courageous man; he never gave in and fought to the end even in the most frightening battle, a character trait which saw him through many more horrific and tragic events in his future years.

In Koenigsberg, he found no one ready to risk this dangerous operation either. It was too late, the boy was going to die they told him. With my father at her side my mother had managed to keep some kind of composure but when the last hospital gave them the same negative reply, her nerves gave in and she collapsed into a hysterical fit. My father was still carrying my brother as she lay on the floor convulsed with grief. Werner, too, was screaming with pain. The scene must have been one of such pathos that one of the surgeons took my father to his side while nurses were struggling with my mother to calm her down. This doctor suggested that father telephone the former head of surgery who had retired many years earlier.. When this man had been in charge of the department, his reputation for his many successful experimental operations had spread beyond the boundaries of Prussia. If he thought that my brother was going to die anyway, he might come out of retirement for this one more experimental operation. It was certainly worth a try.

Father told me that the next part of the story was the most amazing. When he and mother reached the professor's house and entered the hall, a very old gentleman came towards them, reaching out his hand to shake hands with my parents. The professor's hand was trembling so badly that my father's hopes were finally dashed completely and he was close to collapse himself. The professor stayed very calm while listening to my father and then examined my brother. All he said was:
"Let's go back to the hospital at once. I cannot promise you anything but I will do my best to save your son."

He allowed my father to attend the operation, something which was most unusual in those days. Father's nerves began to settle when he saw the calmness and professionalism of the staff around them mixed with considerable deference for the old professor. He was, however, still very worried about the professor's shakiness until he saw him take the scalpel into his hand. To father's utter amazement his hand became completely still. A miracle was unfolding right in front of his eyes. The professor's total focus and concentration transferred itself to father and he suddenly knew without doubt that the old surgeon would succeed. He knew it even before the scalpel had entered the scull just above Werner's left eye. When it did, the pus shot out of the point of incision with the force of an erupting volcano, shooting right up against the ceiling as well as spluttering all over the professor and the assisting theatre nurses. In the early 1940s surgeons did not have the skills they have today, except for the odd exception like the venerable old surgeon. He saved my brother's life. We always asked ourselves later why my father had been given those two days of leave. Had God had a hand in it? Of course, he had, how else could one explain such a miracle?

Ever since this traumatic event my mother seemed to dote on my brother with all the passion only a mother can give and, rightly or wrongly, I began to feel less loved. I was too young to understand all of this and the ugly head of jealousy began to rear itself. If Werner got his food first at lunch I would kick his legs under our very own children's table. I would lie to my mother about things Werner had done knowing full well he hadn't, just to see mother scold him. It was in the early days of the winter of 1944 that my anger and feeling of not being loved reached its peak.

Snow always fell early in Prussia and my father had brought home (from Riga?) a wooden sledge which we were meant to share. To share, with my brother, when he was older and bigger, and I was only the silly little sister? Of course not, he had several friends who lived in our street and ours was the only sledge. It was a golden opportunity for my normally soft-hearted brother to enjoy some superiority among his peers and to allow them to share the sledge runs with him. His little sister would have to wait. It wasn't 'cool' to let her have her fair share of the sledging runs. She had to learn to keep her place, be patient until he felt inclined to let me have a go by myself. Not a good idea as he was soon to find out.

Our house was situated on the Schlossstrasse (Castle Street) of Insterburg leading up to the ruins of an old Schloss on top of a hill. It was perfect for us kids to sledge downhill all day long. The street was cobbled but the pavements were not, so they made a perfectly smooth run. Little Brigitte waited and waited at the bottom but Werner enjoyed his status with the other boys and kept ignoring my ever more angry pleas. How was I going to get my way and achieve my rightful turn with the sledge? I begged sweetly, I begged angrily, I warned him that I would go and tell Mutti. Nothing worked. Real anger was welling up from deep within me. It grew stronger and fiercer, climbing up from my tummy higher and higher until it had reached my spiteful, clever brain. That's what I would do; I would teach him a lesson he would never forget!

He was coming down towards me on the sledge with a friend sitting behind him and they were both laughing and screaming in sheer delight. If he wasn't going to give me a turn on the sledge now my mind was made up. Surely enough, he didn't! Next time, I hoped, he would come down by himself and if he did I would spring into action. As I said, the run was on the pavement and if, by chance, the sledge had to veer off onto the cobbled street he was bound to fall off and I could snatch the sledge away from him before he could get up. If I positioned myself slightly higher up the road in the middle of the pavement he would have to steer towards the cobbled road or he would drive into me. And he would NEVER do that, I knew. He had much too soft a heart for that and would risk any hurt to himself rather than hurt me. I had guessed right, he landed with a frightful crash; he had cut himself on the elbow and screamed in pain. All his friends gathered around him and no one took any notice of the sledge which was finally mine and mine alone. One of the boys ran home to tell my mother what had happened to Werner. Everyone was shouting at me and calling me names. How could I do such a beastly thing and to my own sweet brother? Werner was still screaming, bending over holding his left arm. My plan had worked but it had also misfired. Poisonous looks were being shot in my direction. My mother was leaning over him scolding me in anguish.

"What have you done now, Gitta?"

My joy had long since evaporated. I was clutching for dear life to the sledge rope as if that could make me feel any better. The run was now clear, the sledge at last in my possession but at what terrible price. Physical pain for Werner, emotional pain for me. Who was the winner now? I had the sledge, but Werner had yet more of my mother's love, the one thing I missed since his illness and now I had surely lost even that which I so yearned to possess. Now it wasn't only Werner who would not forget this accident, it was also Mutti and me. Werner had actually broken his left arm. We all cried a great deal that night and I don't remember ever using the sledge again.

I loved our mother dearly and my brother, too. However much I tried to gain my fair share of love in return from her, in my jealous and hurt state of mind, I felt she did not really love me as she did Werner. Soon I was searching for affection elsewhere, from friends, even from neighbours! My mother told me in later years that I had so endeared myself to a childless couple living nearby that they had asked to adopt me!

I must have missed my father very badly for me to be in constant search for more affection and attention, because Mutti was a loving mother and wonderful to me despite her doting on my brother. Somehow I imagined that I would be feeling less lonely and bereft if we had been a 'proper' family with a mother and a father at home all the time. We needed a father who was at home with us and not always at war in some far distant land. How Mutti must have missed our father during these many years of extreme hardship. All the pressure of raising us rested on her young shoulders alone. If I missed our father so badly, how much more must she have yearned for him. She had no loving man to turn to in times of crisis, so seldom to feel his warm embraces and reassuring strength. The longer we had to exist without Papa, the more we children turned him into a godlike figure who, so we thought, by his very presence alone could magically dissolve any sad or difficult situation into instant sunshine. If only he could be with us for good, then all would be well with the world and our small squabbles and problems would be gone forever.

Chapter Five

Ma was already in the garden when I came downstairs. The workmen had erected the marquee at the back of the house the day before. Now more people arrived to decorate the inside walls with flowers and candles, to lay down the carpet and generally to get everything ready for the reception after the church ceremony. My new mother-in-law being such a keen and talented flower arranger had created several large bouquets for the long trestle table which was to hold the champagne and wine. Another magnificent arrangement was resting on a flower stand next to the table which was to hold the wedding cake. She had worked tirelessly for many weeks to ensure that this was going to be a wedding like none other and certainly one our guests and the village would talk about for years and years to come.

If there were to be only half the glamour and ceremony Ma was aiming for I would have been overwhelmed, but then, who was I to interfere? I was just the little refugee girl from Germany and Ma was in sole charge of this performance, the boss of the show. It had become her life's project. She had always regretted not being able to stage a traditional country wedding as Richard was her only child. Unexpectedly, she had now been given the opportunity and she loved every moment of it and was in her element as never before. She was showering me with undreamt of magic and attention and it was not my place to intervene in any way even though it was supposed to be my wedding. It would have been mean to have argued with her over the wedding arrangements now, but then there was no need to, since all the arrangements had been discussed with us and we had been fully involved in so far as we were able to be. Only my wedding gown had been entirely my own choice. Despite my simple background from the ravages of war I had always had an inborn sense of style which met with Ma's approval and her own inherent elegance and taste. It is true to say we never disagreed on anything she had planned for my special day and the joy we shared in preparing for it remained with me for many years.

I found her inside the marquee gesticulating wildly while talking to some of her flower arranging club friends and at the same time trying to keep her cigarette in a position so that she could still puff away at it, no matter what. She didn't look quite so elegant with the cigarette dangling from her mouth but, wisely, I kept that thought to myself. The majority of adults habitually smoked in those days. Being a non-smoker or a vegetarian almost amounted to an admission of being a bit of a freak, while being a smoker meant that you were sophisticated to the point of elegance.

My mother-in-law was elegant and sophisticated even when a cigarette was hanging from the corner of her mouth. However, in my eyes she would have been even more so if she had stopped smoking altogether. She had a tall and slender frame. Her head was always held high and every movement of her body suggested poise, superiority and confidence.

Right now she was in full command and I watched her with envy and admiration trying to overlook the dangling cigarette and the trail of dropped ash. I acknowledged, with suppressed envy, that I would never be like her. For a start I was short and thus lacked the natural command that being tall gave one over others. Secondly, I was foreign and thirdly I was a German. I could never be equal to Ma in this new world I was about to enter. Any foreigner would have had a struggle, especially if they were German, but all the same one could but try; and this I was determined to do. With Ma's help it would be easier. She was a very capable person with many talents, an excellent cook, gardener and flower arranger as well as an astonishingly good needlewoman. She also played the piano beautifully and had superb taste in clothes. Whatever she put her mind to she did well. In my eyes she was a formidable achiever who would be the best kind of teacher for me as her daughter-in-law.

I have always been a keen learner, one who likes a challenge and does not give in easily (remember the story of the sledge). How fortunate for me and how lucky, too that Richard and I should have fallen in love. Cinderella had slipped into her slippers, marriage had been proposed and an extra set of parents had shown me such a warm welcome; it all surpassed anything I could have dreamed of. My prince was about to carry me off into the security of his kingdom, a world very different from all I had known before. The full transition might take time but whatever help was needed, Ma would give it gladly and to the full. I had no fear of the future. With so much support and encouragement the path ahead seemed smooth and strewn with flower petals. Not just along the walk to the altar in a few hours' time but also for our walk together for the rest of our lives.

My own parents also had done everything possible to smooth our path. My prince had captured their hearts as well as mine when they first met. Although he belonged to the former enemy camp, my father in particular had liked him at once. Any remaining indoctrination and prejudice created in the Nazi era vanished in a flash once personal contact had been made. The realisation that at the human level we are all the same was immediately apparent; my father had experienced this many times during his five long years as prisoner of war in Russia. My father and my prospective husband were the two men who cared for me. When emotions are based on love, any barriers collapse like a pack of cards and my parents had agreed without hesitation to come to England for my wedding as guests rather than hosts and to hand over their only daughter to a family they had never even met before and, moreover, to do so with all their generous hearts.

When my father was introduced to my future parents-in-law during a long and splendid lunch in the marquee the day before the wedding, I overheard my father saying to them how delighted he was about our future union and he told them,

"If there should be any grandchildren from our son Werner and from Brigitte, you will enjoy the English ones and we shall enjoy the German."

He did not mean that they would not have an interest in children Richard and I might have, but that they accepted our children should not be pulled apart by their different upbringing, culture and language. They would never make claims on our children that they might not be able or willing to fulfil. My father could be a very stern man but it was this comment which showed me once again that his outwardly steely armour protected a warm and generous heart. In later years my love for him was often tested but at this moment I could not have been more proud of him. If either of my parents had been upset by my decision to leave Germany and settle in a foreign land, they certainly did not show it nor did they ever express it and I loved them dearly for that.

Equally, my new family showed nothing but happiness and acceptance of the new daughter they had acquired and I was filled with gratitude for the way everything and everyone was doing more than could be reasonably expected to help us start our future together. Ma especially was working constantly, worrying endlessly about my parents and their feelings and ensuring that every small detail was in place. No one could feel hurt, left out or let down. Only harmony was allowed to reign, nothing was overlooked to mar the perfection of the great day, and almost nothing did.

She spotted me at once as I entered the marquee. Her cigarette was stubbed out. She seemed to have forgotten it anyway as all her attention was immediately given over to me.
"Let's go, Bee. We mustn't be late."

She took my hand and we sneaked off like two overexcited young girls. The importance of the event temporarily removed our differences of age and status. We became two happy young girls (or perhaps like mother and daughter). Coming back to ground would happen very much later for us both. Had I conquered another heart, as I had so many times before in my young life? Would I be able to keep it conquered though? Right now it did not matter; I was drifting on a scented cloud. Nothing else mattered except this moment, and this very moment was very sweet indeed!

Chapter Six

After my birthday and the thrilling event of the crumble topped cake our life at the farm settled back into a more predictable routine. Werner and I continued to explore the farm animal world and Mutti worked with Frau Rose learning more and more about their way of life and becoming steadily more useful. My fascination with the milking ritual never waned but I was also intrigued by the many chickens of different sizes and colours. They were running freely around the yard and you never knew whether you were going to discover a cluster of them as you ran around a corner. Then they clucked and burst into a fearful cacophony of shrill noises while scurrying off in all directions, fluttering their wings as if they were trying to fly away. Now, as it was still winter, they spent most of their day inside their chicken coop. It wasn't always snowing and on the warmer days they ran around the yard and beyond as freely as they liked, yet always returning to their coops at dusk.

Another of my favourite ventures was collecting the eggs with either Mutti or Frau Rose; yet watching the cows being milked remained the highlight of my day. The stable doors were shut in winter, keeping the temperature inside warm and the atmosphere cosy. Greta and her assistant milkmaid were a chatty pair. A lot of banter was exchanged between them and with the farm hands that came in for their ladle of warm milk and a bit of a gossip.

Weeks passed. With the arrival of spring I recall my mother leaving with Herr Rose early one morning to plant potatoes in the fields beyond the farm yard. This was very hard work for her, bending down endlessly dropping seed potato after seed potato into the freshly dug furrows the farmer was ploughing ahead of her. Yet Mutti never complained. There was always a shortage of hands on the farm, most men being in the front line or having died or been wounded in action. Mutti's help was much needed and we children eventually had to do some of the easier work to show that we earned our keep. Besides, although Werner had started attending the local village school, I was not due to start until September and so I had plenty of time to spare.

Work also gave me a chance to be around Mutti and to give her a hand as best as I could. That was my greatest joy. I always bore the incident of the sledge in my mind; I needed to make up to her (I wasn't so bothered about Werner; he had deserved it after all) but Mutti had not. If I helped her as much as I was able to she would surely realise soon enough that I was worth her love as much as Werner was, even if I had not nearly died as he had done. Of course, all these thoughts of Mutti not loving me were a figment of my imagination. Perhaps I had felt more guilt about my nasty action than I had admitted to myself.

A guilty conscience is not easy to deal with. Perhaps Mutti had already forgotten about the incident and possibly she loved me as much as ever despite my nastiness to Werner. I had not forgotten it however, and felt I probably deserved some punishment. I believed that I had lost some of her love and that alone was punishment indeed. Thinking it over now after all these years, it was a complex matter and hard to resolve and I was too young in 1945 to work it out and deal with it sensibly.

In those early years of my life and without the wisdom of later experience, I lacked the understanding of another traumatic event that had affected my poor mother. Two or three years after I was born, she had given birth to a third child; a girl called Renate, who had died shortly after her birth. Renate had caught shingles from one of the hospital nurses and she never came home. She had lived for only two weeks. Renatchen's grave became another playground for us children. Not having had a garden to play in, the local church yard of Insterburg became a substitute and we thought it an area of beauty and freedom. Werner and I had no connection with this dead baby and therefore felt no sadness and had little sympathy for our mother's loss. The soil of the grave was slightly raised from the grass around it. Red busy Lizzies were planted all around the edge of the raised area while the centre of it remained flattened and was neatly raked leaving space for fresh flowers or plants. The area around the grave was also regularly raked most fastidiously. It was a spot of real beauty. While Mutti worked on tidying the area we ran around at will, playing and even singing. She was oblivious of our behaviour as she communicated with her baby and we were immune to her feelings of grief. Everything seemed perfectly natural.

The other graves were beautifully looked after as well with lots of fresh flowers abounding. The entire cemetery was a place of harmony and delight to us, not of sadness. Children see the world as it appears to them, they cannot see beyond their little child's world and neither Werner nor I comprehended the immensity of our mother's loss, even though we understood perfectly well that our sister was buried there. Later on, when Werner had his illness and nearly died, this possibility struck me much more powerfully and I was frightened that I might lose my brother as well. Now he became a very precious brother. I stopped kicking his legs under our table and loved him very dearly, that is until the incident with the sledge! Some months had gone by since his recovery and months are like years in a child's mind. He was safe and sound now, wasn't he? He had *'jumped off death's shovel'*, so to speak. Did he really think he could rely on my sympathy and patience forever?

Renatchen's actual death was quite different. We had never seen her, never touched her and never bonded with her. We felt no grief, no sadness and were too young to ponder on our mother's feelings. It took decades before the real measure of her loss dawned on me. This was why she had loved her son with that extra sense of protection, from which I felt excluded and which had made me feel less loved. Winning back her love, which I wrongly, but strongly felt I had lost, was always on my mind and I helped her whenever I could as one way of trying to make her love me more.

Working in tandem brought us closer together. Her physical presence was the best reward. Surely she would realize soon what a precious child I was as well and how willing I was to be helpful and good. It would only be a question of time!

We missed Papa so badly in our daily lives. We had only seen him a few times since the start of the war, and then for only a few days at a time. In fact, he had never lived with us on a permanent basis since I was eight months old and as an absent father he became an almost imaginary person to me. Then, all of a sudden, here he was again, looking so handsome in his smart uniform. I remember him still smiling a great deal at us then, but most of all I remember his hugs. They were warm and loving. I was so happy and I felt so safe. With each visit I loved him even more. With each departure I felt dragged into a pool of ever greater longing from which it was hard to pull myself out. Only Mutti could rescue me; she had to be both mother and father for me, feed me, comfort me, be the angel of protection and keep me from all harm, hunger, bombs, fear and confusion. She must lift us into a realm of constancy, of warm safety and into a state of contentment. She succeeded most of the time and I loved her so much. If only I could have my Papa back, too; back for good, never to leave us again. I wished fervently for the war to be over and for us to be a proper family, together at last.

It was not to be, the war continued and Papa's absence was felt more harshly at home. Mutti's face turned paler and greyer; more sirens awoke us from our sleep at night, signalling a dive into the underground shelter across the street. Finally there was the escape to Marienburg and from there to here at Herr and Frau Rose's farm, our sanctuary for the time being.

Chapter Seven

One day in early May, the village woke up to a great deal of commotion and noise. A column of soldiers were entering the village, marching along the main road towards our farm and further along towards the next village and, possibly, towards the Russian front. My brother and I rushed out to watch them march past. People were streaming out of all the neighbouring houses. White sheets were fluttering from open windows like doves' wings. A carnival atmosphere had gripped the village. We quickly joined in cheering and waving not knowing whom we were cheering but, I hoped, my father would be among them!   It surely would be our German soldiers; why else would everyone be so excited and happy? Little did I know about the mood of the country in 1945.

The consequences of war had not been kept from us children. We had experienced the loss of our father in our daily lives. We had learned the hard way about shortages and hunger. We had lived through air attacks, and the flight from home before the Russian advance. Yet the finer intricacies of the politics behind this terrible war were beyond the capacity of our childish comprehension. Mostly I had heard the adults discuss their terrible fear of the Russian Army's inexorable advance deep into German territory. They were the ones everyone feared, they were the ones on everybody's lips for as long as I could remember. If Germany was going to lose this war, then the Russians were the soldiers to fear the most as they would have no mercy. At that time we children did not know of the atrocities our own army had committed inside Russia. To us the effects of this war were only one sided, we only considered how it was going to affect us. We knew vaguely there were other countries involved, yet Russia was the only one we feared. The adults knew the war was lost long before it became hinted at by the official propaganda. Snippets of hushed conversations reached our curious little ears quite often and it became clear the Russians were expected to overrun our part of the country quite soon. Fear had begun to paralyse everyone, even to some extent the farmhands and milkmaids working at the farm as well as the community around us.

The ecstasy of the villagers in welcoming these marching soldiers meant that they were certainly not Russians. If not the Russians, then who else could they be other than our own men? As Werner and I were running towards the tumultuous scene of hundreds of booted legs marching past us along the street, the hope that our Papa might possibly be among them drove me, half-awake in the early morning, faster and faster in the direction of the new troops, not wanting to miss a second of this great event. As we got closer to those marching soldiers, we realized they were not wearing German uniforms.

"It's the Americans! The AMERICANS !" excited voices gasped in disbelief. "They have liberated us! We are free. Hoorah, we are free!"

From somewhere there came music. White handkerchiefs were thrust into our hands and Mutti, who had followed in our footsteps, shouted:

"Wave, Gitti, wave! Werner, you, too! We have been liberated! The Americans have freed us. Thank God, it's all over! Thank God it's the Americans! Not the Russians! Not the dreaded Russians! Thank God, thank God!"

I had never seen her in such a state of exuberance and joy. Her deep brown eyes, which had looked so sad for months on end, were now sparkling like freshly peeled chestnuts, transporting her back to the very young mother and woman she actually was; she would be twenty-six in a few days.

Crowds of villagers were running towards us, all smiling and shouting and waving their arms ecstatically and cheering from their hearts the soldiers who had freed all of us from the dangers of this hateful war. These were the Americans, not the dreaded Russians! They had crossed the river Elbe only a few hours earlier. Six kilometres further north they were now entering our village to a reception they must have experienced many times over as they advanced towards us. This was a day of such joy, nothing could ever wipe it from my mind. Neighbours, who had been too preoccupied with the business of survival, fell into each other's arms, hugged and kissed and tried to grasp the hands of the soldiers as they marched by to squeeze them in gratitude.

"Thank you for liberating us!" "Danke schoen! Danke schoen! Hoorah, hoorah!"

Caps were thrown into the air. Some soldiers smiled embarrassed smiles, others beamed wide all over their faces. All of them looked extremely tired but happy and friendly.

Following the marching soldiers were some jeeps and one or two tanks, then came some more soldiers. It was a very long column and it seemed to go on forever until, abruptly, it came to a halt. For a while the soldiers remained standing, looking confused and awaiting orders. Officers on horse-back rode up and down the long village road until someone gave an order for the soldiers to relax and settle down where they were. All of them collapsed in relief down onto the road or along the grass edges for a long awaited break from the torturous march to an unknown goal. Some of them smiled in reaction to the rapturous welcome these enemy folk were giving them, but mostly they appeared to be cautious in response to our welcome, trying to avoid eye contact and instead closing their eyes for some much needed sleep, even if it were only to last for a few minutes. It was obvious they had orders not to be too friendly to any of us, much to the disappointment of the villagers and us children.

After an hour or two of gaping at them without much else happening, we gradually returned to our homes for our lunch and the inevitable work which was waiting for us.

Later that afternoon the soldiers were still sitting and sleeping as they had done in the morning and some villagers approached them again to show they bore no bad feelings towards them, rather the contrary. Eventually, it became clear they were going to spend the night here in our village. Some of the villagers offered them their houses to eat and sleep in. This they must have refused since, when Werner and I went out again the following morning to see what had happened, some of them were still asleep in the ditches on either side of the road, their rucksacks serving as pillows while others were making fires in small portable stoves. After months of uneventful life on the farm, watching these soldiers became an irresistible attraction. They spoke another language. This in itself was more than enough to draw us nearer and to inspect them with our insatiable curiosity.

Mutti did not like us spending too much time with them. They had 'freed' us and were therefore our heroes but they were also strangers from another world, unknown to us, and she was fearful of what they might do to us. This was a fear we children did not share through our childish ignorance. They smiled at us, stroked our heads fleetingly as they walked past. We had nothing to fear from them but loads of novel entertainment for us to watch and enjoy.

As we became surer of them we drew closer still. I don't know anymore how many other children had clustered around them. If there were others, they did not matter, for out of the blue I became the centre of attention. Hands held me up, passed me on to another set of arms, on and on until I landed on somebody's lap. I was cuddled, fed pieces of CHOCOLATE and stuffed with sweets! Men's hands stroked my hair, my cheeks. They took me to their chests, hugged and loved me as if I was their own child. I was showered with something extra I had dreamed of for ages and could never have enough of: showered with LOVE. My Papa was not with me but for a short blissful time, the accumulated love of these soldiering fathers for their far away children enveloped me in a way that I shall never forget. I was blond and cheerful with a cheeky smile, small enough to be lifted up like a little, living doll. I smiled back at them with sheer delight as I was gently and safely thrown from one set of arms to another. For those brief moments I became everybody's little daughter; the epitome of all their daughters back home in America with whom they longed to be reunited. No need to understand one another's language, my laughing eyes and intoxicated giggles made language obsolete. The chocolate, the sweets, the pieces of bread and cake all added to the joys that lay ahead for me; this was what peace was going to be like. I had heard this word uttered so frequently around me by the adults, always in hushed tones, mingled with fear; their eyes searching whether anyone was in earshot.

Talking of peace was obviously considered treachery during the fascist era, yet it was something everyone desired. We little ones, who had never known life without war, felt peace was an elusive word, something we could not fully grasp. Was peace a part of what I was experiencing, or was it merely a *'Fata Morgana'*? Of course I did not know the meaning of this word at that time, but I had become familiar with the feeling it engendered and I dreaded the moment this delicious experience might cruelly end. But end it did. Sadly, sadly, sadly!

When we woke up the following morning, the ditches were empty and the street deserted; the Americans had gone. The streets looked as if they had never been there. Fear and disappointment assailed us, no more chocolate, no more sweets (in fact, no more of those for many years to come), no more strong, friendly soldiers to throw us into the air either. As is its nature the *Fata Morgana* had disappeared. What would happen to us now?

The village collapsed again into its state of dread and fear. Life on the farm was gloomy and silent; only the animals remained the unaffected. The cows still needed to be milked and the horses to be worked and fed at night. The necessities of farm life kept everyone going but I never stopped wondering what had happened to my wonderful American soldier friends. Would they ever return and keep us free? They had made me feel like their little princess; to the community they had brought hope and relief beyond imagination. For forty-eight hours our lives had changed from drudgery to ecstasy and I wanted this marvellous feeling to return.

"Please, God. Let them come back. Please God, they have been so nice! I liked them, God. Please God, please….."

But we never saw them again. What I had not realized, of course, was how lucky and privileged I had been to have met them and to have been treated with so much love and affection by so-called 'enemy' soldiers. To me they seemed like kind uncles, only nicer. They had shown me a little bit of heaven, of almost fatherly love and these wonderful feelings remained the foundation of what I felt all Americans were like: an expression of goodness in contrast to the feared Russians, whom I imagined to be the epitome of evil (never actually having met any). At that time I did not know that their people had precisely the same opinion of our German soldiers. It was not until I lived in England and read and heard more about the Second World War that I learned about the 'no fraternisation' orders to all Allied Forces concerning the German population, including and particularly with the children. Apparently the American soldiers had strict orders not to speak or smile at children, stroke their hair or give them sweets. Yet MY soldiers had given me all of those forbidden gifts. Their humanity had won over the orders of their commanders and by doing so had given me hope of more joy and happiness to come in the future. Over the course of that summer all prohibitions against the German population were loosened by the American Government. Only a ban on marriage between Germans and Americans remained.

Chapter Eight

Nearly twenty years on I was to be a princess once more. We had returned from the hairdresser's and Ma was saying good-bye to her flower arrangers. The marquee had received the final touches and the caterers had arrived while we had been away. There was a constant buzz around the house and garden, laughter and jokes rippled through the air; the sun was shining ever more brightly and there was not a cloud in the sky. You don't get days like this one in England often, not even in June but here it was in all its magnificence and the relief on everybody's face was palpable. The service in the church was to be at three pm; not long for us to get ready. First we had some lunch, Dad had made us some sandwiches but nobody felt like eating much. I was too excited for anything but Ma quite rightly made me eat at least half a sandwich while we all sat nervously around the dining table.

"I wonder what Richie is up to now," said Ma, whereas I replied: "I hope he's eating some lunch or he'll be very shaky in church later on."

I missed him badly. He had gone to stay with his best friend and best man three days before. This was the custom at that time if bride and groom normally lived under the same roof. We had both moved in to Cowslip Cottage a few days earlier, each from our own London flats. This separation turned out to be much harder than I expected, even though there was plenty to divert me during the wedding preparations. Richard was allowed to come over during the day and, of course, he was at Cowslip Cottage the previous day for the celebratory lunch with my parents and brother. In the evening he had to return to his friend's house again. On the day of the wedding we were not allowed to see one another until we met at the altar.

"Don't worry, Bee. He will be fine. Julian will keep him amused and make sure that he turns up on time."
"Yes, of course, you are right, Ma. I only wish it was three o'clock already!"

"Hallo, my daaaaalings! How are you?"

Maggie, the French dress-maker and friend of Ma's had arrived and thankfully interrupted my trail of thought. One always knew when she was around; she was such an exuberant character. Her strong French accent added to the attention she attracted. She was neither tall nor beautiful. Her lips were always painted bright red and her face caked in powder which emphasized her middle-aged crows' feet and wrinkles rather than hiding them. Altogether she was a theatrical-looking person, yet today she looked rather elegant in a full wide skirt with a matching tailored jacket and a small black lace hat on her auburn curls.

Dad had made us his speciality mug of fresh coffee and when this had been finished Maggie and her 'daaaling' could go upstairs to perform the best part of today's preparation, to dress the bride. Shortly after Maggie went upstairs with me, three more girls arrived with their helpers, the bridesmaids, two of whom I hardly knew. Ma had insisted that I should have two adult and one younger bridesmaid. As I had no girlfriends of my own in England she had chosen them from among her own friends. However, the eldest of them I did know a little and liked a lot. Gayle was Richard's first cousin from Kenya where she had been born. When her parents divorced, she had left her home with her mother, who was Ma's only sister, and come to live in England to start a new life, staying, for a while, at Cowslip Cottage. Ma and Dad had given them shelter and Gayle soon became the substitute for the daughter they had never had. By the time of the wedding she had moved across to the other side of the village and was now living with the parents of a new friend of hers, which suited everyone very well. Because her new home was in the same village we were able to see a lot of each other and get to know one another so that I was more than happy to have her act as my principal bridesmaid. By then she had become my new friend anyhow.

In a way we were both refugees, both having had to leave our homelands for a new life and in a strange country with different social values. We came from different social backgrounds, but we had both lost our roots, and had to learn to integrate into the English way of life. Gayle had lost her security a while back, I was about to gain mine that day. Yet the loss of our childhood homes and the lack of security which went with it created an unspoken bond between us. Her role as my principal bridesmaid was one of mutual support and bonding. She had become my first new friend and it was comforting to have her by my side. The other two bridesmaids I had met only briefly before. They meant little to me but were essential for my mother-in-law as they completed the tableau she wanted to create.

As I had mentioned previously, Maggie was a top class couturier-dressmaker. On meeting her for the first time, apart from being delighted with my slim figure, she also seemed to LIKE the fact that I was petit, perhaps because she was rather short herself. Furthermore, and to my utter surprise and delight, she also rather liked the design I had chosen from a weekend edition of The Daily Telegraph. If she had not approved, she most certainly would have declined to accept the order, substantial though it was.

"I make everything with luuuvv – you understand? Without luuvv, it does not work. Therefore I don't do what I don't love. C'e va."

And luckily she loved what we were asking her to do for us – at, no doubt, an enormous fee! Money was not discussed in my new parents house, so I never found out how much they had paid for it, but I knew this much: a small fortune! For there were also the dresses for the bridesmaids which were to be made of the same silk organza and in almost the same style but in the shade of dark pine! Prior to our wedding Ma and Dad had been invited to two other weddings and they had hinted to their friends that they wanted Richard and me to be invited, too, so that I might acquaint myself with an English traditional wedding. In each case the dresses of the bridesmaids had been in pastel shades which I thought to be a bit too sugary for my taste. Clearly Ma wanted a sensational wedding and that is what she was going to get! We looked for a long time at Peter Jones, the well known department store in London, for the right kind of material and colours to satisfy us both. When I spotted this magnificent pine green among the many swatches of silks and organza my mind was settled on it straight away.

Organza being see-through, the sleeves in particular would give the gowns an air of lightness despite the dark colour. They would make a wonderful and elegant contrast to the ivory of the bridal gown. To my surprise Maggie was happy even with this controversial choice of colour, which was almost revolutionary for the sixties. I could hardly believe my luck. Weeks and weeks of creative work later the long awaited moment had arrived when all four of us could finally slip into our organza dreams, ready to enter the magical stage!

The bridesmaids' mothers had arrived to help them get dressed. Maggie insisted in helping me with my gown. She had worked for weeks getting it just right, had altered it twice because of my weight loss. She was not going to take any risks with it being less than perfectly fitted and my veil to be attached to my hair just so. The front of it was to cover my face as I walked into the church on the arm of my father. It was to be lifted by Richard after we had taken our vows when the vicar was going to tell him that he may now kiss his bride!

Just before Maggie and I went upstairs, my parents, brother and my girl-friend Ursula from Germany arrived from their hotel rooms in town. The tension was building up. I flung my arms around my mother and then left them to their fate as by then the excitement of everything had pushed me into a state of strange detachment as if I were a top spinning at incredible speed in my own universe, barely noticing the action all around me in the real world.

Probably Papa was given last minute instructions on his role in the ceremony and Dad was told to brew some more of his delicious coffee for everyone who wasn't busy upstairs. Maggie had known exactly how much time to allow for getting dressed. After all, she had a lot of experience with this kind of occasion.

When I was kitted out to her exacting standards it was precisely the right time to leave for church. The house sounded strangely quiet as I descended the stairs when suddenly my mother ran up towards me, looking agitated and nervous, quite unlike her normal self.

"Oh, Brigitte. Da bist Du endlich! – There you are at last. I feared I might not find you." She only glanced briefly at my dress. Just searched anxiously for my eyes and grasped my hands with both of hers.
"Mutti, wie gefalle ich Dir? Ist mein Kleid nicht wunderbar?" How do I look? Isn't my gown wonderful?"
The tension softened in her face and she agreed that I did indeed look wonderful but I could see there was something urgently pressing on her mind.
"What is it, Mutti?" I had become slightly anxious by this stage.
"Nun, mein Kind," she said with a gasp of relief welling up from her heart. " You know I have never interfered with your life in any way nor ever given you any advice. But I want to give you one today and before you take this momentous step." There was a long pause. I waited pensively. But then it shot out of her: "Liebe Deine Schwiegermutter! Love your mother-in-law!"
Her dark brown eyes bored deeply into mine and she squeezed my hands even more tightly to emphasize how important these words of advice were to her. A mother's last words to a departing daughter. She sighed heavily and I could see the relief on her face that she had managed to catch me in the nick of time to snatch these last few seconds on the stairs with me to say her good-bye before she lost me to my new life in this foreign land and this foreign family.
My heart ached for her as I realized much more intensely the sacrifice my parents were making for me, how mixed their feelings must be, feelings of joy but also of fear for my future and my wellbeing and I flung my arms around her and hugged her warmly.

"Oh, Mutti, Mutti! You must not worry about that one bit. I do really, really love her already!"

With relief she took my left elbow ready to help me down the remainder of the stairs followed by Maggie who was holding the long train of my dress. I was mighty glad Maggie did not understand German and that this touching intimate moment had been preserved for the two of us alone. We gave each other a knowing smile. My parents had never been the over- emotional types. Hugging and kissing was not part of my upbringing, but this smile said what the missing words would have done had they been spoken, that we cared deeply for one another and our welfare.

My father was standing by the front door which led into the garden, looking more than a bit impatient:
"Komm, Mutti. They are waiting for you. Komm schnell!"
And he rushed out to meet my parents-in-law who had a car waiting to take them and Mutti the few hundred yards to the church.

These days my father was not a man of many smiles any more. Life had treated him very harshly and the loving smiles I remembered from the few visits he had made to us as a young soldier on leave had all but disappeared. Not so now. As I entered the sitting room where he had been waiting for me by the door to the garden, his taught and nervous face relaxed into a gentle smile, one of admiration and, yes, approval. I saw he was searching for words and the right ones simply did not seem to come. Nerves, I suspected. His smile did not stop though and instead of saying anything, he kept nodding with ever more warmth in his eyes, nods of approval, making words completely unnecessary.

Maggie was still floating agitatedly around me, straightening the veil, opening up the full back skirt so that the strait front skirt was shown off to best effect for my father's appreciation. As if he had any idea of fashion! But he did know his daughter did him proud and I think it lessened some of the tension he was feeling. He had never expected to have such a pivotal role at his daughter's wedding. In Germany it was not the custom to walk your daughter down the aisle and to hand her over to her new husband. The bridal couple always took that walk together. Therefore, performing this task was a slightly unnerving experience for him. He looked anxiously at his wrist watch:
"We have three more minutes before we go to the car. It's already waiting but we must not be too early either so that Richard's parents and Mutti have enough time to take their seats in the church. We must not rush, Brigitte. Be patient!"
His right hand, fingers spread out, pushed against an invisible bouncing ball at waist height, indicating to keep it calm.

"Oh, Papa, let's at least start out and watch the girls get into their taxi. I want to see them in their beautiful gowns. Look at Maggie bossing the little one! I hope she is not upsetting her! She is only little!"

But no, the tiny pale face smiled at me from inside the car as she saw me walk up the path towards the gate and my waiting taxi. My excitement grew with every step.

The tension inside me was heightened by seeing the village green totally empty. Not a single person was walking there, or dogs crossing it chasing a ball. The village street to the right of it seemed unusually deserted as well for this time of the day. There was a kind of eerie silence surrounding us and the Green beyond, similar to the atmosphere just seconds before a theatre curtain rises. One has waited for weeks or even months to see this performance or hear this opera. A famous star is taking the lead. The anticipation has lived with you for a long time and now, now the moment has arrived! There is electrical tension in the air.

When Maggie had helped to dress me earlier, I was able to look sideways through the window and across the Green watching the many festively dressed wedding guests stream towards the church, gesticulating while talking excitedly, laughing or smiling. All had a certain spring in their step. There was a sense of elation on the Green. It was lovely for me to watch, elevating the thrill of it all.

I was being prepared for the high point of the day, separate from the guests out there and yet not separate. Like peeping behind a curtain to get a glimpse of the performance about to start.

Everything outside was vibrant and alive, an ever changing scene of ladies in elegant dresses and hats, gentlemen in their morning suits and children festooned in pretty smocks and with ribbons in their hair. Boys in smart blazers and long trousers. One of them even wore a boater.

All this colourful life had now converged into the church and the Green in front of it was swept clean. A virgin stillness enveloped the scene and I was glad I did not have to walk through it but was driven the 200 or 300 yards to the gate of the church which looked out onto the village Street.

Gayle was the last to get into the car and she looked stunning. Gayle was a beautiful young girl, dark-haired with slightly olive coloured skin. My fear, the dark green colour might not suit her skin was quite unfounded. If anything, it complemented the shade of her skin. Hopefully it meant that she, too, was happy with the way she looked and would enjoy the glowing glances of surprise and approval from the waiting guests. It was important to me that she should feel special, too, and get as much admiration as was her due. And watching her now I felt certain she would.

The sun shone still as brightly as earlier in the day, the air was balmy and warm. My heart began to pound as the car set off for the church. At last the moment had arrived when I was turned into a princess once again. This time not being the little war- time princess handed from arm to arm and from lap to lap by my lovely American soldiers but to be carried splendidly in a gleaming black taxi decorated with streamers of cream ribbons and matching flowers and with my father sitting beside me holding my trembling hand; the grown up princess being driven to her wedding and to her husband to be. I was delirious with happiness. Life was very wonderful indeed! And so very exciting!

I savoured every second of this glorious feeling. I was in love with Richard, was in love with life. And I loved both my new parents-in-law. Indeed, miraculously and unexpectedly, my entire life had turned into one of love and well-being.

Chapter Nine

Our lives had reverted to fear back in Heiddorf. The elation whizzing through the air from house to house and man to man, to woman, to child had been so exhilarating that when the American soldiers had gone the disappointment was crushing. For me, watching the stooped posture of resignation of the adults walking back into their houses or returning to their work in the fields turned into a terrifying fear, which clawed itself to every fibre of my little body. It took hold of me like an eagle's grip of his innocent prey that he had caught in an unsuspected nose dive. Back we were in a state of cruel uncertainty which even the arms of our mother could not assuage. Nor could kind Herr and Frau Rose, nor their lovely animals or their milk maids. This time we were all in it together, suffering the same grip of fear. The war might be over, but what would the future hold for us? Who would arrive next? No one could tell. "Please, God, not the Russians! Anyone but them! Please God, please!"

In comparison to Germany, Russia was a backward country. Historically though, it was a country Germans feared, especially the East Prussians as they were geographically the closest to this vast land with huge armies of peasant soldiers, easy to ply with alcohol and to indoctrinate by their superiors. In peace time they were kind and lovable simple people, but get them into uniforms and involve them in conflict, their love of Mother Russia could easily turn them into the most brutal, savage army. East Prussians had experienced this during previous conflicts, under Frederick the Great in the Seven Year War (1756 – 1763) and again during WW1 (1914 – 1918), when the Russians temporarily conquered parts of East Prussia before they were eventually beaten back again. During the Seven Year War the Russians had occupied the town of my birth for four years.

As it was the East Prussians who had experienced their brutal fury more than any other German province, the fear they had unleashed in them was deeply rooted in their psyche and we children had sensed this dread of the Russians as soon as it looked likely that they might overrun East Prussia once more.

As intensely as I remember this fear as quickly did it abate, at least for us children. Whatever may happen or not happen in the outside world, the world on the farm had to continue along the same routine. Everyone had a job to do and this fact alone was a great diversion from inner turmoil. Mutti spent more and more time helping in the fields, mainly weeding the potato fields, a particularly hard job if you weren't used to farmhand labour. Later, when the first new potatoes were ready to harvest, we children were asked to help as well. Everything had to be done by hand in those days. Still, we actually enjoyed collecting all those luscious looking potatoes, some big, some small and selecting them to be put into different baskets, according to their size. Everyone on the farm was involved in this task. There was a lot of chatter and laughter and I loved being part of it.

A few weeks on and the corn grew taller and stronger. Werner and I had never seen corn being grown before and to watch the changes in colour and growth never lost its fascination for me. Oh, for the wonderful smell of it when you walked along the edge of a corn field to pick corn flowers or red poppies to take home to mother! Nothing could compare with it and I roamed around the open fields a great deal that first summer, sometimes with Werner or my cousins but often alone. I loved being close to nature, being able to watch the bees and butterflies, listen to the humming of birds and flies, lying in the grass and watching the blue sky and the floating soft clouds above me. The freedom after life in the town was a great excitement and compensated for being friendless, an unwanted refugee child , far away from home.

If I didn't have many other children my own age to play with, Herr Rose's increased friendliness towards all of us made up for it, especially towards me, the little hobgoblin, who was always here, there and everywhere. I was allowed to follow him wherever he went, just watching or asking if I could help, which in most cases, naturally, I couldn't. But sometimes he let me lend a hand with something easy. Perhaps holding a gate open, feeding the chickens, bringing some hay for the horses to feed even though this job was more a hindrance than a help. But he allowed me to think that my little help was of real value to him. So I became fonder and fonder of him and it appeared these feelings were mutual. He still never spoke much, just a faint smile from time to time and a silent tolerance of this little weasel frolicking around his legs, except when he was in the court yard with the open cart and horses. Then I kept well away. Horses still made me nervous. On one occasion I got nearly hit by one as I ran behind it crossing over to the other side and being much too close. Not having grown up on a farm, I was not aware of the danger and got scolded badly. "Don't ever do that again!" And I didn't. Made huge circles around horses from then on and gave them the respect they deserved while at the same time never losing my fear of them.

This fear increased one evening when Herr Rose was feeding both horses in their stable. They were kept in one box with each of them having their own feeding trough, separating their part of the box from the entrance walk alongside the stable block.

The magnificent white horse was closest to the door and got his food first, brownie was further down waiting behind his trough. As usual I was looking for something to watch and ran towards the stable to join them. The "Schimmel" was starting to eat his food and Herr Rose was just pouring the grain into brownie's trough when I reached the entrance to have a peep. I remember eating something special, I think an apple (a rare treat) and was therefore particularly happy and excited, jumping from one leg to the other in a kind of dance, singing and intermittently sucking at my apple to spin out the pleasure of this delight when suddenly, Schimmel 's head pushed over the trough and his teeth snapped angrily into my left shoulder. The instant I felt his hot, snorting breath behind my left ear, I threw myself to the ground, screaming hysterically which did not exactly settle "the beast", rather made him more angry and trying harder to reach down towards me as I lay petrified and writhing on the floor, envisaging Schimmel jumping over his trough to make mince meat of me. Was this how I was going to die?

"Mutti! Mutti! Hilfe, Hilfe!!" But it was Herr Rose who came to the rescue. With great skill and strength he managed to push Schimmel's viciously fighting head up and back over the trough, holding him sufficiently still for me to wriggle myself along the floor towards the safety of the door, trembling, shaking with fright and still screaming my head off while attempting to get up to run inside the house for comfort. But Herr Rose wasn't having any of it. I deserved a good telling off and that is what I got.

"Was faellt Dir ein, hier so herumzutanzen? Du machst die Pferde nervoes und die sind kein Spielzeug! Marsch, raus!" (What on earth makes you think you can dance around like that in here? You are making the horses nervous and they are no toys. Out with you – march! And don't do this ever again!)

In all the time since our arrival at the farm I had not seen him so angry with anyone and now it was ME who had incensed his fury. Me! Who had wanted nothing better than be loved by him or at least LIKED! And now this. Was it my fault that I did not know about the sensitivity of horses? I had not grown up with them, had not intended to do Schimmel any harm. So why did he try to bite me, turning on me viciously when all I was doing was being happy. I had an apple to eat, an enormous treat, and I was innocently watching dear Herr Rose feed his beloved horses. I could not make any sense of it.

"Why? What have I done? I don't understand!" I yelped between crying. "Please don't be angry with me! I did not mean any harm!"

"You were playing too closely to his trough and he probably thought you wanted to take his food away. That's what!"

I was shattered. One minute all was cheer and happiness and then terror, pain and tears. As quickly as his temper had flared Herr Rose calmed down again, especially after he had checked out my shoulder and realized that the bite was not as bad as he had feared. There were some teeth marks but no blood - yet. Not even a teeny weeny bit or a broken shoulder! Damn! All this terror and deathly fright for merely a few teeth marks without blood when Werner had been so lucky to break an arm when he fell off the sledge! I had lost quite a bit of favour with Herr Rose and Mutti might not even feel very sorry for me either – life really wasn't fair!

In the end Mutti did, of course, take pity on me. She took me in her arms and pulled me up onto her lap while she was singing to sooth me with her beautiful voice. Singing together with her were then and always remained thereafter the most treasured memories of my childhood relationship with my mother. I could not have asked for anything better. Nestling so close to her body was all I could wish for and everything I needed. Life was well again. Werner soon stopped mocking me – "Girls!" – Herr Rose was kind and smiling gently and Frau Rose got out some extra sausage for our bread at supper time, a real treat! Everyone was my friend again – except Schimmel. He had taught me to be thoroughly scared of horses and I remained shy of them for the rest of my life.

Chapter Ten

In my memory, the next momentous event of that summer soon followed. By August the corn had ripened in the fields and had been harvested. I was out there again either picking left-over cornflowers from the edge of fields or looking for mushrooms in the adjoining meadow in which the cows normally grazed. I was not quite alone this time. Who was with me I can no longer remember, probably one or two of my cousins with whom we had fled from Prussia and who were also still living on the other side of the village. So we usually met up with them when we were roaming around the edge of the village, mainly looking for something to eat rather than to play.

It was a glorious summer's day with lots of sunshine. I remember that we were happy as could be. As usual I had spent some time away from the others, lying by the edge of my favourite field, breathing in the scent of the cropped corn, gazing at the bright blue sky and dreaming little girls' dreams – with the buzz of bees and the flutter of butterflies around me. It was afternoon and very peaceful when, with shocking suddenness, I heard my brother's voice from a far distance. He was shouting something incomprehensible. He came from the direction of the village and was waving his arms in the air like a mad thing, while running as fast as his legs could take him towards us in the field. His shouts became more agitated when he saw that we were staring at him but not moving, since we could not hear exactly what he was on about. The way he was running towards us suggested, however, some sort of alarm.
Then we heard it:
"The Russians!
The Russians are coming! Come home at once! The Russians are coming, they are nearly here. Come home! Come home as fast as you can! Quickly, quickly! Don't just stand there!"

His face was contorted with fear, he was nearly in tears and we realized instantly the urgency of our safe return home. When fear sits in your belly you can run faster than normally and we ran as if a vengeful bull was chasing us, all the time closing in on us. Werner yelped terribly, gasping for breath and tumbled down once or twice with exhaustion from all that running without stopping for breath. But we made it home somehow and in time before Herr Rose had locked all the doors to the house, having made sure the horses were safely in their stable. The cows were left in the fields, at least until milking time. But they were not really our concern. We just wanted to be safe with mother, safe in the house from the beastly Russians who might do God knows what to us.

As I explained before, fear of the Russians was endemic throughout the entire population of Germany. As six and seven year olds in 1945 we did not understand why this was so, only that it was thus. Everyone had been absolutely euphoric when the Americans arrived. And they were enemies, too. We learned later that the English and French had also been fighting us but none of those were dreaded. On the contrary, everyone prayed we might be freed by them. The Russians, however, were an enemy dreaded on par with a sentence of death. Many, many years later, not until I had lived in England for quite a few years, did I begin to understand why the ferocity of the Russian revenge and the fear of this revenge was putting the wrath of God into everyone. And now this wrath was drawing near!

Our army had committed unspeakable crimes during the invasion of Russia and, little by little, stories had trickled out when soldiers had returned home for visits. Soldiers, who had become traumatised by the horrors they had been forced to commit. Not all Germans were born butchers by any means. At times, to stay silent to spare their relations grief was simply too much for them. However, back then, in the summer of 1945, we children knew nothing of the atrocities committed by our own army in occupied Russia and I do not think that even our mother knew the full extent of what had happened there.

But we knew the fear these terrible deeds had created, knew the panic on everyone's face when the word "Russians" was uttered and it had instilled a terrifying fear in us.

Herr and Frau Rose, with their black cat for comfort, shunted themselves into their kitchen while we fled into our bedroom with Mutti's arms around us like an eagle protecting her young. There we cowered on her bed awaiting our fate. Werner on one side of her, me on the other, we snuggled up against her warm, soothing body as closely as we could, not realizing that she might be far more afraid than anyone else in the house. I do not know how long we waited; it seemed like forever. Would we live to see the next day? We really believed that we might not. Yet, no one said it out loud.

After that fearful night in our mother's arms all other memories of the entry of the Russians into our village have faded. I only remember that they did arrive and, worse still, that they stayed! At the time I was still much too young to realize exactly what had happened to Germany after the capitulation, only that the Americans had arrived to liberate us and then disappeared as quickly as they had come and that this meant the Russians might eventually take their place. Why everyone feared this would happen remained a mystery to me.

Years later I learned (probably at school) about the famous Yalta Conference held in February 1945 where the leaders of the United States, England and the Soviet Union had met to discuss, in anticipation of the German Capitulation, how the defeated Germany should be
divided : which parts of the eastern areas should be given to Poland in exchange for other areas of Poland that the Soviet Union had incorporated into their own republic. Later, in July of the same year, the discussed demarcation lines for each occupying zone were officially recognized and the Oder-Neisse Line confirmed as the new border between Germany and Poland. The territories east of this border, like Pomerania, Silesia, Bohemia and West and East Prussia went to Poland. Only the upper part of East Prussia was annexed from the larger southern part and given to the Soviet Union to grant them access to the Baltic Sea. This was the part of Prussia my family came from and which we had been lucky enough to escape from in January 1945. A vast number of the population, especially those living in the country and owning horses and carts, had tried to escape via the frozen Baltic to reach Sweden. Most of them drowned when being attacked from the air, thousands and thousands of them. Others simply walked all the way to central Germany in deep snow and exceptionally harsh temperatures and with almost nothing to eat.

One of my friends whom I met much later when living in England, was born somewhere along such a route. Her mother had already walked with her two brothers as part of a trek for many weeks, when Heiderose was born , literally on a snow covered dirt track somewhere in Bohemia. A lot of these refugees aimed for Dresden, a city large enough to give them shelter, so they thought. They had trekked through deep snow and ice without much food or shelter for more than two months before reaching the safety of the city. Tragically, they could not have aimed for a worse place in which to hide for survival. During the night of February 13th 1945 the Allied Forces attacked Dresden from the air in one of the most brutal and sustained bombardments anywhere during that war. It destroyed practically every building of the inner city and killed approximately 30,000 inhabitants, many of these were the refugees still living in the open streets, always hoping to be rescued by the Western forces since the end of the war was nigh, very nigh indeed. Instead of being liberated, they were slaughtered.

The commander-in-chief of the American battalion arriving at Heiddorf that certain May morning clearly did not realize the river Elbe had been designated as the border between the Soviet occupied area and the one having been assigned to British administration. I assume that the general adult population of Mecklenburg and our village must have known by the end of the war that their area was going to be administered by the Soviet army and thus the Russian government. But we children knew nothing of those assumptions. Therefore we spent the weeks between the withdrawal of the Americans and the arrival of the Russians in blissful ignorance of the horrors to come. They dawned, little by little, as contact with the new occupying force became unavoidable and life on the farm was no longer what it had once been.

Chapter Eleven

The farm house, having a large and attractively furnished but unused drawing room, became the headquarters for the Red Army soldiers in our village. The commanding officer, a young, tall and very handsome dark haired man (even my six year old little brain registered his good looks at once!) was initially quite pleasant. He spoke a few German words, just enough to ensure that we would understand his orders, especially Frau Rose who would now have to feed yet another mouth and sometimes more than one. Food had been rationed for many years and continued to be rationed after the war was over since most of what was produced by the farmers in the Soviet Zone was confiscated by the Soviet administration, together with everything else useful they could lay their hands on. This plunder of an already deprived land was called "rightful reparation payments". How dear Frau Rose managed to get us all fed I do not know, but although the meals were simple and not overly plentiful, we did not starve while under her care.

As mentioned earlier, the officer was not the devil incarnate we had expected him to be. He even ate with us during the initial few days. Until everything changed. Perhaps his job of keeping his battalion in check turned out to be more difficult than he had expected. Or else other problems were weighing him down. But soon after his arrival he started to drink and sessions of dreadful shouting and screaming at other soldiers, who were coming and going, became the order of the day. There was never a minute of peace in the house. Werner and I were able to escape into the yard and to the animals or the farm workers, never now into the fields or woods and meadows where we had roamed so freely before. Drunk and brutal Russian soldiers might be anywhere. Even the farm was not necessarily safe, but at least here there were plenty of our own people keeping a watch over us. The adults did not find it so easy to get accustomed to the goings on. Their house was no longer their own. First they had to share it with us, now with half of the Russians in the village. Or at least that is what it felt like since orderlies kept coming and going, shouting reports and receiving noisy and often angry orders from their commander.

Night time was the only part of the day when a little calm descended on the house for the officer left every evening straight after supper to the only hot spot in the village,

the local pub! On his return he was singing and shouting, slamming doors in his drunken stupor, waking the whole house and terrifying us children. But worse was to come.

After the first two or three nights at "our" house he was no longer content to sink onto his camp bed in the drawing room which was also his office. He had not failed to notice that our mother was young and attractive and without the protection of a husband. He was now the boss of the village and what he wanted he was going to get. And what he wanted was right here in the house – our mother! Quite what he wanted from her we children did not comprehend. Life had not educated us in this respect. We had endured many ghastly experiences in our short lives, none of them had anything to do with the relationship between man and woman behind closed doors. We knew about kissing, but that was the extent of our sex education. We also knew, instinctively, that Mutti would never want to be kissed by this loathsome creature, handsome though he was when in a sober state. Werner said he had seen him trying to embrace Mutti and kiss her when she was alone in the house, peeling potatoes in the kitchen. She fought him furiously and he had got very angry but stopped molesting her when Frau Rose walked into the room.

From then onwards Mutti was no longer safe from his advances. He grabbed her whenever he could.

"Komm, Frau. Du mich brauchen!" he lulled in his broken German ("Come here, woman. You need me"!).

All adults on the farm tried their best to ensure she was on her own as little as possible as our mother appeared to be the one he was obsessed with. When his drinking increased at night he got fiercer in his attempts to get hold of her. We were very frightened for our beautiful mother. He would rattle on our locked bedroom door, shouting menacingly and threatening to break the door down with a hammer if we weren't willing to open it voluntarily.

"Aufmachen, Frau! Sofort. Ich bin Kommandant! Aufmachen! Ich schiessen!"he shouted in his pidgin German.
("Open the door, woman. At once. I am commander. Open up. I shoot!")

Poor Mutti was in a terrible state. Her lovely brown eyes wide open in horror while strenuously thinking how to escape the clutches of this drunken brut and also trying to comfort us as we were both in hysterics by then. If he threatened to shoot, he might actually do so. You never knew with these Russians. Stories of trigger-happy Russians were abounding. Stories of mass as well as individual shootings had followed us ever since we had fled Prussia. Although most atrocities had been committed by primitive soldiers from the depth of the Russian countryside, even officers had been known to forget their status, especially when they were drunk and obsessed with their desire to rape. Clearly this man, too, was no exception and his bullish behaviour petrified us almost beyond endurance.

At the pit of her fear, our mother had an idea. Her eyes fell on our wardrobe which was standing fairly close to the door. It was a heavy piece of furniture but the combined effort of the three of us managed to push it in front of the door, blocking the entrance in case he would succeed in opening the lock and hammer or shoot his way into the room. The extra blockade would give her more time to jump out of the window to hide, hopefully, somewhere in the other farm buildings. His threats and angry shouts continued for a long time. Eventually he gave up and slouched into his room where he must have fallen unconsciously to the ground as we heard a loud thud followed by total silence for the rest of the night.

We, however, did not fall asleep, not for the entire night. While Mutti tried to calm us down there was an urgent knock on the window pane. Herr Rose beckoned Mutti to open the window. Not surprisingly, he had heard everything that had gone on and he told Mutti to escape out of the window and into their bedroom in case the officer should attempt to get hold of her again. They would leave their window open every night for her safety. Hopefully we youngsters would be left unharmed. Mutti had to make use of this offer many times while the officer was stationed in our house. The wardrobe was pushed in front of the door night after night (Herr Rose helped with this job leaving via the bedroom window afterwards). But night after night, the drunkard tried his luck and night after night he tried in vain!
Sometimes, in his fury, when he threw himself with all his physical might against the door, we could hear the wood creak as if it was to break apart any second and our little bodies stiffened with terror. We wanted to scream but could not get a sound out of our throttled throats as if we had strangely turned into stone. These were the worst nights I remember during the early occupation of the village.

Many hundreds of thousands of women got raped by Soviet soldiers during and after the war – thanks to our wonderful hosts our mother was spared this horrific experience even though she had lived with the threat of it for a very long time.

The commander stayed on the farm for several more frightening weeks. In his drunken state he continued trying to assault our mother. Yet, the next day, having slept off his stupor, he often appeared quite normal, even kind of friendly as if he had no idea of his behaviour the night before.

Needless to say he was not the only one attempting to rape or succeeding in raping the women of the village – it was a common place occurrence preceding the capitulation, as well as for some considerable time afterwards throughout the Soviet occupied areas. Precisely how many girls and women, young as well as old, were raped was hard to establish, but the assumed figures ranged as high as one to two million.

By June 1945, I learned later, all four military occupation powers had assumed the administration of their zones. The commander, therefore, had not truly been in charge of our district and probably just needed to find accommodation for his soldiers while awaiting orders from his superiors about the fate of his battalion, whether they were to stay in Germany or to return home to their families in deepest Russia. Whatever was decided about them, our "guest" eventually left together with his battalion, never to be seen again, Thank God indeed!! At last we could all get some proper sleep again and also had a little more to eat since the officer no longer needed to be fed from farm produce which the farmer and his wife were allowed to keep for our consumption. Any other farm produce, meaning the bulk of it, had to be given to the Soviet administration to feed the general population of their zone and their army personnel and also, as part of the reparations the Soviet Union was requesting.

The plunder of agricultural produce and the disassembly of remaining German industry continued for years afterwards and hit the people of the Soviet occupied zone harder than the German population in the western zones as Russia had sustained greater losses during the war than the other allied countries and therefore made hugely larger demands for reparation.

In the summer of 1945 these measures were still in the future; yet they were nonetheless times of extreme hardship. Each farm was assessed as to how much produce they had to produce and return to central administration. If they managed to grow more corn or get more milk from their cows, then they were lucky. We had enough to eat but it was only just sufficient to keep us going. For as long as we were on the farm we thankfully did not have to go to bed with that awful gnawing feeling in our stomachs which made going to sleep so very difficult.

Later on we would often think back of these days at the farm as the glory days in our new world. We had some simple but nourishing food every day, the protection of Herr Rose and the kindness and care of his wife, warm hearted Frau Rose. I remember looking upon them with as much affection as I had felt for my maternal grandparents in Peitschendorf or those in Goldap.

Chapter Twelve

Unfortunately, not long after the Russian soldiers had left, our time on the farm came to an end. First though, in early September, it was finally my turn to start school. I was 6 ½ years old by then and more than ready to have a crack at learning to write and read.

My brother had started school way back in Prussia for a very short time and continued his first year at school soon after our arrival at Heiddorf. That must have been quite difficult for him as the other children all knew each other while he and one or two other refugee children entered the class half-way through their first year, having missed out most of the first half as a result of the flight from Prussia.

By custom, the first day at school was always a day of huge celebrations for the family. You wore your best clothes, ribbons in your freshly washed hair and clean white socks and highly polished shoes, if you were fortunate enough to own any! And I believe I still did – then!

When you came out of your first lessons your parents or, perhaps, even your grandparents were waiting outside for you with a very large cornet shaped card board box in bright colours full of sweets, cake, biscuits or other heavenly delights. Usually, you then went off to a photographer who would take a photo of you holding this fantastic giant "Tuete" and proudly carrying your "Ranzen" (school satchel) on your back.

I had neither. My first day at school was so uneventful that I cannot even remember it.

Firstly, there was no money to buy either satchel or sweetie bag and secondly, if you had any money, you were not able to buy any of these things anyway. The shops, such as they existed, were absolutely barren. If anyone of my year had a satchel, it would have been bought well in advance of the event, perhaps one or two years before the end of the war. I probably went to school with nothing in my hands and came out with nothing as well – other than my newly found enthusiasm for the mysteries of learning. Of one thing I am sure though. My mother would have made certain I looked absolutely spotless, with my cream coloured ribbon in my hair; my hands clean, nails cut, clean white socks and polished shoes. Mutti was the nurturing mother par excellence. Somehow she always managed to ensure that we looked pristine even if we only had the utmost minimum of clothing to wear. Cleanliness and friendliness were her maxim. It helped us enormously in surviving those early years in Heiddorf where the native population would often be quite hostile towards the refugees who had been forced upon them.

While we lived with farmer Rose and his wife, however, we did not suffer too much in this respect. But as I have already hinted, that period came to a very sad and abrupt end some time after my schooling had begun. If our existence had been challenging for Mutti up till now it would become an almighty struggle for our daily bread after our forceful expulsion from the farm.

The reason we had to leave and find a place of our own was due to a most sickening and tragic circumstance, one which still distresses me to this day (and this is more than sixty years on!) when I think about it. Having been so horrifically tragic, the memory of what happened to kind and loving Herr and Frau Rose still returns to haunt me at unexpected moments.

It turned out they had a son who had survived the war serving in the army and he was about to return home. To my knowledge, he had never been spoken of while we were living with the Roses. Mutti never truly explained to us why we had to move out of the house and find our own place to live. Was it through shock that the events around this move are extremely blurred in my recall? Was the room we occupied needed for the returning son or was there some other reason for our departure? The true reason may never have been discussed with us children or else I would be clear of it in my mind, even after this long period of time. Yet I do remember very well that the son returned to his parents fairly soon after our moving out. Everything else that happened afterwards I know from hearsay, but the gist of it would definitely be true. Rumours spread through the village like wild fires. People whispered to each other in hushed tones, stopping abruptly when us kids got anywhere near earshot of them. Still, we found out in the end. Pretending to be steeped deep in our play and not looking at them when they gossiped, we picked up the sorry tale soon enough. This is what was spread about:

After having worked for his father for a short while, the son wanted to take over the running of the farm by himself while his father was not yet ready to succumb to his demand. Not long thereafter I heard that the son had denounced his father to the Russians, claiming his father had been a Nazi and was now vehemently anti communism. It worked: both parents were imprisoned and the son installed to run the farm. Whether the farm was confiscated and the son allowed to manage it or whether ownership of it had actually been transferred to the son, I'm not certain. But does it matter? What kind of a son was he, betraying his own parents in such a bestial way? How was it possible that a kind and caring couple like the Roses could have produced such a monstrous son? Five agonizing years of waiting for his safe return, full of hopes of building a new future together with him until, perhaps, he would have found a wife and was ready and able to take over his inheritance when his parents were getting too old to run the farm themselves any longer. That was the traditional way farms were handed down to the next generation.

Not so for this young man, this fiend. The entire village was shaken to the bone. No one could remember a scandal of this kind ever having occurred in this village before. Mutti and I were devastated for we had really liked this couple, had become very fond of them. How could any son live with such a betrayal on his conscience? Such callous selfishness surely could not be the result of brutalities seen and executed during the war!? It had to have been lodged somewhere deep inside the man right from the start . The hunger and turmoil of those times may have contributed to lingering brutality coming to the fore in him. Soon after this event we were to realize, however, that communism focused on such flawed people. They were an ideal prey for their cause.

When I had grown older and while attending school lessons we were certainly encouraged by the communist elite of the area to spy on our parents and to report them to the head of our school – no pupil ever did so to my knowledge, but the pressure of telling what our parents said at home and what they did in their spare time never abated despite the lack of success during all those years my family lived in Heiddorf. Perhaps the case of the Roses had helped to ensure that no other parent in the village was ever going to suffer such unthinkably bestial betrayal again. Not a single member of the village was left untouched by this traumatic event. The shock waves spread like a bush fire and the memory of this catastrophic family drama became firmly embedded in everyone's mind. The communists had achieved this one coup but at the cost of extreme resistance to their cause for as long as we lived there and probably for much, much longer.

Chapter Thirteen

How Mutti managed to find our new home when the village was already overburdened with other refugees puzzles me. But she did. Perhaps the Roses had helped her since they knew everyone and everyone else knew them. It was not much of a home, only one room under the eaves. All three of us had shared one room at the farm as well. So we were not complaining, except this time the room had to serve as sitting cum bedroom and kitchen as well. We had moved to a plain straightforward looking house of red brick with two front entrances. The major part of the house belonged to a young family with two children of roughly our age. The smaller part of the house on the right was occupied by the elderly grandmother. She also had a back entrance to her part which meant that we were given the front entrance as our own. From there we were able to easily go up the stairs to our little room under the roof without having to disturb the grandmother. At the end of the entrance hall was a door leading to her kitchen. That door was permanently locked so that she had her privacy and we had ours. I remember feeling so proud to have our own smart front door which we did not have to share with anyone.

There was a small wood and coal burning stove in the room which was also our cooker! It was only large enough for one pan which meant we had never anything other to eat than vegetable soup or fried potatoes. These fries were really disgusting as Mutti had no fat of any kind for frying. Potatoes or the odd fried egg had to be fried in Ersatz coffee. Ersatz meaning "substitute". No one was able to purchase real coffee, only a substitute made from roasted corn. It tasted awful, but, of course, we only knew this from the adults as we children only drank tap water or, if we were very lucky, some milk. But the adults complained a lot about the awful tasting coffee they had to drink then as well as using it instead of frying fat.

At first all three of us had to sleep in one bed as the room could not accommodate more than one. After some time when the owners of the house realized that we were clean and decent folk they did all they could to help us extend our living space. They arranged for the sloping roof space on either side of the room to be made habitable. Two doors were created, one on each wall leading to the sloped roof area and a small window each built into the gabled wall so that we could use the eaves as proper small rooms with sufficient daylight. One area became a bedroom for my brother and myself. The other was turned into a kitchen with a real cooker, if a small one. Mutti's bed stayed in the central room and Werner and I shared another bed in our very own new bedroom. One of us occupied the top end of the bed, the other slept at the foot end . We were thrilled with this new arrangement as we could tickle one another's feet if we felt like it and yet had the entire width of the bed on either end to ourselves. If I was angry with my brother – usually because he had been too lazy to do something   – I could indulge in my old habit of kicking his legs in fury just like I had done at home in Insterburg when we sat at our own little table having our meals. No wonder I earned myself the nickname "the little beast"! But it was said lovingly with a twinkle in the eye. Expressions like: "Na, Gitta! Kommt das kleine Biest wieder zum Vorschein?" (Well, Gitta. Is the little beast coming to the fore again?). Or "Schau Dir mal das kleine Biestchen an!" (Look, there's our darling little beast again) made me realize I was being chastised , yet in no hurtful way. Everyone knew very well the little beast in me only reared its head when there was some justification. In actual fact, I loved my brother very much and sharing a bed with him was really fun and brought us closer rather than the contrary. So now having our own little room meant that things were definitely looking up for us.

The downside of our new home was the lavatory. It was outside at the end of the garden area which we were allowed to use. It had been hastily erected for us refugees and was, of course, a small wooden hut just large enough to accommodate a bench with a hole cut into the seat. Underneath this cut out stood a large bucket for our excrement. There was no lid, of course, and the smell was not exactly inviting. There was also hardly ever any paper. Toilet paper was not available to buy for a long time in the Eastern part of Germany and we had no money to buy newspapers either which, when available, were cut into very small squares to be used as toilet paper. In the summer we used large leaves we had collected from the roadside. In the winter we often ended up with dirty underpants!

Before you got to the toilet hut there was an outbuilding on the right which, among others, housed a laundry and wash room. The laundry room had to be shared with everyone living in the house. Apart from the grandmother and the young family, there were also my mother's sister and her three children, our cousins, living somewhere on the owner's side of the house. So we were practically 4 families, all using this outdoor laundry, each party on certain appointed days. A washing line ran along the entire length of the backyard, nearly always full of washing flapping in the wind to dry except on hot autumn days. Then this line was used for drying slices of apples. The young owner family had several apple trees in their garden, meaning loads of apples were usually left over, which had to be conserved for consumption during the winter season. Consumption by THEM not by us, of course.
 Since we had no bathroom, this laundry room also acted as our bathroom. There was no proper heating in there and, naturally no bath!

 However, it did have the luxury of a large wash basin with hot and cold water. Once a week we were properly scrubbed, our naked bodies shivering standing shoeless on the icy cold stone floor. My hair was also washed in that basin. Being only a pint-sized thing I had to stand on a small stool, bending my head over the sink while Mutti poured fresh water from a container over my hair. It must have been a dreadful job for poor Mutti as none of us children were meek little zombies and hated our bath times like nothing else.

Still, there was no escaping this torture. Mutti was determined not to lower her standards, never mind how difficult it was to sustain them.

Being refugees we had to prove to the villagers that we were not some kind of gypsies, but were at least as civilized as they, if not more so. The only difference being that we had lost all our possessions as well as our homeland while they had kept everything. You could say we refugees were the Germans who had to pay more than anyone else for Germany having started and lost this menacing war. The only possession no one could take away from us was our determination to prove to the world we were as good as anyone else even at this low point in our lives. Cleanliness was one way in achieving this and Mutti was not going to let us off the hook when it came to our ablutions, even if we half froze to death in the process, especially during the icy cold winters. Politeness was another one.

In this regard we must have come up to scratch, since right from the start we had good relations with the people around us. Food wise we struggled. Everyone else did, too, except, of course, the farmers of the village. Decades later, when living in England I had befriended several German women who had also fled from the east but had ended up in the Western part of Germany. They told me they had indeed been given food by the farming population who treated them with much kindness and compassion. This had not generally been the case in Mecklenburg.

Chapter Fourteen

More than fifty years later I returned to Heiddorf with an English friend by invitation of the local vicar to attend a Golden Confirmation celebration . During this visit, just as in the olden days, I did not feel any real warmth extended towards either me or the other former refugees. Later my friend Buzz and I travelled further up north to explore the lake area around the

Mueritzsee. During our tour we discovered a beautiful church in one of the pretty country towns in the area. Although it was early evening there was happy activity noise drifting towards us which drew us in. Various people were preparing chairs for a concert which we were told was going to take place later that evening, a concert entirely dedicated to Mozart.

We must have been in quite loud voice bemoaning our regret that we were unable to stay on for the concert when the vicar of the church came towards us. Presumably he had heard us mentioning that we were tourists from England, which, in those days, was still a rare occurrence. He engaged us in an animated conversation, asking us why we were there, what we had seen and what our impressions had been. One thing led to another and eventually I mentioned I had come to live in the south of Mecklenburg as a small refugee child and that this was my first return after more than fifty years. His face fell serious and he expressed genuine warm sympathy with my fate saying: "That must have been a terrible time for you. Many of my parishioners have shared their experiences as refugees with me when they felt they could trust me. The farmers of this northern part are and always have been known to be tight fisted, which must have been particularly severe during those early years after the war. I feel really sorry for you!" And then he added more quietly:" I can say this because I am not from here and have experienced their – let us say - lack of generosity at first hand myself over and over again."

I was stunned to hear this. A lifetime later nothing much had changed. The Rose family and dear "black" Johanna of whom you will hear more later clearly were exceptions to this claim. In fact, as my story reveals, over time, we befriended several more kind and helpful villagers, but most farmers of the area were the least generous and helpful; in some cases decidedly unhelpful and selfish.

So our beginnings in a home of our own were not the easiest. Poor Mutti must have had many sleepless nights with worry about her responsibility for us and with concern about how to feed and clothe us, to keep us warm and happy. She did have one good source of help, however, and that was from her relatives who lived in the same house with the young home owning family. My aunt had other relations who lived not so far away in a side street from our road. Thus we were quite a clan of displaced people, all helping one another with the different skills and contacts we had made. I don't believe my darling mother would have survived without this moral support.

Gradually though we did put down our roots. As I have mentioned earlier, our host family helped us extend our living space and at school I made friends with a girl called Gerda who lived next door to us. That was a real stroke of luck. Eventually I also befriended the family owning the house opposite us. I have always chatted very freely and in a friendly manner to everyone around me. Consequently it did not take long before I had befriended the entire family of the Moellers, husband, wife, son and their younger daughter who was a year or so older than myself. Little by little Ingetrud became an even closer friend than Gerda. Not a day went by without me running across to spend most of my spare time after school homework with Ingetrud and her family. Yet in that first summer and winter and possibly longer Werner and I were still quite lonely and only had our cousins next door to play with. The girls were even younger than I was and I did not really bond with them well.

However, there was school and I LOVED school! During my first year there and probably also during part of the next one we had no books or paper to work with, just small slate boards and chalk with no other teaching material. If any child broke their slate there was no replacement. Therefore we guarded them like our life depended on them – and indeed it did. Our slates meant education and a better future for us. I wanted to become a doctor when I was grown up. To achieve this goal I had to learn to write and read and then become the best in the form so that I could go to university. However, during my first school year I had not quite formed these ambitions. I loved school simply because I enjoyed learning. It made me immensely happy and whenever I had managed to write my alphabet just that little bit better I showed off my skill to my mother with huge pride and excitement and was so pleased to see her smile and pat me approvingly on my head.

School was not far from the pub with the large forecourt where we had arrived in January the previous year. When we still lived on the farm I had to walk along the main road as far as the pub and the school was in a road leading off to the right. Of course Mutti took me to school on my first day, but soon thereafter I had to walk by myself. Everyone did that in those days. It was expected of us to become independent as quickly as possible.

Therefore, after my first few days I usually met up with one or two other girls who lived along the main road and we marched off cheerfully together. In those days we had, of course, no television; not even a radio. As we had to leave everything but the most important clothes behind in Prussia, my brother and I had no toys either. All our entertainment came from the activities on the farm. Therefore school was the most exciting diversion of my early life. My enthusiasm for learning made me forget whether I was hungry or cold. It also helped me over my shyness, which I did have to struggle with at the beginning. Having been shunned by the village children up to that stage made me quite scared of them. They seemed way up above my station in life, coming to school with thick slices of bread and sausage to be eaten during our breaks, whereas I had nothing to eat at all. While we still lived at the farm I had at least had something for breakfast with a cup of milk. But later after our move to our nest under the roof we were left to fend for ourselves. For years it seemed I had nothing but a dry piece of bread for breakfast. As time went by there was sometimes some milk, but never any butter or sliced sausage to go with the bread. In fact, never even a second slice. Bread was so severely rationed that nobody could eat more than one slice per day.

Werner and I woke up badly starved every morning. We screamed for our slice as soon as we woke up. More often than not Mutti gave us our bread while we were still in bed! She had to keep a strict diary about who had been given the end piece of the loaf last time as we were always fighting for it. Somehow we imagined there was more bread to it. Sucking the crust extended the eating period and psychologically we felt better fed afterwards. So we regularly fought bitterly over it. Mutti never ate the end piece; she often went hungry to let us have more as we needed energy to learn, she said.

Watching the farm children parade in front of us eating their "Pausenbrot" (break snack) filled with delicious smelling sausage or cheese during our morning break was the hardest part of school life during the early years. Their mean and spiteful behaviour towards us hungry lot reflected perfectly the attitude of their farming parents towards us "invaders". If the ghastly Nazis had regarded Poles and Russians as inferior human beings (Untermenschen), some of our own people demonstrated a similar attitude towards us war victims. A lot of hatred and callousness pervaded the school yard. Not everyone gave out these vibes. Nonetheless, they were there and spoiled what should have been a carefree and happy playtime during the breaks.

Gradually the food rations were increased and we also had a sandwich to take to school. Filled with margerine, if we were lucky, never with sliced sausage or cheese. At least we finally had something of our own to bite into which stopped us ogling the other children's snacks with hungry, jealous eyes. Despite this improvement, we never felt properly satisfied for years and years. You never forget this type of hunger nor the respect for food you developed during those years.

Recently, on a trip to Berlin with an American friend of mine, we visited the Kaethe Kollwitz Museum near the Kurfuerstendamm. Kaethe Kollwitz was a painter and sculptress and the first woman artist to become a member of the German Academy of Arts. She had a very distinctive style of drawing, mainly in black chalk and only very occasionally introducing a bit of other, but always dark colour and only, if it was essential for the theme to do so. Her entire work depicted the struggle of the poor even though she herself did not come from an impoverished background. If her theme was not that of hunger or hard work on the field or in mines, she made death the main character of her story, often showing death as a figure that was alive but menacing. Sometimes he would embrace the body he was collecting, almost in a loving way. They were immensely stirring pictures, disquieting and deeply moving.

There was one picture which touched me more deeply than any of the others, powerful though they were and desperately sad and shocking. Only three figures filled the canvass, the back view of a mother, her head bent forward towards the ground in a despairing fashion and two little children, pale faced with huge hungry eyes looking up at their mother's hiding face and pulling at her long skirt in a vain effort to convey to her their extreme hunger and their lack of understanding for being starved day after day. The picture was entitled in Kaethe's own handwriting simply with one word: "Bread".
No other piece of art – and I have seen many in my life-time – has ever stirred such violent emotions in me, tears were starting to fill my eyes and I had to make a huge effort to control myself so that my friend would not notice the emotional reaction this picture had evoked inside me.

"Bread": one word, but it contained volumes of unspoken ones of thousands of starving people in Germany and probably the world over before and definitely after the First World War and then once more after the Second. My brother and I had been given at least that one slice a day; these little mites did not seem to have had any! Who had been these children with their desperate mother? Had they survived like we had done? Had they become adults, despite the obvious lack of food, and had they experienced at least a glimmer of happiness as they grew into adulthood? Of course they were merely drawn, but their situation was expressed with such a convincing sense of reality, you could be forgiven for believing they were indeed real.

"Bread" – sustenance of the ages! The lack of it: death.

However, as I said before, the acquisition of knowledge at school made up for the hunger and, in the winter, also the cold. Slowly the local children began to allow us refugees to play with them during break times and I began to have fun outside the classroom as well. By the end of my first school year I had become good friends with Gerda. We often walked home together along the dusty road where we both lived.

Chapter Fifteen

The winter of 1946 must have been the most depressing and challenging period for our poor mother as well as her sister and the other relatives who were scattered across the village. We were generally still not liked or accepted and therefore none of us got any real sustaining help from our neighbours. To keep our spirits up the grown-ups often came to our room to sing and to talk until Werner and I had to go to sleep. They would bring a log of wood or some coal because while they were with us they did not have to heat their own accommodation, just kept the cinders glowing. These evenings were very nice for everyone as we snuggled together in the more than usually warm room, everyone feeling almost happy and enjoying the company of equals –

equally poor, equally deprived of much local contact, equally concerned about our bleak looking future.

Mutti had a particularly lovely singing voice. Werner never sang along with us. Boys did not do that. Today you would say singing isn't cool for boys. How wrong he was. The music making with my mother or together with my aunt and cousins was the most uplifting experience during the drabness of our lives. It was manna for the soul if not for our stomachs. If only Werner had joined in! Much later, when he was a young man living in the West, he became an ardent fan of popular music. He even recorded his own voiceovers of the current major hits. Sadly, he never sent them off to recording agencies, as otherwise, he might have made some success with his extremely beautiful voice. Often I thought that his recordings were far better than the originals. But he could not be convinced of it. Or he lacked the confidence. For lack of confidence was the most gripping and lasting evidence of a childhood spent as a deprived refugee. Somehow we never felt quite "good enough". We may have come home with the best school reports at the end of each school year and the farmer's boy from next door might not even have been passed on to the next class, yet because of who they were we still felt strangely inadequate, almost inferior to them. For some of us, remnants of these feelings stayed with us for a very, very long time. If I am honest – in my case - until now.

Chapter Sixteen

My bridesmaids were waiting for me by the entrance to the church. They looked somewhat tense and serious. However, when I had climbed out of the taxi and Maggie had rearranged my dress and train to the perfection she desired, we all relaxed and gave each other little twinkles of encouragement. Father was positioned to take my left arm and the littlest bridesmaid, holding a basket full of rose petals and flowers, was to step out in front of me, strewing the flowers along the aisle. They were to symbolize the happy route Richard and I were going to walk together.

There was a solemn silence coming from inside the church while we were waiting for our sign to begin the procession. My mother–in-law had chosen the music to announce the entrance of the bride, "Trumpet Voluntary", a magnificent stirring piece of English Baroque music, which, together with Richard Wagner's Bridal March from his romantic opera "Lohengrin" or the Wedding March by Felix Mendelssohn-Bartholdy from his "Midsummer Night's Dream " are the most popular processional pieces of music chosen by couples for the entrance of the bride. I had plunged for the "Trumpet Voluntary" as this was totally new music for me and very stirring and appropriate. Also, I wanted to please my new family and their friends. England was going to be my future homeland and I wanted to start on a good footing by delving into English culture rather than hanging onto German traditions. However, I did feel it was essential to make my dear parents feel that they, too, were an integral and important part of the event and I chose the hymn "Glorious things of thee are spoken", among others to be sung during the service. This hymn is sung to the melody by Haydn, which is also used as the German National Anthem. Thus my parents could hum the melody and enjoy the beauty of it.

The church did not have a trumpeter but a good organ and we were now waiting for the first sounds of this instrument, a sign the procession was due to start. While my father had shown no nervousness up to this point, I could feel a slight tremble of his arm now, while I myself was suddenly quite calm and self-possessed. The short part of my veil covered my face but it was still possible to see whether my smile showed signs of strain or a radiance of happiness. Mine was certainly the latter.

At last the first organ notes were ringing majestically through the tiny church – our moment of entrance had arrived! We had been instructed to walk slowly to allow the congregation a good look of the bride and her entourage. Papa and I had practised this walk only briefly the day before. To my surprise we walked in complete harmony the short walk to the place where my groom was waiting for me, supported by his Best Man Julian, who was standing next to him. And who was in charge of the ring!

I did not look at any of the guests in particular, just at Richard whose tall, slim figure was standing there, still looking straight ahead to the altar rather than turning around and looking at his beautiful bride walking towards him. I was just starting to get worried when he did, at last, turn around giving me his well-loved nervous smile, yet looking pale and pensive.

He cut an extremely handsome figure in his morning suit, elegant and aristocratic, but shy and nervous. His hair was greasy – he had clearly forgotten to wash it! Another sign he must have spent the three nights in the house of his Best Man's parents in a state of apprehension and nervousness. I felt disappointed about the hair, but also felt sorry for the boy for the state of anxiety he must have been in leading up to this moment. I wished I could have hugged and cosseted him the way I used to whenever his depressions took a hold of him. But we had to perform and I just hoped that seeing me so radiant and happy would somewhat calm him and steady his nerves. I searched for his hand to give it a squeeze. We had known each other long enough for me to know the inner turmoil he often suffered. Yet I also knew a mere stroke of my hand could make all the difference to his composure. And I hoped not to fail.

When we looked at each other to say our vows, his smile was beginning to lose its tightness, slowly turning into the soft, diffused smile I love so much. He had found himself again, all was well. As the vicar began the famous words:
"Do you, Richard, take this woman to be your wedded wife, to have and to hold, from this day forward, for better for worse, for richer for poorer, in sickness and in health......." His smile was steadily deepening and yet radiating seriousness. Here we were making a final and total commitment to each other. Nothing else mattered any more, love had conquered and would prevail.

Chapter Seventeen

What do I remember of the first few years at our own little flat under the roof top, apart from those memories already described?

Undoubtedly – first and foremost – the harsh, arctic winter of 1947. People said it was the hardest winter in living memory and we were extremely fortunate to have survived it without any major and lasting damage. Except for the damage done by yet another year of hunger and deprivations caused by the exceptional bitter cold temperatures and not having the right clothing, shoes or warm food to combat the severity of this near eternally long season.

At the start of my second school year we were told that the school in Heiddorf would be closed for our year and that we had to join the second year form in our neighbouring village of Neu Kaliss.

This meant a much longer walk for me and my friend Gerda. It took approximately half an hour. In the winter it took longer since the roads were slippery with black ice or the massive amounts of snow were not always cleared and we had to search for foot prints of adult size to jump into in order to save our shoes and tights from being completely soaked well before we had reached our destination. I had to be exceptionally careful as my shoes were new, but sadly made of stiff cardboard rather than of leather. Firstly, as usual, we had practically no money. Secondly it is true that in the autumn of 1946 there were no leather shoes to be had in the entire Soviet Zone of Germany, nor of imitation leather either. Adults continued to wear their old shoes, never mind how worn or shabby they were. They were still better than new footwear made of cardboard!

For growing feet, though, there was only one alternative to cardboard shoes: wooden clogs. I had those for the summer, but for winter they were simply not suitable. I was wearing a pair of socks over my tights inside my shoes, but when the temperatures dropped to well below zero, even extra socks were not enough to keep my feet reasonably warm. They felt constantly icy, even during lessons.

In fact, it did not take long and I had caught frostbite in some of my toes. Mutti was very worried that I might lose one or two of the smaller toes because there was no medicine of any kind we could buy or organize. There was no chemist for miles. Besides, medicines, like most other products, were a luxury and not available at any cost.

The neighbours in front of our house owned a small farm. All of their land lay away from their house, but their animals were stabled around their courtyard. They had pigs, a horse or two and quite a few chickens. The couple owning the farm were quite elderly and ran their establishment entirely by themselves. Outside help was called in when needed at certain pressure points during the year. Otherwise, the old couple slaved away from morning till night. I have forgotten their surname but the farmer's wife was called Johanna. We were very naughty and called her "Black Johanna" because she always looked unwashed and untidy; the demands of her working day did not allow her to look after herself. Because she looked so messy, was chubby and bent like a very old woman, we gave her this nasty nick name, never realizing she would become a friendly and really helpful neighbour.

I assume it was she who gave my mother the tip to mix chicken droppings with my own urine and to put this mixture on my frozen toes. We did not know anyone else nearby who had chickens, so I am probably right in my assumption. Anyway, throughout this long winter my mother made up this concoction and applied it every evening to my toes on my right foot. Chicken droppings and my urine had to be fresh, meaning Mutti had to concoct this revolting ointment daily. Although I hated the stench of this vile mixture, the pain in my toes was strong enough to allow any kind of treatment to be applied ; never mind how disgusting it smelled or looked.

By spring time my toes got better. The fear I might lose my toes kept us going on with the treatment and miracles of all miracles, my toes were indeed saved! Saved, but not completely healed. For years afterwards they remained slightly swollen and hyper sensitive to the cold. For several winters running I had to wear really thick socks and warm slippers in the house to avoid the effects of the frost bite returning. We had heard of several cases where people had lost some of their toes during this particularly bitter winter and I counted myself very lucky indeed to have kept mine. All thanks to our "black Johanna", to her old wives' tales and to her lovely chickens! Bless them.

My poor feet weren't the only body parts giving me concern. I only possessed one pair of home knitted gloves. Someone must have given us the wool and one of the other relatives nearby probably knitted them for me because our mother could not knit. These very gloves were a further most precious item of clothing to prevent more frost bite, this time in my fingers. They alone would not have been enough, but they were better than nothing on my hands to keep some of the chill off. For this reason alone I loved them more than anything. Not having any toys or dolls to play with and to love, my thick woolly friends for my hands took the place of a treasured doll or other plaything. Most nights that winter I took them to bed with me instead of a doll to hug them and squeeze them lovingly against my face!

As I have already said, my new school was in Neu Kaliss, a neighbouring village which was divided from our village by a small river, the Elde, a tributary river of the bigger river Elbe. To get to the crossing to Neu Kaliss one had to walk or drive through a huge private estate of farm buildings and a large industrial mill consisting of two very large buildings, several storeys high. There were also some cottages for the farm and mill workers of the estate. Bordering this private area with public right of way stood a drawbridge over the river Elde, a miniature Tower Bridge of London, if you like. Or better still like the drawbridge at Langloise outside Arles in France in the famous painting by Vincent van Gogh. It looked very picturesque and during the warm season I loved crossing it. The banks of the river were lush with green and on the Neu Kaliss side several back gardens sloped down to the river's edge, adding colour and interest to the river scene. Often boats were waiting for the bridge
to be lifted or a horse and cart were waiting to cross over if too many people were crowding the bridge. There was usually something intriguing to watch around the bridge. It was my favourite spot along my daily route to and from school.

Yet in winter, and particularly during the bitter winter of 1946/1947 I was scared crossing the bridge since I was terrified my beautiful and only pair of gloves might suddenly slip off my hands and fall down into the icy water! This fear had taken such a strong hold of me, I even felt it when walking in the middle of the bridge and not, as I should have done, on the pavements on either side of it.

My gloves were actually mittens, meaning I could clutch the inverted top of the mittens with my pointing and middle fingers to make sure they could not really drop off my hands. Yet even doing so would not lessen my anxiety, such was the importance my mittens had in my life that winter.

Luckily, no evil spirit succeeded in ripping my precious mittens off my hands and I was able to wear and love them passionately for another year or two. And take them to bed to cuddle!

Bedtime was the best time that cold winter and all the others, too. Thanks to the foresight of the train driver from Marienburg who had seized the lavatory in order to keep the several sacks full of clothing and our duvets safe, we did not have to freeze too much during the bitter nights. The duvets were rather heavy in those days as the winters in Prussia were notoriously cold and long. Therefore all bedding had to be warm enough to cope with the extreme temperatures. Our lives were literally saved by still owning them.

Usually we would go to bed straight after our meagre supper to save on heating. Everything was rationed. Coal and wood were always in short supply. Since my father was still in Russia, there was no man about the house who could have tried to secretly steal some logs from the woods. Felling trees was strictly forbidden by the authorities but people did steal wood nonetheless. Survival was more important than any punishment meted out.

Needless to say, many times during this exceptionally cold winter our thoughts wandered to our father, hoping he might still be alive somewhere in deepest Russia. Most likely, if he was still living, he would be in a Prisoner of War Camp, where conditions would not be good at the best of times. And these were the worst of times. Obviously, with my limited experience of life I could not possibly imagine the life our poor father was enduring, but I did know he would be hungry and he would be cold. During this exceptional winter the weather in Russia was bound to be considerably worse than it was here. After all, cold winter weather always came from the east and Papa would be so much further east than we were; perhaps even as far east as Siberia! I had already learned in geography class or from hearsay that winters in Siberia were so cold, the population there hardly ever went outside. If they did, they were clad in enormous fur coats and boots and hats all lined with yet more fur, scarves covering most of their faces. Their breath would freeze in the air as they exhaled it!

Father would not be so lucky. He would perhaps still be in his shoddy army uniform, wearing his old boots with loose soles and old rags wrapped around them for extra warmth and to hold all individual parts of the disintegrating boots together.

Even if Papa was not in Siberia living out his days in those infamous labour camps, he would still be poorly dressed for the Russian climate, be even hungrier than we were and definitely much colder, too! Thoughts along those lines made me feel very depressed and lonely. I often ran away somewhere to hide where I could cry my eyes out without Mutti knowing about it. She had enough to worry about as it was. I did not want to add to her sadness. Letting the tears flow really hard always made me feel better. Why this was I could not tell. But perhaps God had seen me cry and had heard my prayers. By making me feel better he was trying to tell me:

"I have heard you, Gitta. Let me see what I can do for you!"

It was very strange, but after these lonely cries to God, apart from feeling better, I was also convinced that our father was still alive, that he would return, staying with us forever. And he would love us so very much! And we would love him!

Chapter Eighteen

Soon after, we moved to our own accommodation and thus to self-sufficiency: the local Council had given every refugee family a small plot of land as allotments. It was only a tiny plot but enough for Mutti to start realizing that she had green fingers! She grew lettuces, spinach (horror of all horrors!), radishes, carrots and even some potatoes. Not enough to feed us properly but at least it was a small supplement to our poor diet.

Part of our food supply for the winter months was a few sacks of potatoes which we were given some time during the autumn. Wonderful, but where was Mutti going to store them during the long winter months? We had no outbuilding, no use of a cellar and only a tiny shed. There was no other solution but to copy the farmers. They would pile all their potato crop into a big heap, cover this with lots of straw and finally add a really thick layer of soil on top of the straw. This method protected the potatoes from frost during normal winters, even cold ones.
Our allotment became the place where our potatoes were prepared for the onslaught of winter in precisely the same way. Heaven knows, who gave Mutti enough straw. Perhaps Johanna again? I wouldn't be surprised. Like squirrels preparing for winter, we beavered away at building our potato mound and Mutti was really proud of her achievement and immensely relieved knowing we would at least have some potatoes to eat, if not much else.

Tragically, she was proved wrong. All our potatoes were caught by frost. And not just ours. Everyone who had had to solve their storage problem in this way lost their crop. If you haven't ever had to eat frozen potatoes in your life, be very grateful for it! They were revolting, to say the least. Yet they were all we had, together with a slice of dry bread. So Mutti had to cook them, she had no choice. And all of us had to try to keep some of them down, if we were able to swallow them in the first place. Extreme hunger makes you do anything. Werner and I squeezed our nostrils together so that some of the stench at least was lost to us and with eyes closed we succeeded in getting some of that horrendous grub down our throats. The smell was almost worse than the taste. To think this was going to be our fare for months to come, really was too ghastly to contemplate, Yet, by the end of the winter the potato mound was gone and we were alive – barely, but living.

When you have experienced deprivation of the most essential foods like we had that winter, it changes you. The hunger of many childhood years has imprinted an indelible respect for food onto my being. Hardly anything ever gets thrown away. And now that making your own compost has become fashionable again, all peelings of fruit and vegetable land in my two composters, together with leaves, grass cuttings and other garden refuse. I never now waste anything which can be returned to Mother Earth! Or land in a stomach – anyone's stomach!

Something good and exciting did happen some time during the summer of 1946. I was still going to our village school and had just made it home when there was a lot of excited noise in the road. People were running towards the centre of the village and I was smart enough to search for my mother and shout that we must follow the others. Something was happening, something not to be missed.

Fortunately I found Mutti in the laundry kitchen. She left what she was doing at once and both of us ran as fast as our legs would carry us to the centre of the village. Sure enough, close to the square where the pub was situated we saw a huge army lorry laden with old boots and army uniforms, German ones, which Russian soldiers were throwing out among the screaming womenfolk, all of them fighting fiercely to catch something. A scene met us similar to those we see on television screens these days when food parcels are thrown out of aeroplanes in drought affected areas of Africa.

"Run faster, Mutti, we must get some of this stuff. Trautl can make something out of it and may be there will be a small pair of boots for me!" I never ran that fast in my life before. Mutti was trailing a bit behind. The swarm of women were screaming and pushing and shoving. We simply did the same. Being so little I tried to squeeze past some of those adult legs which was not easy. They knocked me back or kicked me. No one wanted to give up their plum position at the front lines. Eventually though we managed to push our way up to the lorry since, gradually, some women simply had to leave for home as their booty was more than they could carry. One of them lost some trousers, which I was quick enough to pick up and run away with.

Later Mutti got some more uniform items. Sadly, no boots. They had disappeared in a jiffy as they were even more scarce and therefore more precious. We knew by then that new shoes made of leather were not available for anyone, not even for any amount of money or food you might be able to offer the shop keeper in exchange. So these boots were worth their weight in gold!

Yet our efforts had not been in vain. We trotted home gleefully with an armful of uniform jackets and trousers. Trautl, the relation who was able to sew, would later cut up the larger pieces of cloth from each item and, incredibly, manage to create a beautiful new suit for my brother, even with LONG trouser legs! She deliberately made the suit a size or two larger so that my brother could grow into it for a few years. Somehow we found a suitable belt for his trousers as she had made them quite big around the waist as well and his skinny body looked totally lost in his new outfit. But who cared about that? He had a smart dark green suit and looked like the perfect young gentleman in it.

Unfortunately he had no shirt to go with it. We would have needed to cut up a white sheet to make him a shirt and that was out of the question. The few we had rescued from Prussia inside those famous old potato sacks were needed more than a shirt for Werner. He did have a vest to wear underneath the suit, and that simply had to be enough.

Sometime in the winter of 1947 but more likely during late spring or early summer of that year our darling mother had saved up enough money to take us to a photographer in the neighbouring town of Doemitz to have a family photo taken, Werner wearing his beautiful suit minus a shirt, me wearing a pretty dress made up of fabric from two second hand dresses someone had given us. Mutti wore a lovely home-made dress designed and made up by clever Trautl. It was astonishing what she was able to create out of ragged old clothes village people gave away to refugees knowing they would otherwise have absolutely nothing to wear. The shelves of textile shops were still completely empty, except if the owners had been able to put away cloths they had acquired pre-war or during the early parts of the war when textiles for private use were still manufactured and sold.

Our village had such a little textile shop attached as an annexe to the pub in the square. They were open for business right from the beginning of our evacuation there. Naturally, you never saw any refugee women making purchases there, only the locals. Refugees were permanently much too poor to buy anything other than the rationed foodstuff which was precious little enough.

I often stood in front of the shop window admiring whatever items were displayed. Never any rolls of fabric. They would be too valuable to be seen. Also they could be bleached by the sun. But there were small displays of handkerchiefs, sometimes ribbons and threads. Even needle baskets. In the spring of 1947 I actually went inside the shop on my own as Mutti had allowed me to buy some white sewing thread, three small spools for my needle class lessons at school. Since we still had insufficient teaching books and materials for our academic education, we had started needle craft lessons from an early age so that by now I was already quite a competent little knitter. We had also learned to crochet, always using sewing thread, as there was no other thread available. For some reason we were able to buy simple white cotton handkerchiefs and by the time I was 8 or 9 years old, I was slowly getting to grips with the art of crocheting lacy borders for these handkerchiefs. In fact, I really loved all forms of needlecraft. Later on when more yarns and fabrics were available I learned embroidery in class as well. I enjoyed knitting and crocheting very much indeed and began to produce simple things which later, when complete, became presents for my mother.

Entering the little shop I realized that I had chosen a busy moment. Who were all those rich people being able to purchase these colourful, wonderful things? Sometimes there were even some knitting wools on the shelves, but they were always gone in a flash. Today the shelves were bare. I had to wait quite a bit before it was my turn to be served. Finally, there was only one other older girl in front of me. I did not really know her. In fact, I had never seen her before. I was standing right next to her listening in to what she was saying and what she did say was most intriguing!

"You told me that I must bring in some old pieces of dress fabrics if I wanted to order the little doll you have for sale. My mother has given me these pieces. I hope they are suitable?"

"Let me see what you have got there", said the assistant, and the girl handed over a small packet of fabric scraps. The assistant checked whether they were clean and strong enough to be reused.

"Yes," she said, "these will do nicely. You see, the factory needs these for the production of the clothes for their dollies. We don't keep it for ourselves, you know!"

She then named the price of the doll and the girl said that it was alright. Her mother had inquired about the price and had said that the shop assistant could hand over the doll to her daughter.
"Please would you make a note of how much we owe you and my mother will come later to pay you."

My jaw dropped in astonishment. Was it really this easy to acquire my heart's delight? A little soft doll, only about 20cm tall with a soft body, but a hard painted face. The doll had no hair, but if there was any, it would be covered by the little pointed hat she was wearing . Ever since I had to leave my beautiful doll in her fabulous pram behind when we fled from Marienburg , I have longed for another doll of my own. Something I could cuddle, make little clothes for from scrap leftovers at school, and someone whom I could pretend would LOVE me. She could come to bed with me and I would sleep next to her feeling the happiest girl in the big wide world.

I had seen an example of the little doll in the window for some time but never dreamed of being able to own it. Now here was a chance to get my darling doll without needing any money! Or, at least, not straight away. Just some pieces of cut offs from the dresses Trautl was making for our extended family and telling the shop assistant that my mother would come later and pay for her. I was so excited, not one minute did I think about the enormous difficulties my poor mother would have finding the money to pay for it. My need for the doll was too overwhelming.
I had seen a way of getting my dearest wish fulfilled and I wasn't going to let this amazing chance slip by.

However, I said nothing when my turn came to be served. Just asked for the sewing thread for which I did have the money and decided to organize the fabric cut offs first and then return with my request when the assistant had forgotten about the other girl's way of getting hold of her, no doubt, legitimately ordered doll.

Despite my outer chatty veneer, I was still quite a shy girl in those days, especially with grown ups. But when it was time to return to the shop I entered it with as much courage as I could muster and ordered my doll as if this was my natural right. My mother gave me permission to order the doll and here were the required scraps of fabric. The assistant glanced at me somewhat doubtfully.

"When might the doll be ready for collection?" said I trying to sound really confident and grown up.

" In two weeks' time". " Alright, I will pop in after school in about two weeks and see if it has arrived. Auf Wiedersehen!"

"Phew. That's gone well!" and I left the shop with a spring in my steps trying not to show the wicked smile on my face. "I've done it; she fell for it." I literally skipped all the way home, singing all the while and grinning like a Cheshire cat!

When the two weeks were up the doll had indeed arrived. She was wearing such a pretty skirt with matching hat. I was over the moon and could hardly breathe with excitement.

"My mother said to put the price into your debt book. She will come and pay you herself. She does not like me to carry any money with me, you see?"

For the next few seconds my heart thumped so violently, I felt I was going to faint.

Was the assistant going to fall for my lie and give me the doll without having paid for it? Or would I be unmasked? She hesitated for a moment.

"What is your name again and where do you live?"

I gave her the information she wanted for her debt book and my long cherished dream was in my hands! I was delirious with happiness and could hardly believe my luck.

I left the shop in rather a hurry before the assistant could change her mind. Once off the main street and on our dirt road I stopped, cuddled and kissed my doll frantically. For a while I loved her even more than Mutti. She was mine and mine alone and she would love me like a real baby would love her Mummy. She would smile her sweet smile only for me and for no one else and nothing would ever separate us again – never, never ever! I was ecstatic with joy and love for my new little wonderful friend.

I had been huddling by a bush while kissing and cuddling my little darling , wondering what I should call her and then wondering, how best to hide her. I did not possess a proper school satchel. They tend to be quite big and a small doll like mine could easily be hidden inside it. But the small cloth bag I had would show her up against my few copy books and pencils. So where to hide her? My summer dress would show up every bulge, too. So dolly could not hide underneath my dress either. Could I leave her anywhere safe outside where no one else could possibly find her? And if it rained, she would be ruined. No, that would not do either. I would have to hide her in the washing kitchen. There must be some spot where no one would discover her.

No, there was no secret place there either. That's for sure. Far too many people used the laundry room, practically every day, Besides, there were only shelves, no cupboard which I could lock up for dolly to be safe in. Even if I could lock one, it would not stay locked as everyone would want to use it and, if necessary, would smash the cupboard door to get at their bar of soap or whatever.

No, I would have to hide her somewhere else. Somewhere like Gerda's house. In that case I would have to tell Gerda how I got the doll and why I needed to hide it. No, under no circumstances could I let her know that I had been a liar, had lied to the shop assistant (although at the time I had considered myself rather clever), had also lied to Trautl when I persuaded her to give me some of her fabric scraps and most of all I was lying to my beloved mother.

"Oh, my God! – Mutti, Mutti! What have I done!?"

Suddenly, the enormity of my action engulfed me like a whirlwind, almost strangling me with my guilt. How could I have been so thoughtless believing I could get away with this terrible lie. A purchase of something just to please ME which I knew perfectly well my poor mother could never afford to buy for me, even if she would want to do so from the bottom of her huge and loving heart.

Why didn't I think of the consequences of this deed before, but only of the joy awaiting me when I would have my beloved dolly in my arms? Instead all I had done was count the days when I could go to the shop and collect my trophy, ignoring how it would affect my mother or even myself, once I was found out!

My whole little body shook and trembled with crying and fear of what I had to do when I got home – confess to my mother! There was no other way out. She had to know. Eventually I had to confess anyway as the request for the money would unquestionably be made – and soon! If I told Mutti straight away and showed her how desperately sorry I was and that I now realized also how selfish I had been, perhaps she would not condemn me for ever and I would not end in purgatory for the rest of my life.

I could tell her that I would try and ask for help in every house in the village in order may be to earn a few pennies to help her pay for my doll. I remember very well thinking that, perhaps, perhaps, I might even find some money in the street on the way home!

As if anyone ever found any money! No one had any money and if they did, they certainly were not so careless with it as to drop it in the street. That's how desperately unhappy I was about my deed, believing God would descend from heaven and throw some money in front of me simply because it was dawning on me how thoroughly bad and selfish I had been. No, God does not and cannot perform miracles like that. Only Mutti can do that – perform miracles – somehow! She has never hit me or been extremely cross with me, even not when, through my fault and my fault alone, my brother fell off the sledge and broke his arm. When she saw my utter distress afterwards she took me in her arms and comforted me, comforted me, when I should have been punished! And she might do just that again! May be not all mothers are so forgiving, but my mother is forgiving – even if at first shock she may shoot her beautiful dark brown eyes into me like poisoned arrows . Very soon afterwards she will forgive me. Oh, dear God, I hope she will and let me keep my dolly, too!

I blew my runny nose, wiped clean the wet cheeks with my arms, gasped a bit for air and carefully peeped from behind the bush to see whether the street was clear so that no other girls or boys from school could see my smudged face and sneer at me. Yes, the road was empty and slowly I stood up, cradling my precious doll into my arm and starting to amble up the street, ever so painfully slow to extend the time it took to face Mutti with my dreaded confession.

Strangely, I cannot exactly remember what happened when I got home. I don't recall being beaten, nor punished in any other way. I was allowed to keep my doll and she became the apple of my eye for a very long time. Like lovers, we became inseparable.

On the photograph I mentioned earlier she rests in my arm. Inconceivable that she should not have been captured for all eternity! I remember knitting her a little cardigan from wool which was much too thick, yet, it was all I had. I was so very proud of my handiwork – school had taught me something useful!

The way I had felt when I started on my way home I must have appeared the most miserable little girl in the whole wide world, unable to speak properly for fear as well as shame and I imagine Mutti realized how much owning this doll had meant to me. She was well aware how upset I had been when I had to leave my adored big doll and her pram behind in Marienburg when Father Christmas, in the shape of my Papa, had given it to me only two or three weeks earlier. I never really had got over it. Losing her had affected me more than losing our home. She probably meant as much to me then as our baby sister had meant to my mother. And the loss of her caused almost as much grief to me as the loss of Renatchen had inflicted on our mother.

What puzzles me greatly, even now, is how on earth Mutti managed to find the money to clear the debt. But she did – which proves: mothers CAN perform miracles almost better than God. At least some mothers can and do, special mothers like mine!

Chapter Nineteen

It was now summer 1947 and I was eight years old, Werner would be ten in July.

Summer was always a wonderful time. The splendour of the sun, of swimming sessions in the river, picking blackberries and mushrooms in the woodlands, the sheer joy of merely feeling warm and full of excitement about the crops growing, of the windfall apples we could steal from neighbouring gardens, of picking corn flowers from the edge of fields and finding more grass and dandelions for our rabbit, of rummaging for left over corn ears in the harvested fields were pleasures to enjoy.

Summer made me feel less of a leper. We were freer to run around with a light and cheerful heart, collecting whatever edible things we could find. That alone created a happier mood in all of us. Sometimes I found a few wild raspberries or strawberries, most of them I devoured straight away, but occasionally I found enough to bring some home and Mutti would bake us pancakes and serve the wild fruit with the pancakes. If we were lucky, she also had some milk to pour over them instead of cream. Oh, what bliss!

Towards the end of July we would all of us make off for the forest to pick blueberries. The sandy soil in Mecklenburg is particularly good for wild blueberry bushes to grow, producing an amazing amount of fruit every year. However, to get the best pick, you had to be early since all the refugee families were out there to harvest them. These berries were the only abundant wild fruit we could find. If all three of us went to pick we could find enough, spread over the day, for Mutti to serve pancakes with blueberries for our supper and still have lots left over to preserve for the winter. She may not have been able to do that as early as the summer of 1947, simply because she may not have had any preserving glasses yet. The shops were still empty of nearly everything which was not the most essential for survival. But in later years, she definitely did have some glasses and we preserved quite a lot of berries each summer..

As I grew older I set off on my own on a school free day as I loved picking berries and also being alone in the forest. As soon as I arrived there, having got out of bed at dawn, an invisible burden seemed to lift from my shoulders. A wonderful lightness of spirit transcended my mood. I could have hugged every tree; blown kisses into the pine scented air towards the wide open sky above me and dance, dance, dance! All the troubles of the outside world fell from me and a soothing peace and sense of freedom replaced the anxiousness which had travelled with me to the forest. Here in the depth of the natural world I felt an equilibrium village life had never offered me. I felt at one with the life of the forest, the endless vista of trees among the carpet of blueberry bushes or pine cones lying in profusion on silver coloured moss. I felt in heaven. To this day, I roam the countryside by myself, liking nothing better than my own company with just the splendour of the fields and woods to enjoy.

By the time I was 10 years old I set off by myself, leaving home around 5 o'clock in the morning before anybody else had woken up so that I would get the best crop which had ripened overnight, ready to pick. The walk to that particular forest took about an hour and a half. Walking there was the easy part, as the bucket was still empty. Walking home with it, even if it was only half full or less, proved rather more difficult. I had to stop many times to give my arms a rest.

When I was 11 and 12 we were proud owners of a bicycle. Then I was in the woods around 5.30 am returning only when my bucket was full to the brim because I could hang it onto the steering wheel. Of course, the weight of it was too much to steady the bicycle and I had to push it home rather than cycle it. But never mind. I was so proud and feeling so satisfied with my achievement, the arduous trek home was almost happily undertaken. My huge bounty would make my mother so happy and that drove me on and on. Besides, I had a full stomach and therefore strength, having eaten blueberries all day long!!!

My brother was never part of this fun. He hated picking as he hated everything else that felt like work. His big passion was football which he played all day long on the dusty road outside our house, surrounded by the younger boys of the neighbourhood who looked upon him as a football god. He infuriated me quite often with his laziness. But if I had not returned by 3.30 to 4.00 pm he would anxiously stand in the middle of the road watching out for me turning into it from the main street quite a way off. Then he would run upstairs or shout from down below if the window to our flat was open: "She is coming! She is coming!" I knew then he did care for me a great deal even though I did boss him around a lot for helping us so little or mostly not at all. But I am getting ahead of myself.....

Instead, let me tell you something funny for a change. I cannot remember whether this incident occurred that summer or a year later, but it doesn't really matter. Apart from Gerda I had started to make friends with the people living opposite. Their youngest daughter, Ingetrud, was a year or so older than me but we became good friends over time. And then there were the children of our local family who owned our house. They had two boys and a girl called Christiane. Our little group had started to go to the river to play in the water and lie in the sun. Some of the children could already swim, but I was still learning, and so was Christiane. Still, we always had a good time. There was an area a bit down the river where it widened and on our side it widened into a small bay with a narrow sandy strip of beach, unusual for a small river bank. The water was very flat at this point, similar to an ocean coastline. In this shallow water we non-swimmers splashed around thoroughly enjoying ourselves. A little deeper into the river we pretended we could swim by pushing off the bottom sand with our feet while throwing ourselves forward into the water and paddling like mad with our hands the way real swimmers do. One foot was kept on the ground to steady us. So we got as much fun out of playing around there as the bigger competent swimmers did. Therefore, on hot days, the river bay was our regular meeting place.

While Christiane and I were having a whale of a time in the river, some of the boys
decided to hide our underpants which were lying in the grass with our other clothes. But I saw what they were up to, rushed out of the water and chased after them, followed by Christiane. Together we overwhelmed the boy who had grabbed both pants and quite a fight ensued. Finally we got them back from the boy, not before he had spotted that Christiane's pants were not clean.

Embarrassing brown spots covered the lower part and needless to say, the on looking boys thought this very amusing, teasing her quite cruelly:

"Look everybody, she's got poo in her pants. She's got poo in her pants!"

Far from being embarrassed, Christiane wasn't going to have it. She pulled her pants out of his clutches, inspected them and said with a most serious and grown up facial expression she could muster and with her head held high in the air:

"That's not poo, you silly. It's chocolate!"

With that she marched off, changing from her swimsuit into her pants and dress behind a bush while the rest of us held our bellies with laughter. None of us had seen or eaten chocolate for years but even if we had, who on earth would put soft chocolate into her pants instead of into her mouth?
Still, one had to give it to her – she stood her ground! Yet despite her composed reaction to being found out about her little accident, she never lived the incident down and was teased about it for ages afterwards – as cruel boys would do! I have thought of her hundreds of times since and still chuckle whenever the incident crosses my mind. I bet you none of the other boys and girls present have forgotten it either!

Chapter Twenty

We had now been in Heiddorf for two and a half years and our Papa was still not home with us.
Something important I have learned about life: children survive traumas and tragedies much better than adults as long as they are fed and some adult gives them a little love and affection. Children live much more in the Now. They do not know yet how challenging and difficult life can be and also how

frightening, especially if you are a woman left alone to fend for small children. The responsibility can feel totally overwhelming and this fear of the future must have been terrifyingly depressing for my mother who had never had to work in her life before. Now, in the summer of 1947, she was just 29 years old. She had married at 18. My brother arrived a year later and a further 18 months on, in February 1939, I came into this world. My father had been drafted into the army from the very first day of the start of war, in September 1939, meaning my mother had brought up her two children practically on her own, even if she had not had to earn her living until after the flight from Prussia.

Since then all responsibilities of parenthood had lain on her young shoulders. We children knew she missed our father, but the true extent of her struggles and pain we were much too young to comprehend. She was probably saved by the fact that her sister Ella, Ella's children and other relations from Ella's husband's side had fled with us on the train and were even sharing the same house with us.. But it was mainly Ella's two sisters-in-law who were the practical people in that family, especially Trautl with her sewing skills. However, they were all available for moral support and often came to us to spend the evenings chatting and singing together with us children. Or telling one another naughty jokes!

I would like to think that by summer 1947 – but possibly somewhat later - Mutti had found out that Papa was alive and a prisoner-of- war in Russia. After his return my father told us it was his prison camp commanders who had somehow established we were still alive and where we lived. This may have been made easier for him since we lived in the Russian occupied zone of Germany.

From then onwards small cards started to arrive from Russia. One half of them was the attached reply card. In small print at the bottom were the stern instructions that this reply card only was allowed to be used. If proper letters were sent they would be destroyed. These cards arrived approximately once a month and Mutti awaited them always most anxiously. However, with each card that arrived her anxiety increased instead of lessening. We could not understand why she often cried and looked so distressed. She would not tell us what was the matter. From being overjoyed when the first card had arrived she soon became more deeply distressed with each new one she received. As soon as one card arrived she sent off her reply card. I know this for certain as she often asked me to take it to the post box on my way to school.

I was able to read printed words but not yet adult handwriting in Gothic script so that the text of these cards remained a mystery to me until Mutti eventually confessed the devastating reason for her distress: Each card from Papa consisted of his anguish why Mutti was never writing to him! Did she no longer love him? Had she found another man because she had not known whether he was alive or dead? All five or six short lines he was permitted to write consisted entirely of his pleas to let him know whether we were all alive and well since the thoughts of us were all he had to keep him going. They were heart rending pleas for some sign from her. I can hardly bear to think about the agony my poor parents must have suffered – Papa despairing about the total lack of replies from my mother. And Mutti 's heart breaking each month a little more on hearing her consistent replies had never reached him. What was she doing wrong?

Eventually his cards arrived less frequently and we all became more worried about our father and whether we would ever see him again. Then his cards started to arrive on a regular basis once more and Papa had given up pleading for replies. Instead he told Mutti about his daily life and how much he loved us and longed to be released so that he could be reunited with us again. We assumed, since the cards he wrote to us had not been returned to him , he was now considering it wiser not to continue asking why she was not replying.

 One day, a year or two after the first card had arrived, my mother was asked to go and see the Buergermeister of our village (the local mayor) as soon as possible.
When she returned from her visit she told us and her sister the mayor had received one of those cards from my father asking him to confirm his family was still alive since he had regularly written as allowed but had never received a reply from his wife. Mutti was in a terrible state. Initially the mayor had been really angry with her, saying she was a cruel and callous wife. Instead of sustaining her husband in his agony she was slowly killing him with her lack of love and compassion. How COULD she be so cruel, so inhumane!?

When Mutti explained the truth of the situation, he was shocked and ashamed for his thoughtless outburst and the two of them decided that he, the mayor, would reply and sign his name so that the camp supervisors could not doubt from whom the card had arrived. They both hoped that this would be the answer to the problem and that the next card to Mutti would contain the good news of the mayor's reply.

With this hope in her heart Mutti was anxiously awaiting Papa's next card, which never came! Weeks went by – nothing. Each time the postman passed our house and Mutti ran outside to meet him, he only shook his head in sadness: "Not yet, Frau Mallon. Perhaps tomorrow!" And so the tomorrows rolled by, slowly, heavily like treacle, week after week until the postman stopped shaking his head and looked away as he could no longer bear to see my Mother's distraught face or my wailing disappointment. Poor, poor Papa! Had he died or had he been sent to Siberia?

Why wasn't he sending us the happy note we were expecting? Something dreadful must have happened to him or he would have written long ago. We knew he loved and missed us so very much or he would not have gone to all the trouble he had.

And we missed him so badly, too. Aunt Ella's husband had already come home many months earlier, so had the fathers of several of my class mates. It felt like our father was the only one who was still out there incarcerated somewhere in the wilderness of Russia. What terrible fate had befallen him now?

While the war was on Papa had at least come home on leave from time to time, always arriving with special presents for us, the lovely fox stole for Mutti, the fateful sledge and my last huge present: the doll's pram with a doll in it including beautiful bedding, the works!. By now we had not seen him for close to three years. Would we even recognize him? But worst worry of all: would he EVER return to us? The Russians were up to something; we just could not imagine what. Not knowing why communication had come to a halt was the hardest to bear. Sometimes we even dared hope he might have been released already like so many thousands of others had been. Then one day he might suddenly stand in front of our door, thin like a rake, bedraggled and blue with cold – a figure of utter misery and desolation. Not a bit like the happy father we remembered, who walked into the house laden with presents and smiles bursting from all over his face, arms outstretched in anticipation of our joyful jumps into his arms. No, we didn't expect such a man this time. Whatever his condition though, our love and happiness of having him with us once more would bring him back to full strength again. No one could long for his return more than I did. Because we children hardly knew him, he had become our big hero .We so yearned to be loved and cared for by him in the true knowledge that we had a saviour in our family, a strong rooted tree whom we could embrace as we also leant upon him. We dreamt of nothing else in those fear stricken days.

The reality was starkly different. The waiting became endless. Mutti was starting to believe the Russians had killed him or that they had sent him to a labour camp in Siberia where he was also bound to die. Perhaps, perhaps he was merely ill and too weak to write. We thought of any possibility which would keep us hopeful. And then our hopes were indeed fulfilled!

Another card arrived full of the same distressing questions. Why was Mutti not writing to him? Why had the mayor not replied to his card either? Why did Mutti torment him so much. He begged and begged for a sign from her as he had nothing else to live for!

I cannot imagine how our dear mother must have felt reading these pleas and knowing now beyond all shadow of doubt that the camp commander deliberately withheld the mail for my father, even withholding the mayor's reply! Somehow though Mutti recovered and my brother and I also learned to live with the shock. At least he had not been sent to Siberia! And there was hope he would be among those soldiers who were released on a fairly regular basis. Eventually Papa might be among the lucky ones.

Hope is a most wonderful thing.

While the cards kept coming, Papa was alive. And they kept coming for ages and ages. In fact, for years!

Chapter Twenty-One

Notwithstanding the agonies regarding our parents' separation, we children enjoyed the summer months. As I said, children live in the NOW, each day was a new adventure. For us, it was not how to fill our holidays with exciting foreign trips, or visits to our friends' houses, having barbecues or shopping sprees and cinemas to go to.

I went in search of other excitements – food mainly. And I learned fast how to exploit nature. I really enjoyed going on these explorations all by myself. In the spring and early summer weeks there was not much to glean except it was easier to find enough grass for our rabbit. Quite a few refugees had managed to acquire a goat which they tethered by the roadside. Consequently, there was not enough grass for everyone's goat or rabbit and I had no choice but to wriggle through barbed wire and onto meadows to steal the grass there. I did this only if the grass was really high so that the farmer could not see me. But often their dogs would smell me and that meant the end of my secret expedition into the danger zones.

Apart from grass I had instructions from Mutti to look for wild sorrel. Together with potatoes she made a nourishing soup from these leaves.

Another source of food supply was the wood nearby. Ingetrud's parents were experts in knowing which mushrooms were edible and which ones poisonous. Over time I learned all I had to know about them and became quite expert myself! Needless to say Werner played football while little me became provider of our summer suppers. Not every day, but often enough. And to be honest, I loved my new role in life. And I did not have to ferret around for something extra to eat all of the time. Gradually I made better friends with Ingetrud as well as with Gerda. Sometimes I even played ball with my cousins. Or hop and skip on the road outside. If I was on my own, often someone came to join in.

Apart from my dolly, our mother had managed to buy a ball for each of us. Football was not my style. I used my ball for more artistic skills – ways of bouncing it back against the house wall, using my head, the right or left arm by throwing the ball from behind my back against the wall or using my chest to bounce it back. These skills had to be learned, mind you, and I felt like an athlete performing these relatively simple tasks. I played like that for hours on end, just as Werner never stopped teaching the little ones how best to improve their football tactics.

At some stage we also had a skipping rope, first a short one just to be used by one person. Then we also played with a large one involving at least three people simultaneously. Two people would swing the rope from each end in a clockwise fashion while the third person would try and jump into the rope at the point when it was close to the ground swinging upwards . That, too, required skill. Once you had succeeded to avoid getting your legs caught up with the rope you had to jump over it each time it reached the ground. Hop, hop. The more hops you managed to jump, the faster your friends usually swung the rope as they wanted you to trip up, of course. At the same time, the faster you needed to jump the more fun it got until you were more than happy to get your feet entangled and thus get out of the game to recover your breath. Sometimes, we were quite a few girls queuing up for our turn and the laughter and screams and giggles were enough to annoy the older neighbours. We didn't take much notice though – we needed a bit of fun after all. Of course, the girl with the most hops was the winner. Oh, what a simple life we led, but what a happy one, too!

During the warm weather, spring, summer and autumn, we spent almost all of our free time outside. And why not? Somehow we always found something interesting or fun to do and not all our activities were strictly speaking legal either! Well, I have to admit, there was definitely one adventure which had not been legal but we felt morally entitled to commit this little crime. It was my brother, who was the actual person committing the offence. Morally, however, the entire gang of our cousins, myself included, bore as much of the guilt as he did. This is why.

It was now late autumn and the weather was still surprisingly warm and sunny. Consequently we loitered about outside but on this occasion with nothing in particular in mind. Until one of us came up with this fantastic idea. Every autumn "Black Johanna" and her husband slaughtered one of their pigs and we had watched the procedure with fascination as well as shock from the windows of our little flat.

Whatever happened in their courtyard we were able to see as there was only a wire fence dividing their house and yard from ours. So we were glued like magnets to the events unfolding in the yard, watching the pig being pulled out of its sty by two men who had put strong ropes around the pig's neck. Instinctively the poor pig must have known what fate was awaiting him as he screamed appallingly while trying to escape the grip of the men, pulling sideways with all his might; then backwards or forwards, whichever way he thought might overpower the horrid men. Ultimately the pig's captors were stronger and the wretched animal landed where he was supposed to be: just in front of another man holding a large axe in waiting to execute the poor pig. . I say "poor pig", yet at the time it was normal to slaughter pigs. Not just then, it's done all the time; only in those days the pigs were slaughtered on the farms and not taken to a slaughter house. After all, from the start of their existence pigs are reared for human consumption and in that respect pigs are doing mankind an enormous service.

I would like to think, Johanna's pigs knew that instinctively. While their destiny was only normal they weren't exactly looking forward to facing their executioner. By the time the pig had reached him, one or two more strong young men were holding it down, keeping it as still as they could so that the axe would fall into the precise spot on the pig's forehead where death would be instant.

We had watched this animal tragedy with both horror and fascination but the screams of the terrified pig stayed with me for a long time. I can almost still hear them now! Once the pig was dead a mass of activity set in. Women arrived with buckets, men with knives and more strong rope. The two hind and front legs were strung together, some incision made in or near the head and the pig was hung onto strong metal hooks in the wall of the house which was facing our windows! Once it hung upside down, buckets were placed strategically to let all the blood flow into them, almost every drop of it, since it was a very useful part of the pig's bounty. The blood was used, as we found out later, for making black pudding and a sort of casserole using prunes for extra flavour.

The first autumn we watched this slaughter of the one pig each farmer was permitted to use for their own consumption, we did not get anything edible from Johanna afterwards. But by 1947 Mutti had got to know her well enough to help, along with other women, making use of every little bit of the pig, even its bones for the production of soap.

Mutti helped with the soap making, In return we were given some black pudding, which was delicious and also some of the less appetising looking blood and prune dish. But guess what? Once Werner and I had overcome our disgust and had given in to our hunger we realized the dish was actually very palatable indeed!

Would I eat it now? I doubt it. Yet then was another matter altogether.

Having witnessed the latest slaughter and knowing more about how every scrap was utilized in different ways, we also knew that a great deal of sausage was made and was smoked and thus preserved to last the entire winter in the farmer's own smoke house. This was situated near the end of our yard, exactly where our wooden lavatory was but quite a bit to the right of it and behind the wooden fence dividing the two properties.. Every time we went to the loo we could see the smoke exiting from little holes towards the top of the smoke house, which was built in the shape of a tower.

Apart from the smoke we could also smell the delicious sausages and we stood there many times inhaling the wonderful smell coming from inside. It made our stomachs rumble even more than usual. How could the farmer and his wife possibly enjoy eating those sausages in the coming months when they well knew their neighbours were still starving and could only dream of something so wonderful as a piece of meat or a slice of sausage! It really was too cruel tempting us with their bounty every time we went to spend a penny! Unfortunately for us, there was no window or other point of entry to the smoke house and all we could do was dream. Ah, but when you dream long enough they say that dreams come true. And ours did!

One day my brother met one of our boy cousins by the lavatory and the two of them were straining their brains, how they could find a way of getting at one or two of the beguiling sausages, when the penny dropped! The area by the smoke house was completely hidden by the building which also housed our laundry room. So one was pretty safe from preying eyes! The boys decided, with the help of at least one other, they could get at the brick sized openings at the top of the tower if one boy climbed on top of the other (since we certainly did not own a ladder!) One of our cousins was a big strong boy. He volunteered to be the bottom shoulder on which the lighter boy would rest, also in a crouching position. My brother then formed the top of the human ladder, rather like the animals in the folktale of the "Bremer Stadtmusikanten". ("The Town Musicians of Bremen " by the Brothers Grimm). Another boy must have helped to lift Werner up. However they did it, he was high enough to reach one of those openings in the tower and with the help of a crooked branch from some tree or shrub he was able to pull out a sausage. Encouraged by his success he tried again and, yes, succeeded in pulling out another one!

But now, quick, away from the scene of crime. We gathered in our usual hiding place, a narrow strip of an unused area between the fence of our house, the part where our cousins lived, and the house of my friend Gerda. There Werner divided the bounty fairly between the five of us, all part of our family, sworn to secrecy in return for a piece of the sausages. Having anticipated this delight for many days, we could hardly wait to attack our share and within seconds or just a minute or two everything had disappeared into our hungry stomachs and we dispersed showing the most innocent faces we could produce to the world. If I remember well they were two liver sausages Werner had "conquered". We knew what he had done was wrong, but the word "stealing" would never have passed our lips. We had "conquered" them, like princes used to conquer princesses from their fortified castles in fairy tales. Or kings conquered lands from opposing kingdoms. If the mean farmers could not readily share some of their plenty with us starving mites, then we just had to do what we could to take some of it away from them. It seemed only fair.

Guilt only set in when the police turned up at our house. We certainly **felt** guilty then and felt especially sorry for the trouble we had caused our long suffering mother.

It was Werner the police were accusing, not me. How on earth did they know it was him? It could have been our cousins who had actually pulled the sausages out. Or even some other boys from somewhere in the village. They had no proof it was us. No one had seen us. We felt completely sure of this. For once my brother and I stuck together like iron and denied we had anything to do with those sausage thieves. How could they believe we angelic kids could have done such a thing. We were well brought up children and not thieving gypsies! Yes, the sausages were missing from the hole at our side of the yard but, hey, that was no proof that WE had actually done the wicked deed.

Besides, the sausage had long been digested in our stomachs which made us feel even safer and stronger in our denials. And the police knew it, too. Short of giving us a warning never to attempt such a crime again, there was nothing they could do and so they departed empty handed.

That night, in the bed we shared, Werner and I could not stop giggling and chatting about our triumph over the tight fisted farmer as well as the police. We had become almost "seasoned" criminals but one thing was quite sure: we had been shaken to the core during the police investigation that afternoon and without saying it we both knew we weren't truly cut out to be professional thieves. No amount of hunger could prompt us to steal from the smoke house ever again. There is a saying in Germany: "Einmal ist kein Mal" (once is nothing at all). But **twice** was another matter!

Not us, never again!

Having longed to get hold of those tantalizing sausages for ages before we actually could make a feast of them, we ate much too greedily instead of banqueting slowly and appreciatively to spin out the pleasure for as long as possible. Therefore the actual pleasure was quite short lived in contrast to the shame, fear and guilt we felt once the police had entered our house. We didn't admit it, but it was nonetheless there. We could not lie to Mutti though. Werner did confess to her and as usual, she was extremely upset and disappointed in us, but she did not beat us. She saw how crestfallen we both were and believed that we would never bring shame on her again.

The rascal that I was when need be, I continued to steal in small ways – grass for our rabbit or windfall apples which I had had my eyes on for days on end and which no one bothered to pick up. Rather than let them rot, I felt I was entitled to take them since none of the locals ever offered them to us. I felt this was most unkind and selfish of them. Did they not see how hollow-eyed and hungry we looked? Obviously not. Everyone thought only of themselves in those days – we might have been the same had the roles been reversed. Luckily, no one ever caught me in the act and my reputation as a sweet and hard working girl was preserved. Only Mutti and Werner knew – and now you do, too!

Indeed, most of the time I was very hard working and conscientious. Any help I could give our mother was all I wanted to do. From 8 years of age onwards I slowly turned myself into another mother figure, Mutti's right hand, so to speak.

Apart from the local butcher, a village shop opposite and a baker in the road leading to my school, there was eventually a new shop in the main street where one could buy food items without ration cards. Unfortunately, 90% of the time the shelves were bare. In **theory** you could shop there, in **practise** hardly ever.

These shops the new government had set up were called HO shops, short for Handelsorganisation – trade organization. Here the populace was supposed to shop for anything over and above the allocated food one was permitted to buy on ration cards, except these shops remained mainly empty. Yet from time to time there was indeed a delivery of some food stuffs. As soon as anyone in the village saw a delivery van, the queues started. Whatever it was that had been delivered, people wanted to buy it.

Sometimes it was sugar, sometimes margarine. One thing was sure, the delivery was never enough for the entire village population, so as soon as you saw someone queuing outside, you dropped everything and ran to join them. It could be your lucky day!

Thus, on my way home from school, on entering the main street, my first look was always to the right where the HO shop was located. If there was a queue or women shoppers returned back to their home from that direction, off I went to see what I could get. If it was sugar which had come into store, then I needn't bother – we could not afford it. But if it was margarine, I stayed in the queue never mind how long or how hopeless it would be. For there was never any guarantee the supply did not run out just when it was my turn to be served. It certainly happened more than once.

Chapter Twenty-Two

Talking of sugar....... I have a further confession to make! Writing down these memories I am beginning to realize what a crafty little thief I had become over time. Once you start you get into a habit of it and since I got away with it so many times

I could not resist acquiring what I wanted or needed by fair means or by foul. The thieving of grass or clover for our rabbit or the half rotten apples from under the trees in neighbouring gardens never gave me a moment's concern. But the incidences of the stolen sugar are another matter. They belong to another class of crime, similar to the event of the sausage haul and I am not in the least bit proud of telling you about them.

Most of the time I really do believe I was a good girl, eager to learn, hard working and friendly but there was a wicked streak to me, too, as we already know from the sledge affair. This wicked streak did not stop with the aftermath from that event, I'm sorry to say!

When this mischievous streak got hold of me, there was no stopping it. It needed gratification even if the outcome could not possibly be gratifying! The following was another such story:

I'm not certain what year this happened but that is really of no consequence. We know by now how hard up we were. In fact, I cannot remember if and how much financial support Mutti got from the new authorities. Certain is that we almost had none. From time to time our mother managed to get some kind of work for which she got paid and eventually she got permanent employment in a clothing factory in the neighbouring village of Neu Kaliss - sewing on buttons!!! Some sort of cottage industry was re-emerging and with it employment – never mind what kind. This must have been the lowest paid job on the shop floor, better though than no work at all.

At the time of the following story our finances were exceptionally poor and the sugar we got with our ration cards was properly weighed out into one pound per bag because Mutti had to sell these to the farmers for money. I say, sold for money, as there were other ways of remuneration: selling sugar for food, for instance. Then the most popular exchange. Farmers did not get any ration cards at all. They had to be self-sufficient. Sugar was the one item they could not produce themselves which meant they were more than keen to buy it off us. If Mutti sold all our allowance she got enough money to pay our rent. Therefore, the three, four bags of sugar we got on our ration cards were our most precious asset. They had to be out of reach of thieving children and were placed on top of our wardrobe – the highest and the safest place in the flat.

Mutti knew her little daughter rather better than I thought she did. And so she also knew my terrific, almost unnatural craving for anything sweet. To this day I could go without meat for the remainder of my life, but I cannot and will not go without my home made biscuits and cakes or my favourite Werther butterscotch sweets. And dessert is almost more important than my main meal! Therefore, to be deprived of practically all our sugar and for years rather than weeks was a truly agonizing experience for me. The less I got the more I craved it. And, of course, boiled sweets were never on our menu – I don't believe that the local shop even had any in store for a long time after the war. Everything was geared towards the most essential foods for survival. And even those were hardly ever readily available.

Very occasionally we did have a little sugar sprinkled on our pancakes but it was the smallest possible amount, merely a hint of sweetness was all we could afford. I believe it is true when I say we never ever had any sweets during the entire eight years we lived in that village. Mutti saved a little sugar for the few very special events like Christmas or a birthday and again for my confirmation so that she had sufficient saved to make some cakes for those special celebrations. The rest of the time the sugar "lived" in those forbidden brown paper bags on top of the wardrobe, tempting me daily more than I could bear. Werner did not seem to be too bothered. Sausages were more his style! But I hungered most terribly for a bit of that forbidden drug, like a real drug addict who will do anything to get his daily fix.

For my years I was rather responsible and grown up in many ways, alert and helpful, a good and dependable household assistant, in charge of it when mother was away at work, making sure the fire never died in the stove, collecting twigs and pine cones in the wood nearest to the village as soon as school was over so that Mutti had enough to keep a good fire going for our supper. Yes, I admit it, I considered myself a **good** daughter, not in a seriously calculating way – helping Mutti gave me tremendous satisfaction and joy. Yet we also know by now that some part of me did hope to earn more of her love of which I never seemed to get enough. Perhaps this was because I missed my father so very badly. I missed the male element in our little family far more than I realized at the time and thus Mutti's approval meant the world to me. But obviously not as much as a little bit of that forbidden sugar! Day in day out my eyes strayed to the top of the wardrobe while my brain worked overtime on a solution to the problem of how to get to the bags when there was no ladder I could safely "borrow" from anywhere. We had chairs but I was too little to reach the top from a chair alone. Mutti knew why she had chosen the top of the wardrobe alright. She knew the temptation the sugar bags created. To her mind this place was as safe as Fort Knox and, of course, she was almost right.

"Ich schaffe das; irgendwie schaffe ich das" . "I will manage it, somehow I will. If I think long and hard and often enough, I'll get an idea. It is only a question of time!" I knew as sure as I knew my name that one day I would succeed in reaching the top. Naturally, when this day came I would not be so silly and take away a whole bag. No, no, we needed the money for the rent and I wouldn't be so mean as to endanger the sale of the bags. All I wanted was a tiny, tiny lick of my wetted finger, one, perhaps two at most, from each bag. That little bit of shortfall in the pound no one would notice, not Mutti, not the farmer's wife and everyone would end up happy, especially satisfied me!

Well, you guessed it, No one ended up happy, not Mutti (she was furious, really desperately angry), not me but least of all my poor, lazy but very kind hearted brother.

After ages of intense contemplation I had worked out a way of reaching the top. It involved a chair, of course, but what else I had used to put either under the chair or on top of it is anyone's guess. The passing of time has wiped that bit of memory out. But it worked. Even better than I had expected. I managed to dip the entire wetted finger really deep into the bag coming out densely covered with the most tantalizing white crystals of sweet delight. No wonder merely one dip was not enough. The moment one finger was licked dry another one went into the forbidden bag, time after time – day after day! Until the day Mutti had to get the bags down to take them to be sold! As soon as she looked up at them she noticed something was wrong. They did not look the way they should. The tops of the bags were suspiciously crumbled and looked hollow, a condition which could not have happened by itself! The penny dropped instantly. Her face turned white with shock and fury and her angry eyes darted from Werner to me:

"Now, look here! Who of you has done this?"

"It wasn't me, Mutti. It really wasn't me! Really, really not!"

I gushed innocently, yet feeling sick with guilt and horror of what was to come. "Werner, was it you? It must have been you then!"

"No, mother, no, it wasn't me. You know it's Brigitte. **She** loves sugar. She cannot resist it. Look at her, she is lying. You can see it in her face she is lying!"

And he was right, you **could** no doubt see it in my face. I was cringing with guilt and shame inside me but still adamant of my innocence. I just could not bear to face up to my weakness and take the consequences of it – ME who was usually so good and helpful with the management of our family's day to day existence. How could I possibly admit to such an act of irresponsibility?

"Werner, you are lying. I know it was you. Brigitte would **never** do such a thing. She **knows** how important this sugar is! Come here, at once!"

And with this she darted towards him, grabbed him and bent him over her knee, beating him as hard as she could until she had no more strength left and all her despair and frustration was drained from her body. Her energy spent.

"So, was it you or not?"

Werner had started to cry wildly, the tears were streaming down his cheeks. He could not believe that his beloved mother could actually think he would ever lie to her. She, who had always overlooked his little misdemeanours was now turning all her fury towards him. He protested wildly but Mutti's anger had not ebbed and she was still shaking him in the hope of pulling the truth out of him. I could no longer bear to watch this gruesome battle between them. The kind innocent boy being beaten for the first time in his life – and for a crime he had not committed! I had not counted on my mother's fury, not dreamt she would actually physically attack us as she had always been so mild and forgiving before whenever we had misbehaved in some other small way. Suddenly, for a brief instant, it dawned on me how difficult adult life was in these hard times. A few grams of sugar seriously threw our existence off balance – and I had been the culprit! Not only been the culprit but a liar and a cheat accusing my innocent brother. Of course, I had never imagined he would be so severely punished,. She had never even been angry with him before – but beating him?

That showed the depth of her despair to me most vividly and I broke down in tears. Tears of immense remorse. With outstretched arms I moved towards my mother, wanting to throw my arms around her neck to show her how much I loved her, pleading for forgiveness, screaming through my tears:
"Mutti, Mutti, I will never do it again. Never, never, never. I promise. I couldn't help it, but I will never do it again! Ever! You **must** believe me!"

I clung pathetically with all my might to her trembling body. I shook all over with shame and horror of what I had done and truly felt at that dramatic moment I could never betray my beloved mother in this way again – addiction to sugar or not. Sadly, I was wrong! A month or two later the scene repeated itself in almost the same sequence. Werner would get beaten again. I would be spared once more despite all the lying. Only the end was different. Utterly exhausted with having beaten Werner with her bare hands, she looked at me. There was this boring question in her eyes – and then they went blank and misty, staring despairingly into nothing. Her whole body sank, almost collapsing over my brother. I felt like the lowest creature on earth, also collapsed into a heap on the floor. All three of us cried, but only I with shame and disgust about my lack of control when the sensible me knew all the while how very serious a crime I was committing. And again Mutti refrained from beating me! I almost wished that she had not. Only motherly love can reach the areas of understanding required to know whether something was done out of naughtiness or a deeper unconquerable need. And mother had reached this stage of comprehension.

Somehow, once again, she managed to scrape the rent together. And I never stole any sugar again! I, too, had reached an inner understanding – of **her** needs, not just of mine.
And Werner? How could I make up to him? Well, I did not nag him for a long while when he wasn't keen to help me with our household chores. At night, in

bed, I tickled him with my legs until he tickled my legs back.. When I did that, he knew that I was truly sorry. We always made up that way!

Despite all our squabbles and my frustration with him, we did love one another. We simply had two very different personalities and in times of stress and difficulties these showed up very prominently. I was much more hands-on, he a sweet and loving dreamer, whom it was impossible to hate but easy to get angry with on a short-term fuse. Not only was he lazy at home, he was also extraordinarily lazy at school. There was a time when I had to help him with his math lessons (although I was in a lower form) as otherwise he would not have been passed on to the next stage which in Germany is a huge disgrace and can mar your career for life.

When Werner was an adult he joined the army where he underwent an IQ-test which proved he had an exceptionally high IQ! So my frustration with this lovable brother was well-founded during those years of struggle and strife. Generally speaking we were very affectionate towards each other and during our teenage years he even became my pin-up for a while! He was very good looking and while in uniform on leave, I was more than proud to introduce him to my girl-friends!

Chapter Twenty-Three

Trying to recall these early years after six and more decades has made me realize that I have no problems remembering impressionable situations, may they have been good or bad, but when life rolled along in uneventful ways, my memory draws a blank. Large chunks of time during the early winters don't bring up anything remarkable to write about.

By 1948 our father was still not home. His cards continued to arrive and Mutti's replies continued not to get to him. We had settled in well into our new neighbourhood by then. Mutti had begun to make good friends with

"Black Johanna" since the slaughter of the pig the previous autumn and her help in making liver sausages and later soap from the bones of the pig. Occasionally, that winter, Johanna would call up towards our window from her court yard and ask whether we would like to have some of her stew or soup when she had made rather too much for the two of them. Those were always celebration days, for she really was a splendid cook. Her soups and stews contained real chunks of meat; something we rarely were able to enjoy on our meagre ration card purchases.

I, too, had made yet another good friend by then. Like Gerda, Benita was one of my classmates. She was very slow in befriending me as she was the daughter of the local gentleman farmer and mill owner. Socially, she ranked way above anyone else in the village while I was considered rather low down the line, being a refugee child. Not so by Benita or later by her parents! By the summer of 1948 we had struck up a good friendship in class and soon I was also invited to go and play with her at weekends or in our spring and summer holidays. This was a very special achievement and was viewed with considerable envy by the local farm children who could only admire the private grounds of the Markurth family from outside their huge iron gate to the private quarters behind some of the mill outbuildings.

Benita had two brothers with whom I also got on really well and they, in turn, were allowed to invite one of their friends each when I came to play with Benita. Thus, most of the time, we were a crowd of five or six, playing hide and seek, messing around the farm and mill and having a wonderful adventurous time.

For several years during the summer Benita and I, and sometimes the boys, too, helped Frau Markurth with the harvesting of the garden produce, sitting outside in the sunshine shelling either peas or beans or hulling gooseberries. Sometimes, when I had been particularly helpful I was rewarded, together with the Markurth children, with a small square of chocolate. But this would have been in later years when they knew me and my family well and could trust me not to talk about it to others in the village. Obviously, this chocolate had somehow come to them from their relations in the West as it was impossible to buy any in the East at that time. We were sworn to secrecy not to tell anyone about this treat as it was dangerous indeed to have any food or other rare products imported from the "Golden West" as the population called the other side; the "hateful criminal West" as our new government described it. By that time we children were already well aware of the danger to anyone who did not adhere to the stern demands of our Communist government and we playmates understood very well that these small chocolate treats could become as explosive as bullets if word got round of their existence.

The occasional piece of chocolate wasn't the only treat, however. Often Frau Markurth gave me a small basket full of the type of fruit or vegetables I had helped to prepare for conserving to take home to Mutti. In this way we all benefited from my new friendship which, incidentally, has lasted to this very day!

Playing in the beautiful grounds of the Markurth estate was only one of the benefits I enjoyed. As the family got to know me better they extended their warm hospitality by sometimes inviting me to lunch in their house, which really was another enormous help in making my childhood in Heiddorf more enjoyable. We always ate in their dining room since lunch was the main meal of the day. The table was beautifully laid out with a white tablecloth, starched table napkins, silver cutlery and, of course, beautiful chinaware on which was served even more beautiful food! Although we lived in a most simple abode at that time, I had started to appreciate beauty wherever I found it. Up to this point, mostly in nature. Now I was introduced to attractive furnishings and good table manners, to books and polite conversation – and I was revelling in this new expansion of my life. Benita's mother, in particular, was a very elegant but modest and extremely kind lady whom I admired hugely and of whom I have nothing but the warmest good memories. She always spoke to me as if she was addressing an adult of equal status, usually accompanied by a smile:

"Brigitte, thank you so very much for all your help today and would you, please, give these few things to your dear mother as an appreciation! And, please, come again soon!"

"Thank **you** very much, Frau Markurth. You are most kind. Mutti will be so very pleased."

And I curtseyed, as I had been taught to do in front of a lady and skipped home joyfully, the happiest girl in the village that day. "Come again, soon!", she had said while waving good-bye. As if **I** had done **them** a favour with my presence and not the other way around! And the food parcel was not charity but a well earned gift for the little bit of fun work we had all participated in.

What a wonderful lady she was! Next to Mutti, the nicest woman in the world!

The most gratifying experience about my contact with Benita's family was that they never made me feel inferior to them in any way. Unlike the stupid farm children who really were inferior to the Markurths, Benita and her brothers had been brought up to treat everyone with equal respect and not to judge people by what they had or what they lacked in the material sense but by what they possessed inside. Even on a few occasions when I was obviously out of my depth they did all they could to make me feel at ease and help me with my problem.

The following incident will show you how gracious a family I had befriended. I had been invited to another lunch. On this occasion Mr. Markurth was also at table. As gentle and good natured his wife was as stern and intimidating he appeared to me. I was aware, sitting next to him, that I had to be on my best behaviour. Unfortunately, as would be my bad luck, we were given cauliflower as an accompanying vegetable, one of the few foods I found really hard to eat. In fact, it nearly made me ill and I was struggling to keep small bits down which I had mixed in with my potatoes. Everyone around the table had finished their meal while I was still struggling with a rather large piece of cauliflower which just did not seem to get smaller as much as I tried! I could sense Mr. Markurth getting very restless and I also knew I could not possibly put my knife and fork onto my plate as a sign that I, too, had finished my meal. You ate what you were given! You owed this to your hosts as a sign of respect. And in these hard times of austerity respect for food came naturally to all of us. And most certainly to me who was always hungry, although not for cauliflower!
I poked around my dish in total despair, not daring to look around me for embarrassment . Still, I could not look down onto my lap for ever, so when I gradually lifted my eyes and glanced furtively around the table, everyone looked encouragingly at me with expressions that said: "Come on, Brigitte. You can make it. We'll wait for you, but don't make it too long!"
Frau Markurth especially gave me an encouraging smile and suddenly the smell of the cauliflower wasn't so unattractive anymore and two or three mouthfuls and my plate was empty as well as my dignity saved. Mr. Markurth had no reason to complain about his daughter's refugee friend and, hopefully,

I would be allowed to attend luncheon again one day! Which I did. And if my memory does not trick me, cauliflower was never again on the menu when I was invited!

Yes, from about summer 1948 onwards my particular life began to take on a much happier frame. I had made friends with Gerda next door, with Ingetrud and her family opposite and now I was also a friend of Benita and her family, who were definitely the grandest family of the community. Wasn't it wonderful to be so lucky? Later, towards summer, there was a further fortunate development: Werner and I became friendly with "Black Johanna" and her husband. Ever since Mutti's help the previous autumn the two women had slowly formed a stronger bond .Johanna's offers of stew or soup meant that I had to go to her to collect the food. Little conversations, which I never failed to initiate, soon convinced her that we children were probably not so bad after all. She became much friendlier to both of us and in return, as well as due to her good cooking, we began to like her a great deal better, too. Much to our relief, the incident of the missing sausages from the smoke house was never referred to. Time and closer acquaintance had vastly mellowed their hearts and we, in turn, began to realize what a good couple of old dears they were deep down, below the dishevelled appearance.

I believe it was during that late summer we began helping them bring in their corn and straw. In the field next to the property of Gerda's mother, which was also a miniature farm, stood a huge thresher for the rental use of all the farmers nearby. We children loved watching the various farmers and their helpers bring in the corn from their fields on horse-drawn ladder wagons which were laden so high with the sheaves of corn that we were certain the load would tip over just before the wagons had reached the place in front of the thresher. But although the load of corn was swaying precariously from right to left , the old farm hands had tied the load so carefully to the ladders they never had an accident and we were bereft of the excitement of seeing the whole lot collapse onto the field around them.! Pity, that, but we still had a lot of fun watching this, for us, new experience of harvesting farm work. If the piles of corn sheaves had broken up during the transport to the thresher then the women who had built up the wagons layer by layer after the sheaves had been lifted up to them by the men folks down below, would have fallen down as well. And although it might have been fun to watch the odd skirt or two fly high into the air, together with a few bare legs, we would not have wanted them to get really hurt . As it turned out, they never did.

Once each wagon was correctly positioned next to the thresher, the women, having carefully built up the load sheave by sheave, now had to throw them down the shaft of the thresher as fast as they could since the thresher gobbled them up at tremendous speed, spewing them out the other end minus their ears, which had been cut off inside the belly of the machine. More strong hands then reassembled the loose straw into sheaves, ready for transport to the various barns in the village.

All this work was executed with a lot of banter and laughter despite the hours of hard work which had preceded this part of the harvesting. The collective work exuded a tremendous energy and the brilliant blue sky and warm sun shine added further attraction to the observer.

The day it was our neighbours' turn to bring in their corn and straw we had an added involvement. Johanna's husband had asked us whether we would want to help him, earning us a juicy sandwich for our supper. We agreed at once, even before knowing what was expected of us. Bread and sausage was a very powerful lure! Luckily, we liked our part of the job which consisted of the following: once the released straw had been collected from the machine and transported back to his barn near the house, Werner and I were meant to jump up and down the bales inside the barn to press it down as hard as we could in order to get as much straw into the available space. This was the fodder for their cows during the coming winter months, together with some hay, while it was also used to cover the floor of their stable for the cows to sleep on. Later, mixed with their excrement, this muck was going to be turned into valuable manure for their garden and fields. In nature nothing gets wasted.

What a fantastic job we had found! Werner was determined to prove he could jump a lot higher and faster than me; having spent all his free time since the arrival at Heiddorf three years ago, playing football with the smaller boys, he had developed strong legs and a strong lung. I had to admit he was better at this job but at the end of the shift he was as exhausted as I was. Sweat pouring down his face, he collapsed into a heap, pumping for air. I had succumbed quite a bit earlier, but the farmer realized we had really done a fabulous job and we both went home with well deserved sandwiches filled with thick slices of Johanna's well renowned sausage!

"Mutti, look at our big bellies! Full of scrumptious sandwiches with sausage and real golden butter!"
 We were drumming on our tummies with delight.
What a fabulous day we have had! That night Mutti had a well earned free evening to herself while we kids snored happily in our bed, dead to the world around us. Isn't life great?

That summer of 1948 was not so glorious for the people of the three western parts of Berlin. Only, at that time, I had no idea about it. In West Germany life was starting to look up because by then the US government had extended the economic aid they gave to Europe to include West Germany. By then the West German government had initiated a currency reform, which the Soviets did not like. As a result they withdrew from the previously established four-power governing bodies and also initiated the Berlin blockade. This meant all roads between West Germany and the western parts of Berlin were totally blocked in order to attempt the destruction of their population by means of starvation. Disillusionment with their former Soviet allies had already set in and the Western Allies responded with an amazing reaction: they started to airlift all foodstuff and other goods to the western half of the city! Aircraft touched down in Berlin non-stop for 11 months, when the Soviets finally ended the blockade!
There must have been some people on our side of the border who knew about this astonishing feat by listening to the western radio stations, but I had never heard of it while living in Mecklenburg.

Chapter Twenty-Four

A similar feeling of heightened elation pulsed through my veins as Richard and I stepped out of the little village church, having taken our vows. The sun still shone brightly; the warmth of it feeling like a welcome caress after the coolness inside the church and the solemnity of the formal ceremony. The lightness of the day reflected so uncannily the lightness of spirit I felt inside from the moment the official part of our marriage was over and we turned towards our guests who were cramming the pews of the little church, all of them looking exceedingly well dressed; the men in morning suits, the ladies wearing colourful hats to match their festive summer outfits. The men, in particular, looked exceedingly elegant. Good looking or not, their aristocratic attire transformed everyone into a princely state. The REAL prince though was at my side and he, in turn, had his princess.

As we proceeded to walk arm in arm, as man and wife, down the aisle towards the same door we had entered the church earlier, every part and emotional experience of the previous 24 years of my life seemed to have fallen away in an instant. It felt as if I had simply not existed before, at least not with the same intensity and lightness which, in some miraculous manner, had taken hold of me. A magnificent butterfly was emerging from the chrysalis. Like the caterpillar, from which the butterfly eventually emerges, and which had spent long periods of its life searching for food (like I once had!) and hiding in the underside of leaves while it consumes them, this human butterfly, like its real counterpart, began to flutter into the sunshine side of life alongside her sweet and gentle husband. A different young woman walked out of the church than had entered it half an hour before. Did Richard sense the mysterious rebirth his bride was undergoing? And did he feel the same about his own self? He looked relaxed now, none of the twinges of nervousness I had detected before. A surge of immense warmth rushed through me. Looking up at him my body automatically drew closer to his in anticipation of bathing in the look of love he exchanged with me once we had left the smiling congregation behind us and now stood within the frame of the door, greeted by curious onlookers and bright golden sunshine.

A photographer was waiting, his camera poised for the all important photos of the newlyweds. We were asked to linger on the threshold a bit longer to give him the time he needed to focus his camera and capture images of which we would all be proud when they looked at us from their glamorous photo frames in the nebulous years of the future. These were only a few extra moments of delicious happiness and excitement but they were the first of our married life. To linger and soak in the immense release of pent-up tension and resulting happiness of these special moments was a most welcome pleasure and delight. I did not know it then but certainly know it now, that brief though these moments were, they were of a most unique kind and would never be surpassed by any other. So we happily lingered, intoxicated with tenderness as well as a hint of bewilderment.

Chapter Twenty-Five

While I almost drowned in happiness in the summer of 1963, some time during the summer of 1948 I very nearly truly drowned – in the river Elde! I have told you earlier how we village children spent most of our spare time during summer holidays or out of school hours messing around by the river beach. Children and teenagers, even adults, regularly met up there on hot sunny days. It was the one place where everyone mingled and had fun together. With luck, the older boys or girls helped the younger ones to get better in their attempts to learn to swim. This year I knew that I was getting better and would be ready to, hopefully, pass the test before the end of the season. "Passing the test" meant being able to swim across the river to the Neu Kaliss side of the river bank and then, after a brief rest, returning to the home side. Naturally you could not do this by yourself – if you wanted to survive that is - and, no, I did NOT attempt this like a reckless fool by myself.

I had just enough sense to realize the risk and, therefore, waited until some adult would volunteer to take care of me and swim across next to me in case I got into trouble. It had to be a man, strong enough to pick me up if I were to drown, but the likeliness of this happening never really crossed my mind in any serious way. Had I not practised like a mad thing all summer long? And did not everybody say that I was really getting on well? Well then, why worry? And I didn't. But I did worry about how much longer I had to wait until some kind and patient young man would agree to take me on for the big swim.

Towards the end of summer my moment had arrived. The young man who agreed to supervise us across the river was someone she knew. I had never met him before. But he looked strong and sensible. There were a few other boys and girls around on both sides of the river. There usually were, which was reassuring.

The other girl was not quite as strong a swimmer as I was, so she was placed to his left and I to his right. All went well for a while, but once we were about half-way across it became obvious that the girl was getting weak and scared and the young man had to concentrate more and more on her to ensure she would not go under while I seemed to have no apparent problems.

Also half-way across I felt the current getting stronger. Now it meant staying calm and making more of an effort to make progress at a point in our venture when I, too, was beginning to lose some strength. The other girl was gulping and groaning in an effort to get ahead. I could hear the young man firing her on.

"You can make it. See, we are getting closer. Don't talk, just keep breathing. Well done! Keep going!"

All the time he was talking to her he also watched her without ever taking his eyes off her, therefore totally forgetting about little me drifting away further and further down the river and away from any rescuing hands, if need be! Although I had drifted away quite a bit, the bank of the river was getting very close and I felt certain I could get there without any help, so I did not cry out for it. My confidence began to diminish though when I suddenly felt drawn down by an unexpected clump of creepers entangling my fighting legs and gradually pulling me down, gently at first and then, inevitably, deeper and deeper into the river. It all happened so fast and unexpectedly, I was losing the battle to extricate my legs within seconds and had literally no time to cry out for help. My entire focus was on staying afloat and on fighting the fear. But I sank. I had just gone under when I came up again only a meter or so away from the bank. Yet, before I could make a sound the vile creepers were pulling me down again, tightening up all around my body. I really began to panic and wonder whether I would make it. All the while I was fighting this battle I could hear voices shouting:

"Where is Brigitte? My God, she is gone! What's happened?" and someone else shouting: "Look, over there! You can just see her hands. My God, she is drowning in the creepers! Quick, run, run before she is gone!"

At that point I came up for air for the second time and someone had jumped into the river and I felt hands grabbing mine and pulling me ashore. It was a steep grass bank; several hands were pulling me up as I had no strength left to help them in any way. The young man, who had been in charge of me, grabbed my legs. Other boys helped him until I was hanging completely upside down. Whatever water I had swallowed could now flow out of my mouth, which was a truly horrible experience, but one essential for saving my life! Everyone involved in my rescue was very kind and anxious. I remember two strong, uncompromising hands pulling my mouth open wide to allow the maximum amount of water to exit my stomach as quickly as possible. Everyone present seemed very experienced in this rescue work – clearly I had not been the first person to very nearly drown crossing this river! When my stomach was empty and a little colour had returned to my cheeks, all the helpers involved plonked down next to me, totally relieved and exhausted from having avoided a tragic loss of life. Only then, when all danger was gone and they could return to normal thought processes did the angry telling off begin.

"Why on earth did you not shout for help, you silly girl! Who did you think you were?
An Olympic swimmer? Why do you think no one is allowed crossing the river unless they are really competent swimmers? The first attempt isn't cat's play, you know! There are lots of patches of creepers and the current can be very strong. Didn't anyone tell you that, stupid girl!?"

Well, what could I say to them? Had I been too proud, too independent? Believing I could cope with ANYTHING? Or was it because the creepers came on so suddenly and so violently that there simply hadn't been any time even to shout for help?

But then, I had been aware of drifting further and further away from the man and the girl. So why had I not called out? I really could not tell you, but it was probably because I did not really know the man and was too scared to give him further trouble knowing he was having a difficult time with the other girl. She was his niece after all. He could not really leave her until he had got her safely to the river bank and onto solid ground. However, a little bit of false pride and over-confidence must have played a role of sorts in my stupid behaviour as well.

Luckily, Werner was not there to witness the scene and I pleaded with everyone else never to mention the incident to anyone, as I did not want my mother to know about it. I had already given her enough other trouble. This incident could have been just one trouble too many, something all those involved seemed to understand without any further explanation. My mother never found out, thank goodness! And I never crossed the river again unaccompanied until everyone, including myself, was sure I had become a safe enough swimmer, and one who knew to avoid all the patches of deadly creepers. And there were quite a few!

Although I did become a reasonably competent swimmer over time, I never really enjoyed swimming that much, never wanted to learn to dive or show off in a pool, other than my good figure or the latest pretty swim suit or bikini (naturally, a bit later in life!). Yet, while living in Heiddorf, the river continued to be a star attraction, simply because there was no better place for boys and girls during the summer months to gather around having fun. In those days, nobody went on a summer holiday. Especially East Germany still lay in total ruins after the war. I don't believe the railway line between Doemitz and Ludwigslust had been rebuilt yet. Immediately after the end of the war the Russians dismantled practically everything useful they could still find and shipped it back to Russia. Railway lines were a particular source of bounty and the line connecting our village with the outlying country towns was certainly dismantled within days of the Russian occupation. This meant our village was pretty well cut off from the outside world. The shops were supplied by lorries, but private cars were never to be seen as there was no petrol. The farmers used their horses for transport and we our legs.

Towards the end of summer, early autumn, I walked to the neighbouring town of Doemitz for the first time, following a path along the river. Mutti was ill in hospital and I wanted to visit her. I remember the season as I was able to steal a few windfall apples to take to her for a present.

The distance to the town was approximately 6 to 7 kilometres, which seemed like a very long walk to me. I had actually been close to Doemitz once before. Johanna's husband had taken Werner and me to his cornfield on his horse and cart. We had taken the road route then and it did not appear to be such a long way. Walking along the river bank was another matter. The path was lovely. I still see parts of it in my mind's eye. It was a warm sunny day and I really enjoyed my adventure. I missed Mutti. The flat seemed deathly quiet without her and I desperately wanted to see her and make sure she was alright. I found the hospital and Mutti and it was such a joyful reunion. She looked very pale but said she would come home soon, which comforted me immensely so that I felt sufficiently cheered to make the long walk back. To keep my spirits up I sang the songs I had learned from Mutti and which we often sang together. Sadly I have forgotten what they were. I was used to running around in the fields and to the woods, but I had not walked such a long distance in one afternoon before and by the time I had reached home my legs were shattered. Yet what an exciting adventure I had had!

My first visit to our little neighbouring town! I had not seen all of it since the hospital was the all important place to find. But I had got some idea of what it was like (it still lay in a fair amount of ruins) and I had made the journey all by myself. I remember to this day feeling very proud of my achievement, while Werner was playing football again in our dusty road with his team of admirers.

Two days later Mutti came home and our world was whole once more. I expect someone must have collected her with a horse and cart. She certainly could not have walked such a long way. It is these finer, more ordinary details of our everyday life that have escaped my memory by now. Therefore, what I am able to recall for you in these memoirs are those events which had made some impression on me personally. These may not always appear so very important or of interest to you who are reading about them so many years later but they left a huge impression on my young child's mind.

Mutti was back home. That was what mattered. Not how she managed to get back to us. In fact, reflecting on these early childhood years makes me realize how limited our comprehension was of the harsh world Mutti and the other adults inhabited in those days. We helped Mutti whenever it was possible in our childlike ways. She was the one who had all the responsibility for our survival, literally for our daily bread which was extremely hard to come by. We often went to bed hungry, yet knowing in our hearts that, somehow, Mutti would find a way of providing something to eat again the following day. Perhaps only bread and potatoes, but it could be a stew from Johanna or the HO shop might have a delivery of some other good thing to eat and we would succeed in getting some of it.

Mutti, on the other hand, also went to bed hungry. Who would be HER hopeful provider the following day when she knew fair well there was only a small piece of bread left for the three of us for our breakfast? And probably not much else other than a few potatoes.

One day, on my return from school, someone stood in front of our door upstairs with a large parcel in his arm. He gave me the fright of my life, for he was in uniform!

A Russian uniform! What was a Russian soldier doing outside our door? I had not seen any Russian in the village for some time, so where did he spring from? He inquired after our mother and when he heard that she was at work in the factory, he handed me the parcel and said it was for us – with his compliments! It was a box full of wonderful foodstuff – tins of meat and fish as well as some dried milk and a large loaf of bread. I had never seen this soldier before and would never see him again either. How well did Mutti know this man? Was he just trying to get to know her and wow her with this food or had they known one another for longer? These were questions to which I had no answer. Although I was shocked about this development, I wasn't altogether surprised. Mutti was a good-looking young woman and she had been struggling on her own to keep us all alive for far too many years. Of course, she needed a little bit of comfort and if this "comfort" also meant "food", so much the better. One thing I did know quite clearly though. Whatever her relationship with this soldier, the main reason for it was the supply of food! This unexpected parcel remained the only one from the

Russian or any other man. At least as far as we children could tell. And we were pretty smart!

Chapter Twenty-Six

Another monotonous winter lay ahead. The dark season never seemed to hold much brightness for us, but that is probably fairly normal for everyone, even nowadays when life has so much more to offer everyone in our Western civilization. Then, our small group of relations huddled together for diversion as often as we could, merely chatting and singing. None of us owned any books, of course, nor radios but we had some playing cards. Simple entertainment, but one in which we could all partake.

There was home-work to do as well and Mutti made sure we did not skip on this important part of our school education. We already know, Werner was not so keen. Therefore our mother had to keep a sharp eye on him or he would happily have gone to school the next day with all sorts of stupid excuses why he had not been able to do any of it! I, on the other hand, loved doing my home-work. It kept me busy and made me more intelligent, something I rated very highly! We still did not have any of our own school books, thus had to borrow them from school and be most careful not to dirty or damage them or we were given "Strafarbeit" (punishment), like a fifty or a hundred lines of "I must not defile the school books"! Needless to say I never got any "Strafarbeit", nor did Werner, as he did not exactly suffer from any overuse of them anyway.

Christmas 1948 came and went as if it wasn't much of a festive season. No one we knew ever had a Christmas tree since it was "strengstens verboten" (most severely forbidden) to fell any trees. Stealing them from the surrounding woods would have been the only way to acquire one – for any villager, not just for us refugees. We had no decorations either, nor Christmas cards. I don't even believe that we made our own cards for our mother. Where would we have got the coloured pencils from? These were luxury items which only the school provided during the appropriate lessons. May be by then you might have been able to purchase such things in towns although I doubt whether even there it would have been easy to buy anything "frivolous" such as coloured pencils.

There was one change though on Christmas Eve from all the other days of the year: We had our rabbit to eat for supper! I cannot recall whether Mutti stewed or baked it in our kitchen oven, which we had by then. But I do recall it was delicious, really scrumptious and much tastier meat than the tough beef we sometimes managed to buy with our ration cards. We did not mind eating our rabbit one bit. It had been reared lovingly for this reason alone and I am sure the rabbit did not mind. I felt certain it must have sensed throughout the year that its whole purpose in life was to give us joy at Christmas. What better way to die! After all, our rabbit (or in later years rabbits) were never regarded by us as our pets. The idea of rabbits becoming part of the family as pets never even entered our heads. Animals were meant to sustain mankind and they were much appreciated for being there for us in this way.

I wish I could tell you something really interesting about the remainder of the winter, alas nothing worth getting excited about happened that season. Sometimes I spent time with my local friends, Gerda and Ingetrud, never in winter with Benita. We were all hibernating indoors as the winters then seemed so much colder than they are now.
So when spring arrived everyone's spirits began to lighten, just like the days. My 10th birthday had passed by without me even noticing it. No one sang to you in those days or gave parties or presents. Everyone was short of food and money. The days of Streuselkuchen for my birthday had not yet returned. Cakes were still something we dreamed of enjoying once more sometime in the far future, together with regular warm and tasty meals, leather shoes, warm clothes, perhaps even a bicycle and a sledge for the snowy season. A bigger doll would have been nice or some books of fairy tales and adventure stories for my brother. None of those we had as yet, but we did have each other. Only Papa was still missing to make our family more complete.

The spring and summer season of 1949 passed by in a similar fashion to the previous year, although there were a few improvements. Our relationship with our neighbours was showing signs of real improvement. Black Johanna became ever more friendly. We discovered she and her husband had a grown up daughter. Where she had been up to that period I cannot imagine. But in the summer of 1949 she suddenly appeared. Yet I do not remember that she actually lived with her parents. She was working and living somewhere else but we began to see her in the yard from time to time. By spring 1949 the couple had really taken to us children and I remember walking in and out of their little farm almost as I liked it, helping a little, often merely chatting with Johanna and watching her make butter or spinning wool in the evenings. I think she really enjoyed the life and chatter I brought into their existence. That summer I was also asked whether I would like to pick all her fruit in the garden as she found it harder and harder to find time for this sort of work. And it was certainly work I was able to do and found really enjoyable to boot. Obviously no one had money and therefore I was paid in kind – part of the crop of gooseberries or black and red currants. Scrummy!

Gooseberries and red currants were my declared favourites. I found it hard not to put more of them into my mouth than into the containers! Johanna knew this, of course, but she never told me off. She was glad she did not have to do the picking since her back was troubling her more and more with every season. And of course, there were still more than plenty of berries left for her to make jam with, using the sugar she had bought from our mother!

That summer my friendship with Ingetrud grew a little stronger as well. Her family often went into the woods to search for edible mushrooms and on several occasions they invited me to go along with them. They were a complete family, mother, father, two daughters and a son. I was very envious of their lovely family life and therefore always exceptionally happy when I was allowed to join them on the mushroom spree, followed by a simple picnic once our baskets were full. One year, probably not until 1950 or even later, their son Horst had taken a camera along and I still have one or two photos he took on that day, all of us sitting in deep yellow grass enjoying the sunshine and just being alive.

The occasional invitations to the Markurth estate also continued as did the expeditions into the blueberry wood. Everything was much the same as the year before, only a bit better. Relationships deepened which led to greater self-esteem and more respect from the villagers towards us. Consequently we were beginning to feel that Heiddorf was starting to be home. By then we all knew we would never be allowed to return home to East Prussia. Our homeland had been carved off from the rest of Germany and it was best not to dwell on what we had lost but look to the future and try to integrate as best as the villagers would allow us to do. And they were faintly starting to accept us more.

School, too, was still a place of happiness. Everyone's favourite teacher was Herr Schroeder. He was still quite young (I guess in his late thirties,) and we girls thought he was handsome, too! He taught us German, mathematics and history, I seem to remember. At any rate, all the most important subjects. He was the only male teacher at the school. Consequently, we were all in awe of him, but not in a fearful way. He was much too kind for that. I don't remember him ever getting angry with us. Perhaps he did not need to be. We adored and respected him in equal measure. For many of us he took the place of a missing father as well as our main teacher and everyone competed for his attention and even affection, especially me. Herr Schroeder, however, was a clever as well as a wise man; he showed no preference to anyone in the class but treated all his pupils with the same gentle but authoritative manner. That's why we all adored him and worked extra hard just to please him. I never looked up as much to any other teacher during my entire school life. He was a very special person as well as an excellent teacher and spiritual guide. Since many children in our village school were still without a father at home, Herr Schroeder made sure that those boys and girls in particular were not left behind in their studies due to the lack of a disciplinarian at home!

He was strict, yet in a fatherly manner, rather than a stern one which worked really well with most of his students – bar one, of course. And we know who THAT was! He showed endless patience with my brother. With my help in mathematics, which I wasn't even exceptionally good at, Herr Schroeder succeeded in dragging Werner into the next educational year. Thank you, dear Herr Schroeder. You must have known he was merely a lazy bones and therefore worth the effort. But at the cost of how much patience!!

More patience than I had with my "dear" brother! While I helped him with his math home- work, we got on surprisingly well. He realized that he needed to work harder and that his final exam result would have to be quite exceptional if he was going to be passed on to the higher form next September. So he buckled down to some work with me and since he was not a bit stupid he picked up things pretty well. Surprisingly, we never even had a row!

Not so with his other duties! One day that autumn I did not go home immediately after school. May be I went to Benita's house. I knew I would not be home first to attend to the fire in the stove, so Mutti had asked Werner to come straight home and add some sticks and pine cones to the embers, which were usually just still glowing under the top layer of ash by the time we returned home from school. Mutti, of course, would not return from work until around 5.30 to 6.00pm. By that time there usually would not be a glimmer left to restart the fire, so it was important to rekindle it as soon as we had reached home. We had no newspaper to help restart a fire and few sticks in reserve for such a purpose as well. However, if we built a nice little pyramid of sticks and pine cones over the heap of ash and then stoked it gently and blew hard at the glowing embers, a flame would lick up towards the mount of sticks and the fire would be kept going and ready for Mutti's return home.

Well, you guessed it. Werner did go straight home, but threw his satchel into a corner, left the stove unattended and ran straight down into the street where his little friends were already kicking the football around playfully, in wait for their trainer and goal keeper – Werner.

When I returned home it was also time for Werner to come up as mother was expected home any minute. I walked into our room and felt the cold the moment I entered. I ran to the stove and yes, it was icy cold. As much as I stoked the ash there wasn't the glimmer of an ember left. By that time Werner realized his carelessness and was standing next to me by the stove anxiously staring into the pile of ash and wishing just to see the tiniest glow of something red. But nothing of that sort emerged. I was furious. More furious than words can explain and in my frustration and anger I swung the poker as high as I could and brought it down as hard as I could onto my poor brother's back!

"Now, that will teach you to neglect the fire, you useless lazy bones!" I was trembling from the effort of hitting him and also from the anger I felt of never being able to rely on him. Play always came before work with him and I had had enough of it.

I must have hit him rather hard for he had tears in his eyes and was doubling over with pain, but I have to admit to his credit and my shame, he did not hit me back as most other older brothers might have done. Instead, he gathered up enough kindling to try and get another fire going which, obviously, took him quite some time. With my help he ultimately succeeded, and a good fire was going by the time Mutti arrived home. Standing very closely together and blowing in harmony into the stove to encourage the odd small flame to ignite properly helped to stifle my anger considerably. By the time the kindling had caught fire and we both withdrew from the little door of the stove, looking at one another in huge relief and exhaling a little bit more of our breath into the air, we both realized the storm was over. To make up to him in a small way, and to relieve my guilty conscience, I promised him that I would not tell on him to our mother knowing that this promise would mean the world to him.

He adored our mother and loosing even a small amount of her goodwill would be unbearable. We shook hands on this promise, much to my relief as this incident had not exactly made me feel happy about myself once the stoker had struck. On the contrary. Sometimes I wished I were as playful a child as Werner was. But I was made of different stuff, much too conscientious and responsible for my age which did not always endear me to my laid back brother.

However, we know by now I was not always serious and domineering. From the very beginning I also had an outgoing, friendly disposition which adults, in particular, responded to. Although I truly believed that Werner deserved my kind of punishment, I hated having to lose my temper like that and was therefore rather glad when he behaved quite normally for the rest of the evening and by bedtime tickled my feet and giggled with me as if nothing had happened at all. This was a sign he realized he was not entirely undeserving of my treatment. I have to admit though, neither of us ever forgot the incident. In later life we talked about it in a teasing sort of fashion, both pretending the whole thing had been a bit of a joke, when we were very well aware it had happened very much in earnest.

It remained the only serious conflict during our childhood, having been brief, but deadly. Both of us learned a lesson from it and respected one another better for what we were. And, of course, we loved each other. He was my lovely big brother, lazy but kind. I was his little Miss bossy-boots sister, always busy and fussing around, but with a big heart, too.

If our father had been living with us as the head of the family I might have turned out to be as carefree as Werner was, leaving all the worrying to mother and father. As it was, Mutti was all alone and unhappy and I felt I wanted to be as supportive of her as I could at my age. I felt so very sorry for her having to bring us up single handedly in such difficult war scarred times. With every year that had passed since our flight from home we felt more incomplete without our father. Mutti had managed to bring some family photographs with us on our flight. A professional photographer had taken them during the various visits Papa had made to us during his leaves from the front. So we often looked at them when we sat together at candle light during the dark evenings, which kept our memories of Papa fresh in our minds.

By now we had not seen him for almost five years, anxious years in which heaven knows what had happened to him out there in the frightening land of Russia. What would he look like now. Would any of us recognize him if he miraculously returned to us? His cards still arrived on a regular basis, but now those meagre six lines were filled with guarded information about his existence, just saying how much he longed to be with us again; begging for Mutti to write to him and enquiring how we are coping with our new life "in der Fremde" (away from home). Poor, poor Papa! It was, of course, impossible for us to comprehend the kind of life he was living in Russia. We children were old enough though to realize that his was a truly deplorable existence. We at least had one another for comfort; he was all alone. Perhaps he had made some friends of the other prisoners of war who were still encamped with him; all hungry, cold and desperately longing for home. His cards told us that he had still hope of being reunited with us one day. One day! How much longer could he survive the torture of separation from his beautiful wife? Of missing out on seeing his children grow up?
Once he had had his own family and so much hope for a brighter and happier future together. Yet ten years on he was still deprived of being with them; of enjoying the nourishment of family love. Mutti, too, needed his love more and more as time went by. She often looked very tired and drawn with eyes staring blankly into space and barely a smile gracing her face. She never complained, but we knew very well what was on her mind.

My father at his beloved Rominten Heath

My family during a visit of my father from the Russian front,
summer 1941

During a Sunday walk in May 1941

With my brother after his life saving operation, August 1943.
The scar over his right eye remained with him for the remainder
of his life.

With the ill-begoten doll in my arms and Werner wearing his first suit
made of a soldier's uniform. Mutti had not been able to get him a shirt!
Summer 1947.

Wearing the much mentioned striped jumper which I had knitted
myself. Winter 1953.

My confirmation 29. March 1953.

Last spring in Heiddorf with Frau Rieck and Ingetrud, 1953

The young couple, Gertrude and Hugo, my parents, in Goldap 1936.

1952. My handsome brother wearing a new suit with shirt and tie.
Taken while my poor father was imprisoned in Saxony.
My mother's face showing the strain!

Reunited once more; the first autumn season in Essen,
West Germany, 1953.

What a difference a year makes! Mutti and Papa autumn 1954.

Aged 18 and wearing my cherished feather printed blouse.

"A Star is Born" - Hampstead Heath, 1960.

Our big day in June 1963

Chapter Twenty-Seven

Yet another drab and lonely winter was slowly approaching. Mutti had been able to keep her job, but some time before Christmas she became very ill again. This time she was taken to the bigger hospital in the district capital of Ludwigslust, 25 kilometers away from our village. No hope of us children being able to visit her, only my aunt took the train to see her just once. She said that our mother was doing fine, whatever that meant and I tried to believe her.

Once more, Werner and I were alone in the flat at night. Our aunt gave us some sort of supper. Otherwise we were left to our own devices. Life had taught us by now to be very brave and cause the adults as little trouble as possible. As we grew older we understood better and better the difficult life situation our parents had to grapple with. It is easier to be brave during day light hours. School distracts you a lot. During the night it was another matter. So it was good we still shared our bed. The closeness helped to steel our resolve to get through this challenge and believe that Mutti would recover soon. Werner was very anxious indeed about our mother. He was a sensitive boy and loved and needed her very deeply. Not really knowing the state of her health affected him even more than it worried me. Not only did I have to be a consoling sister but also a bit of a surrogate mother. I remember being very frightened myself yet had to try not to show it to him or to my aunt who was a fairly nervous type of woman, her husband a useless provider and of no support. I grew up quite a bit in just those few lonely days.

Then something most wonderful happened! News had been announced via the radio that a new wave of releases from Russian imprisonment had been initiated and everyone who had a radio sat next to it nervously and anxiously listening to information about the trainloads of men who were arriving from Russia. It took everybody completely by surprise. Hope sprang up for families still waiting for the return of their loved ones.

The "useless" husband of my aunt suddenly came into their own. He sat next to their radio all day long listening to the names of the released prisoners in the hope he might hear my father's name. Amazingly, after a few hours of tense expectation, he did indeed hear his name! Papa was to arrive the following day in the late hours of the morning at Ludwigslust station, the town where Mutti was still hospitalised!

"Brigitte, you must travel to Ludwigslust to receive your father. We have saved a little money and will buy the train ticket for you today!"

Luckily, the Christmas holidays had started, so I was free to make the journey. My first train journey since our arrival from Prussia almost five years earlier. This time I was not squeezed under the seat, lying on a dirty floor, but sitting almost alone in a compartment, watching the attractive countryside fly by and trying to remember the names of the various stations where the train was stopping. Although I was nervous and excited all at the same time, I was not unduly overwhelmed by the enormity of what was going to happen. After an eternity of waiting for Papa's return, the moment we had begun to fear might never happen, was about to arrive.

"Please God, let this really be true! If Aunt Ella's husband has made a mistake and misheard his name and I will be left alone on the empty platform without my Papa, I will surely die!"

I had heard people mention the large village of Eldena. Once the train had left Eldena station I knew we had made half of the journey. I began to feel more and more nervous. My heart was beating like a drum and in my imagination it seemed the train was now going considerably slower than it had done during the first lap of the journey. It also appeared to stop for longer at the few more stations it was passing through before our final destination. As we got closer and closer to Ludwigslust I remember rising up and down my wooden seat with nerves as if I was riding a horse and wanting it to fall into a gallop. But the train did not get my signals. It sped along at the same speed before it unexpectedly slowed down and then, at last, it came to a complete halt. We had arrived at our final stop.

Everyone around me got up and left the train; some of them shoving and pushing, their cheeks red with excitement, and I knew that they, too, were heading to look for their husband, son or father or other loved one. So I just followed the stampeding crowd, down some steps, along a short tunnel and then up again onto another platform where what seemed like hundreds of bedraggled men were wandering around or looking from windows of a stationary train, in search of their loved ones. It was a tumultuous scene of hugging and kissing, of people calling names, pushing through the crowds and suddenly falling into some outstretched arms, gasping with relief and incredulity.

The platform was starting to get clearer and I had still not seen my father. Had I simply overlooked him because the picture I had of him in my mind did not tally with the man he had become? He must have changed a lot in these years, was probably very thin and bent over like an old man. Only my inner voice told me I would recognize him, whatever he looked like now. Our hearts would surely pull us together however much we both had changed. Yet, we still had not found one another and fear was beginning to grip me. What if it had all been a terrible mistake and he was not on this train but still languishing in this god forsaken place called Russia?

By now there were only a handful of men on the platform. The train which had brought the released prisoners was still standing along the platform and lots more ex soldiers were inside watching the emotional scenes outside with smiles of anticipation on their faces – soon they would be the ones hugging and kissing their wives and children somewhere further down the line; next stop Schwerin, the capital of Mecklenburg and then perhaps Wismar at the coast of the Baltic, and the end of the line.

Despondency was slowing down my steps, my feet felt leaden as if I was walking on tar. "Papa, Papa! Where are you? Surely this cannot be true! We have waited so long, have been promised you were coming home. And now, where ARE you?" it raced through my mind.

I could feel my entire body sinking into dismay, drooping like a decaying flower. A terrifying sense of alarm took hold of my mind:

"This cannot be true! It will kill Mutti. He MUST be here! He must be…."

I wished the earth would swallow me up. The disappointment of not finding my father after all this hope and excitement of his promised return was more than I could bear. I began to feel faint, my legs would not carry me forward. I wanted to be dead.

The lonely figure towards the end of the platform was of a large, really big and plodding man, totally unlike the father I remembered. Slowly, very slowly, every step a visible effort, he dragged himself towards me. As he got closer his steps appeared to speed up a little. Could THIS be our father? I had looked at the body of the man rather than his face and when this became more distinct and he began to smile I realized it really was my father!

"Papa, Papa!!!"

Suddenly, the imaginary tar lifted from my feet and explosive happiness propelled me towards him, faster and faster until I was close enough to jump into his outstretched arms. The jolt of my jump nearly knocked him over. He had looked so big and so strong from a distance. The near fall took me by surprise. Luckily, he did manage to steady himself and plastered the most wonderful kisses all over my face, saying over and over again:

"Brigittchen, bist Du das wirklich? Bist Du das wirklich?" ("My little Brigitte, is this really, really you?").

Tears streamed down our faces. The emotion of this reunion was almost too much for both of us. Papa had to lower me down to the ground. He could not hold my weight, but I did not let go of his neck. My arms were locked there and would not let go. I had my Papa back! The happiness of this encounter was almost as painful as the long wait for him had been. I clung to him like a small child clings to her mother when frightened or needing reassurance. We were both shaking with the emotion of it all, as reluctantly I unclasped my locked arms when I realized that my father needed to steady himself. He did not seem as strong as he had appeared to me from a distance. His body looked swollen rather than big from being fat and strong. His face looked so very tired and drawn and his entire figure was trembling with weakness. He was after all what we had always expected: a broken wreck of a man but at this moment a very happy man, too, who was doing his best to hide his deplorable physical condition.

Once I had released his neck and he was able to stand up straight again, he looked around him in search of something – or someone.

"Where is Mutti? Has she not come with you?"

"No, Papa, she hasn't. She is in hospital. But luckily here in Ludwigslust and we can go and see her straight away if you feel you can walk that far?"

"Of course, I can. I haven't come all the way from Russia to remain on this platform!
Is she very ill? What's wrong with her?"

"I don't know, father, exactly what is wrong with her. But she has had an operation and she has been in hospital for quite some time. She must be getting much better by now."

"And Werner, why is he not with you?"

"Werner had to stay at home. We could not afford the train ticket for him as well."

We had walked all the time we talked and were now approaching the station exit. Once outside it was obvious that the station was not in the centre of town. There weren't a lot of houses nearby and the road seemed quiet and almost deserted despite all those many soldiers and their families who had flooded out of the station. But by the time we reached the exit most of them had dispersed and the quiet scene of a country town lay in front of us.

"Which way do we turn, Brigitte?"

"I don't know, Papa. I have never been here before. But I'll run across the road and ask those people over there. You sit down on this bench here and wait for me. Alright?"

His tired body fell onto the bench with a plonk and I crossed the road and asked for directions. Apparently the hospital did not seem all that far to walk to, so I suggested we sit down together for a while to rest up a bit before setting off to the centre of town. Papa seemed glad to agree.

"Just for a little while. I'm dying to see Mutti, you know?"

Of course, I knew what he meant. And after a short rest we set off together, holding hands, me hopping and skipping next to him and swinging our clasped hands up and down as a result of my exuberance. How wonderful it felt to be walking along a pavement in a town where people could see you and notice that you had a father. A father, who walked hand in hand with you and who seemed so delighted with this simple gesture. I felt so happy and proud I wanted to shout to the world around us: "Look, this is my father, MY father! He has just come home from Russia. That's why he looks so tired and ill and cannot walk very fast. But you just wait. He'll be so strong and fit and better than all of you put together!"

The town was sleepy, it looked more like a big village to me. Eventually we came to some shops; one of them was a baker's. Papa stopped there, staring at the rolls and small cakes in the window and lifting his nose up like a dog inhaling a scent –the scent of freshly baked rolls wafting from the shop's open door.

"Let's go in, Brigitte, buy some rolls." "Oh, Papa, I'm sorry. I haven't got any money! Oh dear, oh dear. Tante Ella only paid for my train ticket. She did not give me any money as we are always so short of it."

Now I really was crying inconsolably. Here was I with my long lost father and I had nothing to offer him as a welcome gift. The way he stared at those displays made me realize he had not seen or eaten anything like this for many years and the sight of these delights made him weak in his knees and I was unable to fulfil his wish! Very gently Papa took me in his arms again, wiping away my tears with his hand:
"Shush, shush, shush, Brigittchen. No need to cry. Who said YOU should buy the rolls?! They gave us a little pocket money. So it will be MY pleasure to buy some for all of us."

 With that we entered the shop, the most delicious smell of freshly baked bread almost dousing us. It felt a bit like entering heaven. There were beautiful rolls, bread and even biscuits and cakes on display, delights I had never seen before in our village baker at Heiddorf, and certainly had never eaten. But it was rolls Papa wanted, and he bought 6 in total.
 "One for each of us. Perhaps I can eat two?
And Mutti, too. She must eat well so that she will get better soon. Agreed?"
"Agreed".

Papa and I ate half a roll each straight away while continuing our walk. It was not well-mannered, eating in the street, but he had probably longed for a breakfast of delicious German rolls, the best in the world in my opinion, and neither of us could wait until we were at the hospital. German bakers bake wonderful bread and rolls. The rolls in particular are exceptional. They are crisp on the outside and deliciously gooey inside and extremely flavoursome. Nowhere else have I eaten more delicious rolls in later years of my life. So it wasn't surprising that rolls were the most tempting items my father was willing to spend his first money on in celebration of being back home.

Nowadays, on a momentous reunion of the kind we were experiencing, bottles of champagne would be cracked or the very best wine served at least. But for us, rolls were the ultimate, the first ones in many years either of us had eaten and they were better than anything else we could have chosen, even better than champagne! Of course, in those days, I did not even know what champagne was or wine for that matter. But had I known these, our rolls could not be surpassed by either of them! The only twinge of sadness about this purchase was the cost of the rolls – they swallowed up almost all the money Papa had been given by the authorities!

At the hospital nurses and staff were thrilled to hear our story. It was not the official visiting time when we arrived but hearing that father was one of the prisoners who had arrived by the first train from Russia only a good hour ago and that his wife was somewhere recovering from an operation, they waved all the normal rules and searched for the ward where Mutti was recovering. One of the senior nurses accompanied us there as if we were dignitaries!

"Through this door, please", she said with a warm smile. I cannot remember what either Papa or Mutti said or what they did. I only remember in my mind's eye seeing her lying in her bed looking extremely pale with her deep brown eyes bulging from her face, looking sad and then, on seeing us walk into the room, coming to life instantly as her face transformed to a radiant smile.

I cannot recall what they said to each other. But obviously, it was a most happy reunion with lots of tears and few words but plenty of hugs and kisses. There were other women in the ward but they were of no importance to us, they simply did not exist. The next thing I remember was eating our wonderful rolls, bar one, which was kept for Werner at home.

The news of Papa's arrival spread through the ward like a wildfire .After a little while, in fact while we were feasting on our rolls, a doctor arrived to welcome my father, together with several nurses, all elated about this happy event in our lives.

Prisoners from Russia had not come home for a long time, so this was quite an astonishing event which everyone wanted to celebrate with us. Mutti should have stayed there a few more days to recover, but when Papa asked if she could come home with us there and then, the doctor made an exception and allowed her to be released that same afternoon. We were even provided with an ambulance to take us all the way home.

It was not often that a car drove up our dusty road. Therefore the ambulance caused quite a stir. All the neighbours around us came out of their houses, cheering us and waving and shouting: "Welcome home!" to both Mutti and Papa. They were celebrated like a bride and groom off on their honeymoon. The reality though was somewhat different. Both of them were weak and tired. Papa was clearly traumatized. He cried a great deal that evening, I remember. I hoped they were tears of happiness as he hugged both his children over and over again, one in each arm, while smiling under his tears at our mother who lay wanly in her bed observing happily this touching scene. At some stage we all went to bed, Werner and I in our separate chamber and Papa for the first time sharing Mutti's bed. I wonder what they both felt that night after so many years of separation? I dare not hazard a guess.

Chapter Twenty-Eight

Precisely how we all spent the following days, which were school holidays shortly before Christmas, I do not recall in detail. We would not have had a celebratory breakfast, that's for sure, as food was still short and simple. The celebration took place in our hearts.

Since Mutti was still rather weak and recovering from her operation, I took over the role of mother of the house for the next few days. Papa needed a lot of sleep, too. He was extremely tired and just as weak as Mutti, if not more so. His rotund body belied a very sick man – he suffered from dropsy! What had looked like stoutness to me was in fact just a collection of water in his body due to deliberate starvation which Papa had started in order to become too ill to work.

How he had mustered the willpower to starve himself in the hope of becoming a useless burden to the prison camp authorities, I will never comprehend. He told us, he had gradually begun to realize the camp commandant had kept back his cards from home with the intention of demoralizing him, breaking his inner resolve. Papa had worked his way up in the camp and soon became the most important worker and organizer. Consequently he had become indispensable to them. Their prisoners of war were an essential work force for rebuilding the country, Papa being the best skilled worker they had. Unwittingly he had made himself much too important to them. If they could convince our father that his wife did not want to know about him anymore – by not replying to his letters – he might want to stay on voluntarily and remain in Russia for good! Obviously, no one spoke German or else they would have known from his monthly mail to us, how much he was yearning to be reunited with us and finally, after ten years of war and imprisonment, to start his family life. May be, among thousands of prisoners, there might have been the odd one who could have been persuaded to remain in Russia if he had no family left at home in Germany. But not our father. He had a beautiful wife and two children whom he hardly knew. Withholding the mail from home had not convinced him of Mutti's disloyalty. So he embarked on the only course to freedom he knew – starvation!

Our paternal grandfather, who had been a small town builder in Goldap, had insisted that all his four sons would go into apprenticeships at other small businesses in the town, mainly because he wanted to discharge responsibility for feeding them any longer. Sadly, my grandfather had turned himself into an alcoholic who would entertain all his pub crawling friends to beer and spirits night after night, steadily reducing the income to feed his family of five children. Our father and another uncle told me on many occasions that grandfather had been an excellent master carpenter who set up his own business and soon employed a number of trained workers. From merely doing carpentry work he began to build houses and other properties and also produced the professional drawings for the best architect in town. Then

145

something went wrong and he began drinking, at first socially, which soon turned into steady drinking and loss of work and reputation. Money for the family was getting tighter and tighter.

My father had turned fourteen in November, 1925, which was still a very desperate time for most Germans due to the heavy load of reparation payments manifested in the Treaty of Versailles at the conclusion of World War I.

So, grandfather's drinking meant extreme poverty in their household despite my grandmother's superhuman efforts to feed the family by getting a cow, a pig and some chickens and using her knowledge of herbs. She collected them everywhere in the countryside to make soup or add them to potatoes for extra vitamins.

A solution to this domestic problem, as grandfather saw it, was sending all his sons into apprenticeships straight after they had completed their basic schooling .In those days apprentices also lived with their master's family which was a convenient way of relieving the domestic problems at home. For my father it meant giving up his dream of going to university and to study forestry. He never really got over his disappointment as becoming a forester had been his ardent dream since his earliest childhood. Now he had to start work at the age of 14. His first apprenticeship was with a blacksmith. He loved the work but not the family. They fed him very badly. As I have just explained, the whole of Germany was still suffering from the heavy burden of reparations to be paid to France and England. The poorer people especially struggled for years to put bread on the table.

Papa learned a great deal in the smithy but his real love was for the motorcar! Therefore, after completing his three year apprenticeship with the local smith, he started another one as a car mechanic, which turned out to be his true vocation in life. He later became a passenger bus driver for the German Post Office. Their buses toured through the entire province of Prussia and Papa really enjoyed this job.

My father was an intelligent man, despite his basic school education. Thus, when he found himself in a Russian prison camp, he soon became an indispensable asset to his captors; one day assisting the camp dentist, the next the doctor or he was building a tractor for them out of scraps of metal. He was amazed himself how inventive he became and how flexible he was in acquiring skills he had never dreamed of attaining. It did not take long and the top brass of the camp as well as the other prisoners called him "The Old Master", despite his young years. He had always been good with his hands and having had those years of apprenticeship helped him to make the most of his incarceration. His work earned him the respect of the camp authorities. Eventually they trusted him so much that they permitted him to leave the camp from time to time walking into the surrounding villages to beg for food from the peasant farmers! Whatever food he managed to get he was allowed to keep and to share with his room mates. During the five years spent in the camp, he remained the only person who was granted this enormous privilege.

So his many talents had helped him to survive the ordeal of capture, physically as well as mentally. What had begun as a blessing – having these skills and natural talents – eventually turned into hell for him. When he did not get a reply to his letter to the mayor of our village it dawned on him what the Russians were doing to him and why. They wanted to break his morale .However, they had not counted on the fighting spirit of my courageous father! From time to time some prisoners were leaving the camp and he assumed that they were the lucky ones to be sent home. He also noticed that none of those chosen to leave the camp were healthy or in a fit enough condition for the hard labour in the fields or on the roads. Many prisoners died of hunger in the camp. The Russian population, too, were close to starvation for years after the war. So to survive under these conditions you had to have your wits about you. And Papa did.

When months turned into years of yearning for his release, he began to understand what his keepers were doing to him and he began the starvation process. Hopefully, there would be a batch of releases near the time of his physical collapse. And hopefully he would stay alive long enough to be among those chosen for the return home. He had no guarantee his plan would work. Death was a real possibility. His desperation to be with his wife and family was such that even the risk of dying was preferable to remaining in Russia for longer or even for ever!
Poor, poor Papa!! We knew how hard it was to live through hunger, but to make his choice and continue with it until he appeared to be beyond a possible recovery was a feat of such immense courage that it was incredulous.

What an amazing father we had! And how very much he loved us! My aunt, her husband, Werner and I did all we could to keep out of the way of my parents for as long as was possible during the day-time to allow them quiet time together, to sleep and rest and to hug and kiss undisturbed and to very slowly recover at least a little from all their ordeals as well as getting to know one another again.

Papa told us his story a little at a time during the quiet winter evenings. He never went into great details of life at the camp as he did not want to depress us too much.

Over time he only told us the amusing things he had experienced or the touching contact he had made with the Russian peasants on his begging trips. Like almost all soldiers who had suffered horrific experiences during their years of war he preferred to regale us rather than to sadden us with his tales, a sure sign that the truth was simply too ghastly to tell. If he wanted to get fit enough, physically as well as mentally, to face and tackle the challenges of the present, he knew he needed to suppress the horrors of the past, whether committed or experienced, only focus on what had been relatively good rather than bad.

That first winter was spent in quiet pursuit of helping our father to regain his health. Black Johanna called more often than usual:

"Frau Mallon, Frau Mallon! Moechten Sie etwas Eintopf haben? Ich habe wieder mal zuviel gekocht!" (Frau Mallon! Would you like to have some stew? I have cooked too much again by accident!)

 By now we knew her kind heart and knew, too, that she had cooked too much stew on purpose so that she could give some to us.

Again, I cannot remember how Papa lost all his excess body water. Did he spent some time in hospital or was he treated by a doctor at home? My mind is blank on this issue.

But I remember distinctly that by the first summer after his return, he was well again and could even have worked again, except there was no work to be found. Luckily Mutti still had her job at the clothes factory. As Papa could not find any paid employment he busied himself in other ways to contribute towards our survival, for survival was the most one could hope for, not comfort. He went fishing, tended our allotment together with Mutti, helped the farmers in the village when they needed a pair of extra hands and by mid summer he had started to go into his beloved forests to search out stumps of mostly illegally felled trees which he then began to dig out to supplement our heating materials for the forthcoming winter.

Digging out the tree stumps was also forbidden by our new government just as felling trees had been. We understood that the trees had to remain or there wouldn't be any woods left, but the stumps? We had never seen anyone else attempting to undertake such hard work during the course of the previous years.

Consequently, the police never searched for anyone doing this unauthorized work. Even if the police had patrolled the woods regularly, Papa would have taken no notice of it. His family needed some wood for heating and cooking. What good were the stumps doing in the ground? No good whatsoever. Yet for his family they were doing a hell of a lot of good.

On dry days he left the house early in the morning and I followed him around midday with his sandwiches for lunch. He told me roughly where he had started digging before he left for the forest. Often it took quite a while for me to find him. Like Gretel following Hansel's pebbles he had thrown along his path, I followed the sound of my father's voice in my search for him. Mostly though I realized almost at once on entering the wood where I might find him; I just had to follow the sound of his singing! When work got really tough, like when he had cleared the earth half-way down the stump and got to the more complicated digging around the strong roots of the tree stump, he would sing at the top of his voice, sweat pouring down his face.

Yet the toughest part of his labour was still to come. Once Papa had freed part of the roots around the outer edge of the stump, he had to cut them with an axe, leaving only those roots attached to the stump which were deep underneath it and extremely difficult to get to. That is when he sang the loudest to fire himself on, not to give up and to loosen the entire stump ready for lifting. This kind of work took many hours and father knew when he would need help from Werner. For when the stump had been lifted out of its deep hole it needed to be divided into much smaller parts so that they could be carried home, usually in a rucksack. Werner then came into his own by working the saw with Papa. I think splitting the stump was even harder than digging it out as the wood was full of resin which made sawing through it extremely difficult. But for that it made very good firewood, the resin adding more power to the flames.

Our ration for coal was still insufficient to get us through the winter. Extra wood was absolutely essential. Now that Papa was home again he made sure we had enough, labouring in the woods all summer!

I remember those weeks as being simply wonderful. I loved being in the woods as much as father did and enjoyed sharing the sandwiches with him. Sometimes we would sing together. He knew some different folksongs from those mother had taught us. His favourite song was called "Aennchen von Tharau", a melancholic love song with a particularly entrancing melody. Papa said it was the most popular folksong in Prussia and he sang it with great passion and emotion. Like Mutti he had a pleasant singing voice, made even more attractive by the echo in the woods.

I often stayed with Papa until he was too tired to go on. While he was digging and singing, I collected pine cones and twigs for our kindling wood as I had done in previous years. Only now I did not have to struggle with the heavy rucksack on my back. It was of an adult size and when I stood up, having struggled hard to get it onto my back, it was not actually on my back but rather lower down somewhere close to the back of my knees! So I had to kick it up higher. First onto my bottom and then, by kicking my bottom upwards, pushing it onto my back. Of course, this meant walking all the way home in this forward leaning position; a good half an hour or more. Now Papa coped with the rucksack and I could walk upright next to him, chatting continuously and happily carrying the spade as he had the axe in one hand and my hand in his other. This was the closeness I had dreamt of when he was captured in Russia. Now at last I learned about fatherly love and closeness. No wonder both my feet as well as my heart jumped and skipped for joy, even tired as I was.

That summer our landlady gave us the use of a shed in their outbuilding. By autumn it was nearly half full with chunks of wood. If anyone of the local representatives of the new East German communist controlled government (the DDR – the German Democratic Republic) had learned about it, Papa would have languished in prison once more. Miraculously, we got away with it. No one denounced us, not this time!

150

Apart from these new work excursions into the woods, my own life continued much the same. My friendship with Ingetrud grew closer, although I was not her best friend. That was a girl her own age, whose name I have forgotten. She was also in Ingetrud's class and lived in a side street not far from us. She was a very thin, tall girl with almost straw white hair which she wore in plaits and which reached down to her waist. I was lucky Ingetrud played with me in the evenings when her best friend had to be at home.

When Ingetrud was not around or busy with home work for school, I hung around her parents' court yard and watched her step father and brother Horst messing around with an old car in their garage. The car was not roadworthy. They worked trying to get it to run for years – in fact all the years I knew them! The garage looked more like a proper car maintenance workshop. There were shelves stacked full with tools and tins of all sorts. There was a work table and many mysterious machines and larger tools I did not know the purpose of, a truly atmospheric place full of action and mechanical noises. Best of all I liked the smell of oil and burning when the two men were attempting to create parts for the car from scraps of metal or steel. You would think, being a girl, I would stay away from such a place, but no. I found it most intriguing and always sneaked across to them when I saw that the door to the garage was open. Then I would be happy to watch them for ages.

Chapter Twenty-Nine

Like the previous summer I was sometimes invited to go to the Markurth estate. Gerda from next door was also still my friend.   During the autumn and part of the following winter Papa began to be more at home. He was still unable to find any proper employment which began to irritate and upset him increasingly. On the plus side he was able to help Werner hugely with his mathematics. Papa was just brilliant at math. He could add up huge rows of sums entirely in his head and at astonishing speed. It was really impressive. Math had always been his best subject at school and he simply could not understand that neither of his children liked it one bit. Werner's work improved greatly under Papa's tutelage and so did mine. I hated math but was ambitious and could not bear to get only satisfactory marks for my work. I simply had to keep my second, or occasionally my third, place in the class. So I continued to put a lot of work and effort into all my subjects, including the hated math. Papa checked my homework and, luckily, most of the time he did not find much to complain about, not praising me much either.

As I am telling you a bit of my school life, I think I had better mention something else, which helped to spur most of us on a little: the school supplied us with a certain number of copy books every month or so, since the production of paper was even now, in 1950, very limited indeed. Each front cover had the following sentence printed in bold letters:

"I am not learning for the school but for my (future) life!"

When you see this sentence day in, day out, year in, year out, you simply cannot help taking notice of it and eventually the meaning of it sinks in. At least, it did with me. Later on I began to realize that producing this sentence on our copy books was a very smart way of communist indoctrination, only as young children we did not recognize it as such. Yet as we grew up we did comprehend how communist thinking was subtly or not so subtly infiltrating the class room. More about that later!

German continued to be my favourite subject. We started quite early learning about the classical poets and writers, such as Johann Wolfgang von Goethe and Friedrich Schiller. Their poems, especially those by Goethe, were also the lyrics for a number of the folk songs we learned in music lessons. Of those, "Heidenroeslein" was among my top favourites. The music for "Heidenroeslein" was written by Franz Schubert who had composed the music for several more of my favourite songs. Schubert was not the only world famous composer who also wrote popular folksongs. One of them was Wolfgang Amadeus Mozart, who wrote the music for "Komm lieber Mai und mache die Baeume wieder Gruen" (Dear month of May come quickly and turn the trees green once more). Felix Mendellsohn-Bartholdy is also among those composers who wrote simple and catching melodies to be sung by children. Our school had no choir as such, but every class had regular music lessons, which consisted almost entirely of singing as the school still lacked musical instruments. Personally, I preferred singing anyway rather than learning to play an instrument. Singing, especially with my class mates, was really fun and uplifting and a marvellous contrast to the intensity of the work with other subjects – like math, for instance!

In the early school years, we learned almost exclusively the many wonderful folk songs of which Germany can be justly proud. Of course, I already knew quite a few of them which my mother had taught me and which we sang together on so many occasions. I knew dozens and dozens with all the verses. Sadly, by now I have forgotten most of them, although I recognize them at once if someone were to start singing them. Then the melodies as well as the words seem to be flooding back, which is rather lovely. I can remember well one little song though and I will give it to you as it has only two verses, first in German followed by my own translation. Here it is:

A,B,C, die Katze lief im Schnee.
Und wie sie wieder raus kam,
Da hatt' sie weisse Stieflein an,
O jemine, O jemine, O je!

A,B,C the cat walked in the snow
And when she came out again
She was wearing white booties.
O jemine, O jemne, O je! (Oh dear, Oh dear, Oh dear).

A,B,C, die Katze lief zur Hoeh'
Sie lecket ihr kalt Pfoetchen rein
Und putzt sich auch das Stiefelein
Und ging nicht mehr im Schnee.

A,B,C the cat jumped high in the air.
She licked clean her cold paws
And polished, too, her booties
And never walked in the snow again.

These were typical simple little verses with an easy melody to remember and I loved this kind of song so much when I was small. Another favourite of mine was a charming song about the wedding of a couple of birds. We sang this a lot at school since it had many verses telling you what the various birds did as part of the marriage between the thrush, who was the bride, and the blackbird, her groom. All conceivable birds played different roles. The geese and the ducks were the musicians or the sparrow who brought the ring; the peacock who was allowed to dance the first dance with the bride and so on and so on. This was a fantastic song to perform by different groups in the class room, some children taking the part of the cuckoos and some the larks or the roosters. So everyone had to pay attention to come in on time when it was their turn. May be that's why I still remember the fun we had with this song.

As we grew older we naturally upgraded to the more adult compositions which are still being performed with great enthusiasm by choral societies or at family festivities together with barn dances or such like. And as my parents both liked singing, we had a lot of fun together performing just for our own pleasure.

At Christmas, too, we sang a great deal. The more popular carols like "O Christmas Tree" or "Silent Night" were standard practice, but in our family we sang many more, which are not so well known outside Germany. However, in recent years I have heard and sung one of my best loved carols here at Horsham where I am a member of a German Group. Every Christmas season a local choir joins us for carols sung in English, French and German and "Suesser die Glocken nie klingen" is part of their repertoire. (The bells never sound sweeter than at Christmas).

By now, I am sure, you get my meaning: singing was a major activity of my young life, at home as well as at school. By the time I was eleven years old I became a member of the local church choir which I thoroughly enjoyed as well.

Typically of me I have strayed off the original subject. I mentioned earlier that German was still my best loved subject at school, not merely writing and reading it, but especially learning about our many classical writers and their work. There still was no library at school. So during my entire childhood I had no access to entertainment books or even fairy tales! Therefore, when dramas by Goethe, Schiller, Lessing or even Shakespeare became part of our curriculum I was in heaven. Reading about kings and queens, their mostly horrid ends, about wars and revolution, about all kinds of power struggles, betrayals and, best of all, about love, well this was exciting stuff. Our own lives seemed ever so dull in comparison and these writings showed us how rich and varied the tapestry of life can be.

Naturally, we lived in very different times, not in the Middle Ages (although very often it did feel like it!) nor was I of royal blood and not likely to encounter a prince. But it made me wonder what kind of experiences lay ahead for me once I had entered adulthood. How many challenges would I have to conquer? How and where would MY adult life unfold? Would it always be a struggle and strife for recognition and for our daily bread? These works laid bare the many highs and lows one may experience; that high birth alone may not protect you from personal tragedy or guarantee a flawless, happy future. Outer circumstances, often beyond your control, could change or strangle the path you had hoped to follow. I had not really considered the future much until real literature was introduced into our school life and I wanted to read more, much more. Only I couldn't. Still not having a school library and no access to other sources of supply than the books we used at school - which we were never allowed to take home for fear of damaging them - I felt hugely frustrated. Even in class we often had only one book doing the rounds from student to student, each reading a passage. We had to grasp the contents by listening to fellow class mates much more than by reading ourselves. When the book arrived at our desk (I shared my desk with one other girl) and it was my turn to read a certain passage, I tried to read this as slowly as possible so that I could hang on to the book for longer than the other boys or girls had done. Most of the boys hated literature anyway, especially those stupid farm yard boys! (Probably an unjust snipe at them. They weren't all totally stupid, but I did not like them because of their meanness and their monosyllabic nature).

Really, I should have been the only girl in class to read ALL of the passages. Firstly I spoke flawless High German and secondly, I was convinced that nobody else understood what we were reading as well as I did! This was very conceited of me, but at the time I did not think so. I really believed my passion for literature alone entitled me to a special position in class and thus to have the book all to myself. Best of all, to be allowed to take it home! Herr Schroeder was a good and very fair teacher. He did not make exceptions and, naturally, he was right in not showing any preference to anyone at his school, leaving me maddeningly frustrated and pining for books of my own.

I believe it must have been around that summer of 1950 that lovely Mrs. Markurth allowed me to borrow the most wonderful book from their own family library:
"Heidi" by the Swiss authoress Johanna Spyri. What a thrilling experience that was!
"Heidi" had been the most loved and famous children's book in the German speaking world for a long time (and probably the world over but I did not know that at the time). It was a story about a little girl, aged about five, who became an orphan quite suddenly and was taken to stay with her grandfather up in the Alms. He was a taciturn man who had been at odds with the villagers down below for a long time and Heidi, though at first not really welcome, soon changed his hard exterior with her cheerful ways, despite the loss of her parents. She also befriends a young goat herd, called Peter, and the story tells of their simple lives over the following three years.

The second part of the book tells us how Heidi's aunt comes to collect her again and sends her to Frankfurt to stay there as a companion to a girl called Klara, who is an invalid. They soon become very good friends. Heidi misses her alpine home and eventually she returns to it and teaches her friend Peter to write and read.
The following summer Klara visits her and soon regains her health due to the wholesome goat's milk and fresh mountain air. In gratitude to Heidi and her grandfather, Klara's parents promise Heidi that she would always have a home with them in Frankfurt if her grandfather would no longer be able to have her.

A very romantic story from tragedy to ultimate happiness and security! I devoured it several times over before returning the book to the Markurth family library! It remained the only children's book I had the good fortune to read while living in Heiddorf!

Reading about Heidi made me believe that lives can change, especially if we stay happy in spirit and cheerful to the world. In that respect I felt a little akin to Heidi. Why then should our lives not markedly improve also? Of course, they would! Of that I had no doubt. I only could not see as yet how this should happen, but happen it would.

Though "Heidi" was the only children's book I had read, it would have doubtlessly remained the only important one, even if I could have read dozens and dozens. It had given me confidence and hope in the ultimate goodness of life. What more could I have learned from other books? I felt a very lucky girl indeed!

Chapter Thirty

One most fortunate turn had already occurred: we had our father back. Having him around made all of us a lot happier and more content. At least as far as Werner and I were concerned. I did not really know about my parents' feelings but they looked happy enough, never showing any disagreements. However, as winter progressed Papa did not look so happy any more. He kept saying he felt useless not being able to earn the money we needed. He was a proud man and capable as we already know. Not finding any employment, regardless of what kind, deeply dented his confidence and one day, I cannot recall exactly when, he left us to take up work in southern Saxony. I was shattered.

Let me return for a short while to the early days of arriving in Mecklenburg . Lucky though we had been living with the Rose family, Mutti's lot was made especially hard by not knowing where any of her family was. She did not know whether Papa was alive and where he was, nor did she know what had happened to any of her six brothers or indeed her parents and sister, who had lived with them and had never married. This concern befell all refugees. Indeed all German families to varying degrees.

Eventually, agencies were set up who helped in the search for relatives. A lot of children got lost during those flights across the sea or during walks on foot for close to two months or longer. Trying to reunite split families and finding out what soldiers had been captured and where in either Russia, England or France they were interned, was a huge task. After many months of searching for Mutti's family they were indeed located. Mutti's parents, their mentally handicapped son Max, their daughter Erna and their young grandson Dieter had started their long arduous walk from Peitschendorf (now Piecki) in the lake district of Masuren (now Polish Mazurskie) westwards shortly before the Russian Army was expected to assault their village. Unfortunately they were of the many who had left their flight too late. This was not their fault but rather due to strict orders from above, not to leave their homes as "Prussia *is in safe German hands!*" Soon after having left their village they were overtaken by a small section of the Russian army, who, when they saw the trek of refugees, pulled away a few of them at random, including handicapped Max, shooting them dead there and then as an act of reprisal. Why they did not shoot all of them, I do not know, as afterwards I heard that the Russians' revenge had been merciless. Mostly they shot everyone they encountered when they first entered Prussia, regardless of who they were, young or old, but especially the aristocratic Junkers. When they saw the first farms and lands, noticing how well kept they were (the houses having running water, toilets and central heating) their fury doubled and trebled in envy of the good life the Germans had in comparison to their own miserable serf existence.

My grandparents and their daughter Erna and grandson survived the tortuous walk, ending up in a town in Saxony called Bischofswerda. Mutti travelled to see them as soon as she could after hearing the fortunate news. The news of five of her other brothers, four of them having been officers in the army, was not good. Only the sixth and eldest had returned. The youngest, called Waldow, aged only 18, had burnt to death inside a tank, due to the exit lid having got stuck! Another brother drowned on his way home from Russia. The one I considered the most handsome one of the gang of good looking brothers was stabbed to death by a Russian soldier when he, together with some of his fleeing comrades, were hiding under straw bales inside a barn. I cannot recall what happened to the other two, but they never returned.

The oldest brother had married a girl from Saxony and returned to his wife and children after the war. Eventually he found work above ground in the only uranium mine in Saxony.

Uranium had been extracted in the Erzgebirge (the ore mountains in southern Saxony) before and during the 2nd World War. In fact a chemist from Berlin, M. H., Klaproth, had discovered traces of uranium in the ore as far back as 1789. This element being necessary for building a nuclear bomb, the Soviet Union was keen to reopen former mines for their exploration and mining of uranium which they bought from the DDR (probably for rather a low price). Their company, called SAG Wismut (Sovietische Aktiengesellschaft) opened the first mine in 1946 in a small town called Johanngeorgenstadt very close to the border with Czechoslovakia. Oddly enough they were able to keep their mining exploits secret from the Western governments for an exceedingly long time. Even people in East Germany did not know about it, other than those miners toiling underground and their families.

I may be wrong but I believe my uncle was either the director of this mine or in a very high managerial position. As I said earlier, the activities of the Wismut company were shrouded in secrecy. However, due to my uncle Erich's influence, our father managed to secure a job in the mine - under ground. As it was dangerous and exceptionally hard work, exposing the miners to very high radon radiation, the pay was somewhat better than for other employment enabling Papa to come home for visits from time to time.

It also meant that, gradually, we were able to purchase some necessary items for our home, the most pleasing of all a brand new bicycle! The importance of this item should not be underestimated for it meant better and further freedom of movement.

As mentioned earlier when telling you about my excursions into the woods for blueberry picking, I was now able to cycle there and walking the cycle back with the near full bucket hanging on the bicycle's handle. Cycling back home along the uneven woodland path would have meant spilling too many precious berries. I might even have fallen off the bike, losing all my crop! So I walked.

The town of Doemitz was now within our reach and Mutti was able to cycle to work, making an enormous difference to her life. Cycling remained a wonderful hobby for both my parents all of their lives. My mother never even learned to drive a car! Yet with her cycling skills she never felt trapped. She used her beloved bicycle almost until she died for shopping as well as for pleasure, cycling for miles around the countryside, especially during the summer months.

As wonderful as it was to have a little bit more money at last, as hard was the separation for my parents. Mining was a rather gruesome job for my father who was still not the most resilient of men physically, although mentally he was stronger and more determined than any other man we knew. Therefore, after approximately a year or a little more, father listened to Mutti's pleas and gave up this gruelling job and way of life and returned home. Having held down this very hard labour and having earned quite a bit of money, father's confidence in himself had returned and he hoped that soon he would find some other employment nearby. Yet, like his previous attempts, his searches remained unsuccessful. The country just could not rise from the ashes of destruction and the plundering by the Russians of anything useful which had been left intact after the surrender in 1945. To quote an excerpt from *East Germany: A Country Study* by Glenn E. Curtis:

> *"Most heavy industry (constituting 20 percent of total production) was claimed by the Soviet Union as reparations. The remaining confiscated industrial property was nationalized, leaving 40 percent of total industrial production to private enterprise. The agrarian reform expropriated all land belonging to former Nazis and war criminals and generally limited ownership to 100 hectares. Some 500 Junker estates were converted into collective people's farms and more than 3 million hectares were distributed among 500,000 peasant farmers, agricultural labourers and refugees."*

So, once again, father had to turn to short-time farm jobs and rooting out tree stumps. However, there were other rewards. Papa could recover from the physical exhaustion of his mining work and have another stab at getting used to becoming a patient father, learning to cope with a completely new role in his life, that of being a father and husband, fitting in to a family who had lived without him through years of extreme hardship and deprivation. He had only seen us for short breaks from his army service. He had re- entered our clan when I was nearly 11 and my brother 12 ½ years old, not the best time to take on the role of a disciplinarian father. We loved him and were extremely happy to have him with us, but for us children Mutti remained the boss, the person we respected and cherished. Father had to "earn" his place in the family set up despite our pleasure in having him back. This was extremely unfair towards him but a situation all returning fathers had to battle with. Once the euphoria of his return had settled down, we slowly began to realize that father was indeed our father and yet he was also a stranger. It took a long time for him to integrate and for us to fully accept him as head of the family despite the years of longing for his return.

Not only did Papa have to learn being an understanding father, he had to relearn being a loving husband as well; something we children were only aware of to a small degree. Therefore, the several months of home time after his return from Saxony helped a great deal in the process of gluing us all together again. The visit of our uncle Fritz was thus a welcome diversion for our father, if not such a great joy for our mother.

Chapter Thirty-One

It was not the first time Uncle Fritz had come to stay with us. He was our father's youngest brother. There were two more brothers, the eldest called Adolf and the second youngest called Ernst. Unlike my mother, who had lost all but one of her brothers, father had lost none. I cannot remember whether we knew their whereabouts by then but all of them lived in "The West". Uncle Fritz lived in the Western sector of Berlin. He and his wife owned a small delicatessen shop near the Hallensee Bridge, off the Kurfuerstendamm, which, before the war, had been Berlin's "Prachtstrasse" (show case street) for shoppers and diners.

Uncle Fritz had been taken prisoner-of-war by the English as early as 1941. Although some of his experiences weren't happy ones either to say the least, he spent a long time in a camp in Spalding where the prisoners were asked to help in the well known nurseries, growing vegetables for the nation. They were not allowed to speak nor have any contact with the population. Nor was the population permitted to "fraternize" with the German soldiers. Uncle Fritz did not mind working instead of hanging around the nissen huts with nothing to do. Besides, he also learned a great deal about growing vegetables and loved working in the fresh air. After four years of captivity though he was overjoyed when the war ended.

However, it did not mean all prisoners were automatically released and he, too, showed great courage and determination, just like his older brother, by escaping from the camp! I draw a blank on how exactly he managed to get himself from Spalding back home to Germany without speaking English or possessing any release papers! Apparently it was particularly difficult to get through Germany back to Berlin without these papers. He knew his older sister Elisabeth lived there. He had no idea at that time where any of his other family members had found a new base or indeed whether any of them were alive or dead.

Miraculously he succeeded, turning up at my aunt's place in the dead of night. The reunion was, of course, joyful, but since Uncle Fritz had in a manner "deserted" and had no official papers he also could not apply for ration cards; feeding him with the little my aunt had was not easy.
However Tante Bine, as she was called in the family circle, knew a great many people in Berlin. One of her friends was a relatively affluent lady who lived in a large house, together with her sister. This lady took in the young man and hid him in the attic. In return for her risk and kindness, he repaired the bomb damage to her house, at first with remnants of wood the two sisters had searched for in the streets of Berlin. Later he rebuilt his work with bricks and other solid building materials.

Unsurprisingly, he eventually married the younger of the two sisters though she was quite a bit older than him! Yet prior to this marriage she had to use her extended high powered contacts to get him legitimate papers. You had to have your wits about you in the large cities after the war and especially in Berlin which had been razed to the ground by the conquerors, the notorious Red Army.

Unsurprisingly, Uncle Fritz and his wife and sister continued to almost "flourish" in the aftermath of the war, in contrast to most of the other inhabitants. Obviously, they were rather clever and positive people, gutsy and enterprising; thus it did not take long before they opened their small delicatessen shop near the Hallensee Bridge. Not far over the bridge was an area of Berlin which traditionally housed the well- to- do people of the city. Grunewald was the leafy district of the rich and famous who somehow continued to be better off than anyone else even in these desperate, desolate times. A new delicatessen shop and the first to be opened in their vicinity meant a certain success for the business from the outset. The difficulty lay in the purchase of groceries to fill the shelves. Once uncle and his wife had sourced enough products, there was no problem in selling them.

A wholesale market had started up again and Uncle Fritz told us he cycled to it every morning, getting up at 4am and cycling back again; the bicycle laden heavily with fruit and vegetables. They both worked incredibly hard, apparently never having had a day off work for years.

I wish I knew how exactly and who succeeded in getting in touch. As I mentioned earlier, there were agencies searching for family members all over Germany and this may have been the way contact was made between my mother and her brother-in-law. Initially this took place by letter. Then, one day, uncle Fritz came to visit us. Shrewd and enterprising as he was, he calculated there must be plenty of farm yards around where we lived, farmers who had good meat products and who were extremely keen to exchange them for sugar, chocolate and the other luxury goods my uncle was able to purchase in the Western part of Berlin. Bartering had become the unofficial trading method ever since the close of war and even prior to it. Whatever our mother still possessed of her precious items of clothing or jewellery she exchanged for food stuff – mostly for potatoes from the farmers. This way she lost her magnificent fox stole and a chain of amber beads, the only piece of jewellery she owned, apart from her wedding ring.

By the time Uncle Fritz came to visit us, he did not need potatoes, but wanted the home made sausages and bacon the Mecklenburg farmers produced so well. And who better than Johanna to supply him with the very best! Involving yourself in smuggling activities like that was strictly forbidden in our Eastern part of Germany. If you were caught it carried severe prison sentences. However, this did not stop the brave going about this kind of business.

In those days it was still possible to travel unhindered between Western sectors of Berlin and into the surrounding countryside. By train, of course, since no one had cars as yet. And there were regular police checks controlling the trains. So the risks were extremely high, but my courageous and shrewd uncle was lucky, every time!

Not until mother was an old lady did she confess to us that Uncle Fritz never gave us any of the many sausages he had acquired. Our suffering was made worse by having his haul deposited in our apartment tantalizing us with the smell of smoked sausages or bacon we had not had the pleasure of eating for ages. It speaks for Werner that he never did repeat his sausage burglary, although he may well have been tempted all of the time. In fact, I'm pretty sure he was since I still remember very distinctly that I most certainly was tempted myself, despite the fact they weren't made of sugar!! Hunger was still a constant companion, but Mutti had drilled it into us never to steal or misbehave regardless of how we were tempted or provoked. We know by now that I did not always stick to this rule. What I stole were things the owners did not want but were too mean to give to us freely. Uncle had brought Mutti some small gift in return for our hospitality and giving up our sofa for him to sleep on, but it was very little indeed in comparison to the gains he made by being able to stay with us. Mutti said as hard as she tried she could never really forgive him for that.

This sort of behaviour was not unusual by any means. The fight for survival and rebuilding some kind of decent life was extremely taxing and cruel for years after the end of the war. It brought out the worst in everyone. It hardened the hearts of even the mildest and kindest person. Selfishness was the natural order of the day, especially by those who lived in the cities and had no access to the riches of the land.

Despite Mutti not being well disposed towards uncle Fritz, I liked him a lot. He was cheerful but more importantly, he was a man and for two or three days replaced our absent father. He may even have brought some sweets for

Werner and me and artificial sweeteners for Mutti which may have helped to make me like him rather well.

He came quite frequently on his "hamster trips" since Johanna's sausages were the rage with all his well heeled customers. Unsurprisingly, they seemed to like her sausages the best of all the produce Uncle Fritz was able to scrounge together from the farmers all around us. We laughed a lot about that and wondered whether his customers would still love the sausages as much if they had known quite where they came from. But it proved without doubt, cleanliness was not essential for the production of superb "Delicatessen"!

If anything, it clearly improved their flavour! Good old Johanna! She really was quite special and a gifted culinary expert in so many ways. She really did not deserve to be derided merely because she was a bit dirty. Her heart was spotlessly clean and golden. We knew this very well by then. And mocked her good humouredly rather than spitefully, which she truly would not have deserved.

Was this latest visit the first time the two brothers had met up again since the start of the war?

I'm starting to realize how many gaps there are in my memory box. My mind is completely blank on this matter. I am certain, however, Uncle Fritz came to stay with us several times. Was his first visit prior to Papa's return from Russia? Or soon thereafter, returning while our father worked in the mine? I suppose the precise dates don't really matter. Important is how we got to know Papa's brother and that the two of them were able to catch up with their individual lives after father had given up the work in Saxony. Having spent a few days together the many years of separation dwindled away rapidly and the two of them bonded really well once more.

We all played cards in the evenings and I remember distinctly a truly animated atmosphere in our sitting room.

It must have been on this particular visit when our uncle suggested Papa should come and stay with him in Berlin and run his shop for a few weeks so that he and his wife could finally have a holiday. Not having permanent employment it seemed an ideal time to help one another. Papa was desperate for work and his brother and wife equally desperate for a first and essential break away from their shop. In the post war era it was still possible to travel unhindered to all four military German zones. Only the purchasing of goods in the Western zones and returning with them to the East was illegal as it showed up the deficiency of the communist system, a crime almost worse than death in the people's republic!

The decision to accept this offer must have been made during those short days of my uncle's visit for Papa travelled to Berlin not long afterwards. Altogether he stayed away for five weeks since he had to acquaint himself with this new type of work, do the buying with his brother and generally learn the way his brother wanted the shop to be run. All of it Papa exercised brilliantly. After surviving Russia, this was kid's play. Uncle Fritz and his wife Tina spent a leisurely holiday by the sea, returning sun tanned and refreshed and finding the shop had been run faultlessly. Naturally, Papa did not want to be paid in money but in kind – he had a hungry family at home. Besides, money was a fairly useless commodity since the shops at home were mostly empty of foodstuff anyway.

So Papa took the risk of smuggling his honestly earned payment back home to us and for a while we were in clover! I remember eating chocolate for the first time since the occasion when Frau Markurth had treated us. We were also gorging ourselves on Johanna's sausages which Papa had "bought" from her with a few bars of chocolate. There was tinned meat and fish and other precious foods we had not seen for years. Once again something tempting stood on top of the wardrobe because Mutti knew, like the bags of sugar, this was something Brigitte would find hard to resist: dried milk! All in all this journey had been an unqualified success. Both sides were most happy with the outcome and it was decided to repeat this enterprise if, by summer, Papa was still without any proper work. It was a highly dangerous way to proceed but if the State could not feed us we had to take matters into our own hands.

Chapter Thirty-Two

By now it was spring 1951. The DDR was 18 months old and I was just over 12, old enough to become intensely aware of the political situation in our part of Germany.

On the 23rd May 1949 the territories of the three western zones had become united to form The Federal Republic of Germany. A small town on the Rhine with the name of Bonn became its capital. This new German republic was allied with the United States of America, the UK and France and soon developed a flourishing economic growth.

Our German Democratic Republic was founded on October 1949 with East Berlin as its capital. Its government was selected by Josef Stalin and remained a Soviet satellite state until the demise of the regime in November 1989. Whereas the western republic flourished and grew ever closer to its western conquerors, the Eastern republic under a single communist party (the SED = Sozialistische Einheitspartei Deutschlands) directed by the Soviet Union confiscated almost all private industry and nationalized it (creating "Volkseigene Betriebe -VEBs, Publicly Owned Enterprises), took away privately owned farmland and thus severely throttling private enterprise in its agricultural and industrial development, while all the while the country was still suffering under extensive reparation demands by the Soviet Union.

Every day at school we were exposed to communist indoctrination, either by having to learn yet another socialist song, praising the wonderful achievements of our new government, our "beloved" workers' paradise! A paradise where such workers who had any work toiled incredibly hard and long hours, but were unable to feed themselves! Every day, at some stage during our lessons, our teachers had to tell us how wonderful everything was in our country and how grateful we had to be to our "friends", the Russian army and to the Russian people for having liberated us from the Nazis and given us hope and joy and a rich and peaceful future to look forward to under the wings of Russian socialism. I felt really sorry for our poor teachers. You could tell they did not believe a word they were teaching us, but had to lie to us if they wanted to keep their job – as well as their liberty!

All the while this was happening, most of the people were still going hungry, perhaps not quite as hungry as a few years earlier but bad enough for people, especially those without employment, to despair. Unsurprisingly, therefore, father made another trip to Berlin a few weeks after the first successful adventure. He did all sorts of handy work for his younger brother, painting, doing repairs, going to the market with him, even making deliveries to the rich clients around the Kurfuerstendamm and Grunewald.

Chapter Thirty-Three

While Papa was working in Berlin, mother got news from Saxony that her father had died. When I was very small in Prussia, Werner and I often stayed with both of our sets of grandparents. I have happy memories of both of them. My father's parents owned a house with some land and a few animals on the edge of the small town of Goldap.

Our grandmother Elisabeth worked without interruption from dawn till very late at night, but we did not need her to entertain us. Father's sister, also called Elisabeth (Bine for short), lived in Berlin. Her son Hans usually also spent his summer holidays with them. Our cousin was a little bit older than us but that did not matter in the slightest. We all got on really well and roamed around the place or in the woods nearby all day long to our hearts' content. Most evenings, when our grandfather returned from work, having first spent some time in the pub, he allowed us to empty his trouser pockets to see whether there was any "Hasenbrot" left for us (rabbit food). "Hasenbrot" was the left over bits of sandwiches from his lunch. But on many occasions we also found boiled sweets in the tips of his pockets which even then were a huge treat and thrill for us kids.

He may have turned to drink but he obviously had a kind and generous heart underneath his stern exterior. We liked our holidays at Goldap. Grandmother was a very good cook despite the shortage of money and ingredients. She also was a terrific baker of bread and cake. She regularly baked Streuselkuchen every Saturday night, a delicious treat we ate for Sunday breakfast, together with a cup of hot chocolate! That was the best meal of the week, made extra special by the presence of grandfather and grandmother, who wore a better Sunday outfit for the Sunday meals. Afterwards she changed again because the animals still needed to be fed, whether it was Sunday or not.

Mutti's parents were quite different. Grandfather Michael was a quiet man, tall and handsome, always wearing his Station Master's uniform. Grandmother Luise was a very grandmotherly looking woman, stout, with her hair in a bun. She, too, seemed a quiet sort of person, hard working like everyone seemed to have been in those days.
She had raised six sons and three daughters, two other children had died in early childhood. They lived on the ground floor of a huge house belonging to the railways. They had a large courtyard which was home to lots of chickens and some geese. We could not run into the woods there, but for that we had the trains to watch as the station was immediately next to the big house. So that made for a lot of interest to us both. I liked grandpa Michael. I did not warm so well to his wife. I think she and their eldest daughter Erna, who lived with them and helped with all the housework and cooking and nursing of little grandchildren, could not cope so well with my adventurous spirit and I remember having to stand in the kitchen corner facing the wall as a punishment for things I had done wrong on more than one occasion. I did not dislike them but I enjoyed being at Goldap a little bit more because there I was never told off for anything! To be fair, Grandma Goldap was simply too busy to see what we little monsters were up to all day long and with Grandpa Goldap being away at work , it was easy to get away with anything at their house.

Now, unexpectedly, grandpa Michael had died. Although I had seen him only once since our flight from Prussia, his death upset me very much. We still did not know what had happened to the Goldap grandparents. We assumed that they were dead, six years having passed since the end of the war.

Gone were the days of holidaying with our grandparents in the country. With our grandparents dying or still missing and Prussia being in foreign hands, those blissful childhood holidays were definitely a thing of the past now whether we liked admitting it or not. Even if our homeland would be returned to us (which was highly unlikely), would we want to return to it with so many of our family now gone and villages, towns and cities totally destroyed? A very difficult question and one that is better not contemplated. Opa's death was starting to put a seal on the past, adding more than his loss to our unhappiness.

Mutti was crying her eyes out. She telegraphed Papa at Berlin who replied by telegram asking her to stop over in Berlin on her return journey from the funeral in Bischofswerda. Werner and I were old enough to be left alone. Besides, there were also the cousins and their father in the other part of the house to call on if there was any real need. Fortunately Tante Ella joined Mutti on the long journey by train giving them the chance to comfort one another on this sad mission. I wasn't scared being in charge of the two of us on our own, in fact I had often been in charge before and fear was something I fortunately never knew. Looking back now, it's clear from whom I had inherited this trait – from our courageous father! Most of the time, at crucial points throughout my life, this characteristic has come in very helpful; yet by no means always, just as it has not always been a blessing in my father's life.

Chapter Thirty-Four

Two or three days after our aunt's return from the funeral, Mutti arrived home as well. I happened to see her coming up the road as I crossed over from Ingetrud's house. I ran excitedly towards her to give her a welcome home hug. She was dragging her feet heavily and looked dejected even from a distance and when I had arrived in front of her, I stopped hard in my track. Something was wrong, badly wrong. Mutti looked so sad and worried and could not bring a smile to her face even when she saw me.

"Mutti, you look so sad! Is something the matter, apart from Opa's death?"
"There is, Gitta. There is. I'll tell you when we get home. How have you been? Has everything been alright here?"

She looked really anxious and her mood transferred itself to me. "Has anyone been to see you and Werner or Tante Ella?" I was puzzled. "Who should have come to see us, Mutti?"
"Oh, no one. It's alright, I am so exhausted". She put her arm around my shoulder and in this way we walked home together. I could sense something terrible must have happened to her but I could not think for the life of it what. As we had reached the top of the stairs to our little nest, Werner must have heard us. He tore open the door excitedly to welcome his beloved mother. We were both so glad to have her back with us but Mutti's mood did not change. Something weighed down on her very heavily and she sank onto the sofa and hastily drank the glass of water I had given her.

I was about to ask her again what was wrong when she looked at us both and said:
"I have had a very frightening experience on the train and I am so worried!"
She sighed heavily. "It is Papa, it is Papa I'm worried about!"

Then she related her story to us. Following Papa's instructions, she had interrupted her train journey in Berlin. Papa was waiting for her on the Hauptbahnhof, the main station of the city. She was so glad to see him and have his support as the funeral and stay with her mother and sister had been rather sad and tiring. The short stay in the city with Papa and Uncle Fritz and his wife Tina was a comforting break. It was her first experience of such a big city. Up till then Koenigsberg had been the only city she had ever been to and not under happy circumstances either, as you will recall.
Originally Papa had decided to stay on a bit longer with his brother but Opa's death made him change his mind. He knew Mutti needed him now, so he planned to go home with her. He had earned a bit of West German money and had turned all of it into food, which, this time, was rather more than one

suitcase could carry. Too much for one person to smuggle through. He therefore suggested that they should not travel together after all but leave Berlin on separate days, each one of them taking some of the food hidden inside their luggage.

The idea made sense, except Mutti has always been a rather diffident person, unlike our father, and she was really frightened to take this risk; yet Papa insisted until she had no choice but to agree. He had worked hard for Uncle Fritz and we desperately needed the food he had earned. It seemed a shame not to try to get all of it home in this way. Papa was used to being daring. He would never have survived Russia if he had not been such a plucky, determined person. Our mother was entirely different. She, too, had survived and brought up two children under exceptionally hard circumstances. Though her courage did not include committing anything illegal. Naturally, what Papa was planning to do was by no means a crime, just another way of trying to feed the family. He had not robbed anyone, had worked hard and bought the food in the West with the money he had earned merely because he was unable to buy the same or any food, for that matter, at home in Mecklenburg. Strictly speaking, he had not even "bought" the food at all, but had part exchanged it for his work. There was nothing immoral in that.

The East German authorities did not see it that way. For them it was a crime and Mutti was not a very confident person. Anyway, despite her fear she finally agreed to do as Papa had asked her to: hiding some of the food among her clothes in her only suitcase.

Police did not always check all the trains or all the carriages. Unfortunately, on this occasion they did and poor Mutti experienced the heavy hand of the law on her shoulder!

Two grim looking rude policemen entered her compartment. Seeing Mutti's frightened expression on her face, they knew at once here was someone with something to hide!

"Is that your suitcase?" one of the dreaded police men asked. Mutti nodded, unable to speak with fear, and starting to feel sick. "Open it", he demanded in his military style. "Quick, quick! What takes you so long?"

They were extremely intimidating, did not help her get the suitcase down from the rack and kept asking her to hurry up. Of course, they saw the chocolate, sugar and tins of meat straight away and gleefully started to get their notebooks out to jot down all the items they immediately confiscated as well as her name, address etc. Mutti feared they would arrest her there and then; instead they asked her where she got these items from. They did not go in a friendly manner about their business.

Mutti was so scared, she told them everything, honest woman that she was.

How Papa had worked and earned the money honestly and since his brother had a delicatessen shop he wanted to be paid in kind rather than in money. That she had travelled from Saxony and had stopped over in Berlin to see her husband and that he had asked her to take some of the food with her so that he could manage to bring the remainder with him when he was ready to return home!

All the while she was telling them everything, she knew she was doing wrong, that she should be lying to save her husband, to pretend these items were merely presents from her brother-in-law which would have been perfectly plausible. Though these ideas were running through her mind, the words coming out of her mouth were totally different, the easier words under the fear of arrest: the truth.

These words did indeed save her. They just took everything away and gave her a strict warning not to do it again, leaving her utterly shattered, a nervous wreck. There were other passengers in the compartment, all of them had turned to stone as soon as the policemen entered the compartment, inspecting everyone's frozen face until their searching eyes came to rest on Mutti's pale face and quivering mouth. None of the other passengers seemed to be alive while the interrogation was taking place, but once the police men had left and mother collapsed into a heap of tears, one of them did at least help her gather her clothes into her suitcase and lifted it up into the top rack for her.

No one uttered a word of comfort or sympathy. Even such little support was too dangerous as everyone living in the DDR had learned by now. Thus Mutti was left alone with the choking fear that she may have, unwittingly, condemned her husband to possible capture when he was coming home on the same and only daily train the following day. No one had telephones in those days and even sending a telegram was impossible – we had no post office in the village either. And Papa was going to take the morning train. If only we could have warned him, but there was no way we could do so. This helplessness was the worst about the situation, knowing the mouse was running into a trap and not being able to stop her.

Whatever Werner and I tried to say as a comfort to her was said in vain. She merely shook her head in total resignation. Deep down even we children knew she was quite right to fear the worst. So we kept hugging her and crying with her. None of us slept that night. And all of the next day each of us spent in dejected silence, locked in our own thoughts of unbearable fear for the safety of our father whom we expected home in the early part of the afternoon. How terribly long even half a day can feel when you are that anxious! All we could do was hope that father had decided to take a later train or even postpone the trip home altogether. But why should he want to do that? For all he knew Mutti's adventure had run smoothly. After all, police spots were random since not many people dared "smuggling" anything useful out of West Berlin on a public train. Perhaps we were worrying quite unnecessarily. They would have to check every single person on the train that day or even the next to find the part-time novice "racketeer" Hugo Mallon. Surely they had better things to do and bigger fish to catch!? Mother being such an unworldly kind of woman always worried far too much about everything and had probably talked herself into this state of hysteria quite unnecessarily.

Chapter Thirty-Five

In my youth, marriage was the ultimate state most young men and women aimed for.

To love and support one another through thick and thin (for richer for poorer, in sickness and in health…!) seemed the very best way to go through life. We did not really think much about what this truly meant in the inevitable tough times. Youth is full of optimism and hope. And I for one was not short of it when Richard and I stepped into the taxi which was taking us, this time together, back to the house across the Green for the champagne reception in the garden.

I think I am right when I believe there were over one hundred guests queuing up to shake our hands and to extend their very best wishes to us for the remainder of our lives. It was the most wonderful party of my life so far. The weather was still splendid, the champagne even better and the finger foods most delicious and plentiful. Young or old, everyone seemed in the best of spirits, Richard and myself being the focus of attention.

The second most glamorous person was, of course, my new mother-in-law. She wore a wonderful chiffon dress in off-white with large dark green flowers printed onto the fabric. She wore a soft hat in a similar shade of green, which also matched the dark green chiffon of the bridesmaids' dresses. A stage designer could not have found a better outfit for her. She looked resplendent, very grand, very English!

My own parents had also decked themselves out well, but being German and not used to this type of wedding, their outfits looked smart, yet somewhat severe in contrast. Mutti had taken my advice and worn a hat and I was very proud of her. Like the day before, so many of our guests spoke to my parents as they all seemed to know at least some German, although they would have denied it at any other time!

Speeches were made, the cake cutting ceremony started. Everyone looked so happy and excited. You could have been fooled to believe that none of the guests had ever attended such an event before, such was the gaiety all around. I drifted on a cloud of elation from one guest to another, hardly seeing Richard or my parents and barely believing it was all real, not a dream from which I would wake up at any moment.

For my part, the day could have gone on forever. Instead I had to go upstairs to change out of my wonderful gown and into my equally fabulous turquoise silk dress with matching jacket, my going-away outfit, which Ma had insisted we buy in London. We had travelled there to a specific shop in Baker Street where we acquired this wonderful outfit from a Norman Hartnell ready-to-wear collection. The dress and jacket were very plain, since I don't like fussy clothes, but the silk was of a superb quality and the colour so brilliant, it did not need any further decoration to shine, except some simple detailing emphasizing my tiny waist!

Norman Hartnell was THE clothes designer in England at that time and continued to be until the end of his life. He had a royal warrant and had designed the coronation dress for Queen Elisabeth II as well as outfits for her sister, Princess Margaret and many other royals as well as the rich and famous of the period. Although my dress was from his ready-to-wear collection, it felt, nonetheless, very grand indeed. I was really glad the tradition demanded to have a special dress or suit for the departure. Who would not have liked being dressed from top to toe like a princess – and not merely for the actual ceremonial part! This outfit, and mainly the dress itself, remained my best occasion dress for many years to come. I only wish I still had it today!

Richard also changed out of his morning suit into a new very smart day suit. Facing the waiting crowd who had patiently stayed on to see us go, we strolled towards the part of the garden where Richard's divine, dove-grey MG sports car was waiting for us. All the while we were heading towards the MG (slowly to spin out the moments, of course!) both of us waving to right and to left as if we were royals! In true traditional style Richard's Best Man and best friend Julian had attached the inevitable sign to the rear number plate "JUST MARRIED". Also attached were several empty tins in varying sizes trailing from strings on the ground and making a dreadful but essential noise as we set off out of the gate and into our glorious future, everyone waving excitedly and shouting:
"Happy Honeymoon!" "Safe journey!" I even noted the odd "Hoorah!"

Chapter Thirty-Six

Papa's journey had not been a safe one. Mutti's fears had not been unfounded. He did not turn up that day or the next. By then there was no denying it: he had been caught and arrested or he would have arrived home by the next day, at the latest.

I cannot remember when the police came to inform our mother of his arrest; they came alright and their tone of voice was not exactly sympathetic. Mutti fell into a deep depression for a long time however much we both tried to comfort her, hugging her, weeping with her and trying to do little favours for her to show how much we felt for her. A nasty, heavy cloud descended on us all which was made worse some time later when we heard that Papa had been convicted of "Crimes against the economy of the DDR" and given a two year prison sentence! Two years!! For trying to make an honest living, although in the West, because in the East you could only survive by dishonest or immoral means! We could not believe the cruelty and savagery of this new regime. Their hypocrisy beggared belief. Our parents had lived through years of fascism, which, so we heard, had also been a dangerous period in their lives; then war and separation, followed by intense relief at the war's end, followed by loss of our homeland, further separation, hunger, hopelessness and despair, loss of dignity, loss of opportunity to rebuild a decent life. And now this massive blow to our hopes of ever being a happy and united family again, simply living a NORMAL life. All such hope gone in an instant! How could our dear father or our lovely mother ever hope to recover from this hammer blow when they had already suffered so much trauma, so much pain and suffering?

I was extremely concerned about our mother. She could barely get out of bed for a while and nearly lost her job as a result of this new tragedy in our lives. But we had to live. Money needed to be earned and this necessity spurred her on to get well enough to restart her job. Little by little she picked up. These were very terrifying times for us all. Even Werner tried not to add to Mutti's worries by helping more and working harder at his school work.

I was now a little more than 12 years of age, but in maturity I was much, much older. It was at this time I began to really hate the political system in our part of Germany. I became intensely preoccupied, how I myself could get involved in fighting the government in whatever small way possible. Unfortunately, in practical terms, I soon realized I could not do anything whatsoever, other than silently oppose them; thus stoking a really deep hatred of everyone and everything communist inside me for the rest of my life. One day in the future I might be able to oppose this tyranny in more concrete terms. Meanwhile I would show my opposition to the communist cause in whatever way I could at school: for instance by not singing the socialist songs we were required to sing daily. Instead I would merely move my lips as if I was singing. No one could force me to utter those hated words of adulation of the people's paradise, no one, ever again!

We were regularly encouraged to join the "Young Pioneers", a communist youth organisation, similar to the Hitler Youth under the Nazis. Needless to say, they were not lucky with me. This was a particularly good opportunity to show my resistance to our poor teachers who were forced, mostly against their own belief, to indoctrinate and educate us in the way of communist dogma. Even then I understood how everyone had to live a lie, day in, day out, just to survive! How our teachers must have hated that side of their job! But that was no reason for me to stop resisting them. I felt sympathy for their plight, of course I did, yet this did not mean I could forfeit my principles. My hatred of the government became so strong I often dreamed at night of wanting to assassinate Ulbricht, usually by strangling him! They were only "day dreams" dreamt at night, a way of releasing the tension and violent hatred which was building up inside me since the arrest of our father. Of course, I wasn't a killer by nature. I had, however, always been a strong individual; someone who knew her mind and who liked to express the thoughts in her head. It was part of developing your own personality, of growing and evolving as an individual. In a communist ruled state this was, however, the very notion which had to be suppressed with all possible might in order to keep control over their people. Well, without me! We clearly were not free to say or do what we wanted. Danger lurked all around us.

In every nation, at every time in history there have always been "Mitlaeufer" (sympathisers) and our village was no exception. No one really knew as yet who the party members were but they were around and spied on everyone because the police always found out who had done or said anything disparaging about the Russians, the communists or the government.
Someone was feeding the authorities useful information. Therefore we soon learned not to express our ideas to ANYONE, not even to our best friends. For you never knew where the danger lay in waiting! Anyone could betray you – we saw what had happened to Mr. and Mrs. Rose. And that had

occurred years earlier. Since then the political oppression had increased measurably and the standard of living was still appallingly low. Why work hard when Russia was still draining the land of anything useful? Stagnation and fear paralysed any attempt for economic growth.

Our school was still badly equipped – no library yet, no sports hall. Sport consisted of volley and hand ball games during the summer term. Our physical and spiritual development was limited at every level; academically we did well, however. In that respect the state provided the necessary text books as well as standard equipment for the science subjects. It was important to educate the young and turn them into convinced young communists and future leaders of the state!

My frustration and anger with the system had started even before Papa's arrest, increasing with huge passion afterwards. I had to be particularly careful to check my "Plappermaul" (my chatterbox mouth); being exuberant and somewhat temperamental I really had to watch myself or else life could become even worse for my entire family – not merely for poor Papa! We were already being viewed with great suspicion by the local party hierarchy. Any false move could damage our future irreparably.

Chapter Thirty-Seven

On a happier subject: Something lovely happened in the village that summer. Our neighbour's daughter, Johanna's daughter, got married! All the time we knew our neighbours, their daughter had lived somewhere else, exactly where we never knew. She was not so very young any more and probably had lived near her place of work. Now she was back with her parents due to her marriage because in those days no girl or woman ever married away from home. It was the parents' privilege to arrange and pay for it – the parents of the bride that is. The groom's parents got off scot free!

Since I had become quite close to Johanna by now she asked me to help her a bit more than in previous years, mainly in the garden. After Papa's demise it was so comforting to have that family and their animals for company and distraction, to say nothing of the food that I earned from my fun work there! What was good enough for the well to do customers in Berlin was certainly more than good enough for us! In fact, anything created by dear black Johanna and honestly earned by me for our supper equalled a slap up meal in a five-star hotel anywhere in the world nowadays! Except, of course, her "Himmel und Erde" which I never grew to like. May be a similar dish might be apple and parsnip soup here in England – one of my favourites now!

Their daughter, the bride, was a statuesque, heavy shouldered, tall, blond woman. She married a farmer's son and would go to live with her husband on his parents' farm not far away. That must have pleased her parents. She married late but obviously the right kind of man. In other words, into the right family set-up, the farming world.

The night before the wedding was traditionally party night for the young in the bride's house. Lots of drinking with their mutual friends. Then, around ten o'clock at night when it got dark, it seemed like all the village youngsters had assembled in front of the house, smashing old plates and crockery against the door step or the walls near the front door as a good luck token. The original villagers mainly partook in this custom – we refugees did not have too many spare plates to throw away. So we just looked on and enjoyed the camaraderie among the crowd. No early night for us that evening but who cared? We were in desperate need of some diversion and something like this did not happen every day.

The church wedding took place the following late morning. A beautifully decorated horse and carriage took the bride to the church, together with Johanna and her husband, both of whom I barely recognized: Johanna was immaculately clean and wearing some smart outfit I had never seen her wear before. Her husband looked very smart, too. You could not believe they were the same couple! It looked to me that their clothes were still pre-war, the quality was simply too good for anything they may have been able to purchase nowadays. The horse, too, had been magnificently decked out: flowers behind his ears, his coat having been brushed to a beautiful shine and

the hair of his tail plaited and tied with a bow! It was not a Schimmel like
Herr Rose's horse who had bitten me, but a beautiful brown horse with a good
carriage.

Although we almost felt like part of the family, we did not get an invitation
which really disappointed me. Perhaps we were not good enough. When it
matters you stick to your own kind. After all, we were refugees, not land
owning farmers like the rest of the guests. We had to be content watching the
departure and arrival of the bride and groom and their guests. The reception
and a festive lunch took place in the pub near the river bank. The lunch took
place in a dance hall attached to the main pub – behind drawn curtains so that
no hungry eyes could look in and spoil their enjoyment of the mountains of
tasty home made food! Werner and I walked home when we realized that we
were even excluded from watching. Around four o'clock we returned; the
time we suspected the dancing would start. We had hoped the curtains would
have been drawn open by then for us to watch. But no, nothing had changed.
However, we could hear the music loud and clear and tried to dance to it as
best as we could.

Some more children had joined us; one of them shouting towards us that on
one of the windows the curtains had not been drawn completely. Through a
chink in the centre one could see just a little of the festivities. Of course,
everyone wanted to be nearest that window. It took quite a while before little
me was allowed a look inside, too. The music was terrific though and we
stayed on messing around to it for quite a while until we got bored and
sauntered home. Besides, it had not felt all that good to be thus excluded from
the fun inside anyway. May be, I comforted myself, one day I will also go to
a wedding although I doubted it would be such a big event as this one had
been. Little did I know......!

Chapter Thirty-Eight

At some time during that summer, something even more sensational happened. During a very violent thunderstorm, of which we had many every year, a barn had been struck. The fire was to be seen many metres high in the air. The fire station in our village was at the bottom of our road. However, the fire was so severe, the firemen were unable to rescue the barn. The corn had just been cut and harvested and the barn was full with this year's hay and straw, the best possible fodder for fire. There was frantic activity to save the barn; to no avail. To us children this disaster was a spectacular sight and adventure, to the farmer a tragedy. At least no lives were lost, also no other properties since the wind was mild and did not carry sparks far enough to light up the surrounding dwellings. Werner and I had never watched such a dramatic spectacle before. It left us with an enormous respect for the men fighting such fires and an enormous fear of it, too.

The remainder of that year bore no more such events for the village or for us. My friendship with Ingetrud and her family deepened and my visits to the Markurth estate continued as before. Werner's football skills had become well known in the village and he was invited to become the goal keeper to the local youth team.

Most weekends I now went to the sports field in the direction of the local forest to watch Werner and his team play against other village teams. Football was not at all my scene and I never learned the rules to appreciate the game properly. But it was easy enough to see whether my brother performed well or not – he either held the goal or he didn't. It was something to do on a Sunday afternoon and more often than not I met up with other boys and girls from my school or even my form.
Sometimes the games were also quite exciting, especially when Werner was in good form and held all his goals, which he did quite often. He actually became a good goal keeper and never lost his love for the game. When he had become a father and his son was growing into a teenager he became the

trainer of the local youth team with Kai-Uwe, his son, following in his footsteps as a passionate goal keeper.

While I had had no time for Werner messing around with the little boys chasing a ball in our sandy road, I did become rather proud of him when he had been elevated to the proper team and supported him genuinely if not always enthusiastically. As I said before: football wasn't really my scene! I preferred good old fashioned work and handicrafts in my spare time.

The upcoming winter was tough without Papa and without the wood he had dug up for us. We had a little left from last winter, but not much and our home was not as warm a nest as it had been the previous winter. Whenever I could and was allowed to I went over to Ingetrud's house where it was much cosier and where there was plenty of cheerful company. My best memories of that winter as well as many others are of Mutti and me doing the ironing. Actually, Mutti hated ironing and I loved it which worked out rather well.

For me it wasn't a chore but a pleasure, a very satisfying job. What I liked best about it was folding the finished sheets together with Mutti's help. She took the two corners of one end and I the other two. Then we shook the sheet in unison to shake out any small creases before folding the sheet into a half width and then into a quarter width. Then came the best part!: we shook the folded sheet again to straighten it out nicely. This done, we walked towards one another, each of us holding the two corners of the folded sheet in order for one of us to hold it by all four corners and then folding it once more before it was the correct size for storing it away.

We always giggled as we walked towards one another, wondering who would pick up the opposite two corners fastest. That person was the winner! These were simple intimate moments with my mother but for me they meant the world. While writing these lines, I can still see the two of us quite clearly in my mind's eye. It was working in harmony and split second unison with mother which made this work such an enjoyable experience.

Another warming winter evening activity was darning socks. This was something else Mutti did not like whereas I loved it!! We had a really good teacher of our needle work classes at school. Darning was a most useful craft to learn since no one had enough money to keep buying new socks just because there was a hole in them or the back of the foot had rubbed the sock thin. Everything had to be repaired. An item would only be replaced when it was no longer possible to repair! So my love of needle craft came in very handy, making me feel proud and happy. Sometimes I took the socks in need of repair over to Ingetrud's in the evening.

After supper the entire family usually gathered in the sitting room around a large table, playing cards, knitting or darning or merely relaxing in happy chatter.

Chapter Thirty-Nine

I remember nothing else special about that winter nor the following spring or early summer for that matter. The first anniversary of Papa's imprisonment arrived and a day or so later Papa stood in front of our door! He had been granted early release from the infamous Bautzen prison due to exceptionally good conduct and been spared half his term. We were overjoyed and kept hugging each other for ages. There had been no indication of this amnesty, turning our reunion into a very uplifting, exhilarating event.

It was early summer 1952 and fate had given us another chance to rebuild our lives with Papa as the head of the family. His physical condition was not at all bad. After a short recuperative period Papa set out once more searching for permanent employment. This time he was lucky. While he had been in prison a new colliery had opened in one of the neighbouring villages, raising brown coal. Only this time father did not have to go underground. He did all sorts of useful repair jobs above ground. His training experience in his youth as well as in Russia came in most handsomely now. His skills were much needed and for the first time since his return from Russia we felt some kind of security underpinning our existence. Papa's pay was enough for us to get by. Therefore he wanted mother to give up her job – no more sewing on buttons for her! Luckily we had bought our bicycle before his arrest, giving him a means of transport to and from work. With Papa's return and his steady employment and income a new hopefulness entered our lives. Also renewed

184

pride and dignity. We no longer needed Johanna's left-over stews. We still accepted and welcomed them as a gift from a friendly neighbour, though no longer as part of a necessity for survival. By today's standard we were still rather poor. Even by the standards of the local farmers and other inhabitants we were still poor. But to us it felt as if we had started a new era of something almost akin to prosperity, not knowing what prosperity truly meant, at least not us children. We had a regular income and could afford to buy the food on ration cards and some extra in the HO shop, if their shelves had something to offer!

Mutti was once again home, where mothers should be. Supper was on the table when Papa came home from work. Heating materials were still short in supply but on the whole life definitely showed some improvement day by day. We could not afford to change our home for a larger one, but we did not really want to move anyway. We loved the home we had and gradually Mutti was able to buy new items such as bedlinen, towels etc. Every new acquisition, however small it was, felt like a huge leap forward!

Like before his arrest, Papa spent most weekends in the wood digging out tree stumps. Life was by no means a bed of roses. You needed a regular income to buy the essential foods but anything other than that was still a struggle. No amount of money could guarantee you sufficient amount of coal or wood. Seven years had passed since the end of the war and the "workers' paradise" could still not provide the necessities for a simple life.

Chapter Forty

Papa had changed after his release from prison. We had some idea what kind of life he had to endure during his incarceration but our imagination came most likely nowhere near to reality. No doubt, having been a so-called "economic criminal", thus an enemy of the State, he was probably treated rather differently from other criminals, like murderers, sexual abusers, burglars etc. Criminals against the economy of the DDR were ordinary people, yet with the wrong political attitude since they had disobeyed the orders of the government: not to bring anything from the West back into the eastern part of Germany: no product of any kind, no foodstuff, no newspapers or magazines; nothing indicating that life "over there" ("drueben") was clearly much better than in the glorious DDR. These so called "criminals" were no danger to other people but considered to be so to the totalitarian communist state governing our country, at least that was the opinion of the higher echelon of the party and our current government. In reality these "criminals" were ordinary people trying to feed their family or to continue a business in a stalemate economy. Who would deliberately starve when they see an opportunity of getting something to eat for their family? Of course, those new rulers themselves did not starve, on the contrary, they lived very well indeed. In my opinion, therefore, *they* were the true criminals.

They filled their stomachs and their pockets while the rest of the population starved or lived close to starvation and were certainly deprived of anything which was not essential for bare survival.

Enterprising people like my father were considered political enemies. Consequently, they had to be re-educated. I do not remember Papa telling us much about his time in the "Knast" (prison) or his treatment while there. He would have told our mother, but we children were unaware of the finer details of his imprisonment. Yet, from having lived under this new political system for some years now even we children were conscious of how oppressive a government we had, one that suppressed any expression of free thought and speech most cruelly. I can easily imagine Papa having had to undergo mental torture of various kinds every day he languished in his cell. He was probably exposed to intensive indoctrination of socialist/communist ideology. Knowing how father hated any form of totalitarian regime, these twelve months of incarceration must have been unspeakable torment for him. Despite having had to work a long daily shift behind bars, his time spent there must have felt even longer than those years in Russia, especially since he did not know he would be released early! Remember? His sentence had been for TWO years!

Yes, Papa had changed. He did not smile much, if ever. It was hard to feel really close to him. He usually carried a stern expression on his face. His mouth was tightly closed, two lines on either side dragging it down and making him look much older. These were the visible outer scars, those inflicted on him inwardly we could only guess at. While in Russia, he had kept himself alive with his dreams of a better life once he was back home with his family and in his fatherland. Now these allusions had proved to be false. The mental torture and hardship continued, even the separation from his family! No wonder he was turning bitter and hard and building a wall of stone around his heart in order to gather enough strength to keep it beating and giving him a glimmer of hope for a better future.

Seeing her husband changed and bitter must have been really distressing and difficult for our mother. She had married a young, cheerful and very positive man, full of vigour and zest for life. On his return from Russia she had found a very different man: ill, weak, estranged from ordinary family life. She could not even be sure he would ever regain normal physical health. Papa had endured so many traumas and there was no one other than our mother to help him through the after effects. No psychological help, as soldiers often receive nowadays, was available for him. You pushed all your pain into the deepest recesses of your heart and hoped it would stay there and not show on the outside. But, of course, it did.

We did try to give him as much love, respect and understanding as we were able to. Often it wasn't enough. I cannot speak for my brother or my mother but I can speak for myself and have to admit that, sometimes, I did long for the softer side of our father to re-emerge more often. Yes, the struggle had changed him. On occasions, for instance when I got home from school with particularly good marks that I proudly told him about, he never said: "Well done!, Gitta". If he said anything at all it would be something like: "I expect that of my daughter!" That sort of remark was the closest I ever got to receiving a compliment from him. Doubtless, this new sternness had nothing to do with either of us. He adored our mother, we could see this very clearly and he loved us children in his undemonstrative way. There was only one explanation: his past imprisonment had pushed him almost to the edge. At least, while in Russia, he had a certain amount of freedom of movement due to his special standing he had acquired with his skilful work. Even his so called masters respected him so that he never lost his self-esteem. The Russians had regarded him very highly indeed, in contrast to a select bunch of his own countrymen who, no doubt, looked upon him as a dangerous individual, enemy number One. Either he had to be crushed or re-educated. Better still, both!

Father was released early from the clutches of the new elite due to good conduct. They were unaware he was PRETENDING to embrace their ideology. Inwardly though he must have gathered an explosive amount of hatred for their system which gnawed away at him colossally. Even his eventual freedom and reunion with us did not shift this hatred. On the contrary, it increased with every day since life outside was only marginally "freer" and less bleak than life had been behind bars.

On lovely sunny weekend days in the wood I did still sometimes hear him sing when I was taking lunch to him which Mutti had prepared for the two of us. Those moments were rather special. The sun and his songs had brightened his spirits and we ate our sandwiches in harmony close to intimacy. He always called me "Brigittchen" or "Mausi" (little mouse) during those short fiestas, despite my having grown into a teenager by then, if a short one who looked nowhere near her age. I was still his little girl and I loved it.

It was during that summer, after Papa's release, that our parents began to discuss openly with us their hope of escaping to the West as soon as a good opportunity presented itself. One heard of more and more people fleeing the misery of life in the DDR. Some of them, who had made it across, were from our village or villages nearby. These were mainly the original "Vertriebenen" (exiled) and refugees from the eastern parts of the old Germany, Pomerania, Silesia, Prussia, who risked their lives during their flight. Their homeland was gone and by then everyone knew that these lands would never be returned to Germany again. Why should these refugees not seek a better life than the drudgery and poverty they had to endure here? Struggle and strife was shared with practically everyone living in the DDR. Yet unlike the indigenous population, the refugees suffered the added burden of the dispossessed with no hope of ever acquiring a home of their own. In addition, the lack of personal freedom was much worse than it had been under Hitler and it was hard to see how this eastern part of devastated Germany would ever yield a happy life for its inhabitants.

We spent many evenings talking about the possibility of escape. My parents did not hide this from Werner and myself. We were intelligent enough to understand what was going on anyway. Including us in their plans was also a way of preparing us for the eventual daring escape. Of course, we were sworn to utter secrecy. No one was allowed to get the slightest hint of our plans as this could end in both our parents being arrested once more. What would happen to the two of us then? As with any hugely disrupting life change, like a house move or emigration to another country, the thought required germination and slow but steady build-up of will-power to execute the plan.. The lives of four people were at stake and Papa wanted to ensure a successful outcome. He had lived without his family for far too many years to risk losing all of them forever.

Chapter Forty-One

A terrible incident in the river near Doemitz demonstrated to everyone in our village and the surrounding area that the dream of escape from this oppressive regime was on the minds of many people.

I never knew the name of the girl nor did I know her family personally except that they were also refugees from Southern Silesia. She was approximately five years older than myself which explains why I had only known her by sight. She had gone to our village school but I only ever saw her from a distance during break times. She was tall and very beautiful, probably the most beautiful girl in the village. Her most outstanding feature was her blond hair which she wore in plaits. They were thick and extraordinarily long, reaching almost down to her knees! We always wondered why she did not cut her hair shorter. It must have been so much work keeping it clean and drying it after a wash or a swim in the river. She seemed to plait her hair daily as it always looked absolutely immaculate. She was clearly very proud of her crowning glory as she walked tall, knowing all eyes were set on her. Despite that she certainly did not appear to be conceited, merely conscious of her extraordinary beauty.

To everyone's shock and horror this young woman – she had left school the previous autumn – had tried to swim across the river Elbe at Doemitz to the western side of the river bank which was in the newly founded Federal Republic of Germany – "The Golden West" as we in the East considered it to be. The border dividing the two Germanys went straight through the middle of the river. Consequently, the entire river area was very heavily guarded by river police on boats and from watchtowers. The girl had attempted to cross over in the middle of the night. She had almost reached the halfway point when police heard her screams for help! Had she not needed to shout for help she might have made it across as the guards had not seen her up to that moment. Tragically, her long heavy plaits having soaked up too much water, pulled her down even before the police could reach her. The shock wave of this terrible tragedy spread through the village like wild fire. Everyone living near the river knew how well guarded this border was. No one before had ever attempted to escape this way. She must have been extremely desperate for a better life to have considered this fateful route.

This was not the only tragedy befalling a family in the village. One of our aunt Ella's sisters-in-law who had been part of the group of people fleeing Marienburg had a son who had joined the People's Police when he turned 18. He had been unable to find any kind of work after leaving school, aged 14 or 15. Unfortunately he had not realized the unbearable stress this decision was going to place upon him. The constant hateful indoctrination of communist ideals, coupled with the total lack of any personal freedom of expression as well as the demands required of him to denounce anyone of whom he had the slightest suspicion, regardless of who they were, whether father, mother or any other family member, became completely intolerable for him.
He simply had to try and get out of this oppressive trap. Although he knew it was severely frowned upon by the authorities to ever leave a job with the police, he did just that!
The following day his mother had a visit from the Head of Police informing her that her son had had an accident and, sadly, had died! No details were given, except that they were exceedingly sad to have lost such a promising young recruit! Therefore they had made arrangements for a special funeral in the local cemetery in three days' time at no expense to herself! I never knew what reasons they gave the distraught mother, but no, she was not allowed to

see her son again. The coffin had already been closed to save her the distress of seeing him once more!

With the exception of Papa who was at work, all family members went to the funeral which was the most sickening spectacle imaginable. The coffin was carried into the chapel by eight young police men, his former colleagues. After the short service was over they carried the coffin to the allotted burial place. More police had gathered around the open grave, all carrying rifles but one of them carried a gun. When the coffin was lowered into the ground, twenty salutes were shot into the air as a mark of respect for "the beloved colleague" who had so tragically lost his life! We all felt sick with disgust about this hypocritical behaviour. As if we did not know they had killed him and why! His mother was in a terrible state, screaming her thoughts towards the officer who had visited her and who was obviously in charge of the brigade and the shameful pretence. She made it quite clear to him what she thought of this disgraceful performance, even hitting his chest, if I remember correctly. She did not care what they would do to her, she wanted to be dead and with her son anyway. But nothing happened to her there and then or later for that matter. They must have considered it wiser to keep up the pretence of "honouring" a well loved and accidentally killed young recruit and his grieving mother rather than taking any measures against the distraught woman. Any disciplinary action could have tipped the balance in her favour and swung public opinion even more against the hated police. By ignoring her accusations they probably thought the population would actually believe this death to have indeed been accidental.

All these incidences that summer could only strengthen our resolve to leave this horrendous deceitful system behind us where no one was safe and anyone could find himself being arrested or even murdered for no other reason than wanting to have freedom – freedom of thought and speech, of action and personal development. One day, surely, we would be able to escape this tortuous "paradise". Meanwhile we had to be extra careful not to give the slightest hint of our thoughts away to anyone. We had just witnessed how doing so could end!

Not only was this system spying on and eradicating important people who were, in their opinion, working against them. No, the small man was just as dangerous an enemy and had to be brought to heel. In their evil pursuit, any means justified the end. One false move and our family would be next on their hit list. We had to be extremely careful from now on, lie low until a chance for our escape would hopefully present itself.

Chapter Forty-Two

For me personally, life continued much the same as it had done in previous years. My friendship with Ingetrud had deepened over the years. I did not see as much of Gerda outside our school lessons although we still walked home together most days. We were still friends, but Ingetrud and her family had the greater fascination for me. The invitations to the Markurth estate continued and school life got more interesting. The school had somewhat better equipment by now, especially for Biology and Physics, both subjects I did not care much about. Physics was saved by the experiments we did in class, but my heart was never with these subjects.

We had started to learn Russian at some stage, but because I hated the Communist ideology so deeply and did not have pleasant memories of the occupation forces, learning their language was a bit tough for me as well. But I did what I had to and forced myself to do as best as I could to get a good mark in this subject, too. My best loved subjects remained German, also Geography! It was wonderful to learn about the outside world, countries I might never see. So at least I wanted to learn about them and visit them in my imagination. We had only school atlases to work with. Therefore a great part of our lessons consisted of copying the maps of the various countries, often from memory. I enjoyed creating my own maps tremendously as I loved working with coloured pencils, creating mountains, rivers, agricultural land and woodlands using my own shades of brown, green or blue and yellow. I had never had the slightest bit of talent for drawing as such but working with colour was a craft I became really good at. Later this talent expressed itself in my love of needlework and very much later in life of interior design, soft furnishings and gardening.

However, my love of German and literature remained my unchallenged favourites.

Classical literature in particular had developed a special fascination for me – and this, in part, is why!

I cannot remember exactly when we began studying Goethe's works, probably earlier still than 1952. We had begun studying his poems years before. The one I remember best of all was "Osterspaziergang" (Easter Walk) which was part of his drama "Faust" . In this poem he describes the changing of the landscape from winter to spring, fields and trees slowly turning green once more and the towns folk streaming into the countryside for their Easter walk, dressed in colourful clothes and adding colour to the virgin land. They are celebrating the resurrection of the Lord but also their own resurrection from a long and icy winter in the narrow confines of the town. Here, and not in church or town, they feel the true light of heaven and the joy of human existence.

Another of his poems I still remember is "Erlkoenig" (King of the Elves), a sad and very touching story about a father riding through a stormy night with his very sick son in his arms to reach home and help for him. Throughout the ride the son tells the father of the King of the Elves enticing him to come with him and how afraid he is of him. The anxious father tries to calm his son, suggesting it is only the dense fog and noise of the storm rattling through the leaves of the trees that makes him believe he hears voices. Yet, in his feverish state the son continues to express his fears of the King of Elves, ending, just as the horse reaches the farmstead, in a fearful cry: "Father, father, the king has done me a great harm!" As the exhausted horse comes to a halt in the yard, the child in the arms of his father is dead!

The profoundly touching way Goethe succeeds in relating this tragic story is something to experience in the original language in order to appreciate the impact on the reader – a unique and unforgettable poem!

We learned many more wonderful poems by Schiller, Heine and other famous German poets, which we had to learn by heart and recite in front of the class, an unnerving experience but precisely the reason we had to do it so that we should learn to speak and perform in front of an audience, therefore gaining in self esteem and confidence.

Following this period we progressed to the drama works of Goethe, Schiller and Lessing, another great writer of the classical period around the eighteen hundreds. The only work by Shakespeare we studied was "Hamlet" in the German translation by Schlegel and Tieck. These two men were superb poets and translators from the English and "Hamlet" lacked none of Shakespeare's beautiful language in the German translation. In fact, their rendering of "Hamlet" is considered one of the best translations into any language. No wonder I loved our studies of this drama and wished we were learning English rather than Russian in our language lessons.

And yet, it was Goethe who fascinated me more than any of the other great writers. Not only did he produce a huge amount of poems and many dramas; he also wrote novels. One on which his entire future fame rested was "The Sorrows of the Young Werther". This was a very romantic and tragic love story and the first one any of us had ever read. Remember, we lived in a farming community where books were hardly to be found in private homes, other than at the Markurth household. And new books were also extremely hard to come by, even in 1952. It would have been different in towns, but here in the wilderness of Mecklenburg you could only dream of finding books to read for pleasure. Certainly no love stories! Thus our school books remained the only access we had to good literature.

Reading aloud in class from "The Sorrows of the Young Werther" was a wonderful experience for me personally, but for many of my classmates (and for myself as well) it was also a rather embarrassing experience. Twelve and thirteen year olds in those days were pretty inexperienced in the realms of romantic love. There was no sex education at school, least of all at home! These subjects were totally taboo and I cannot even remember how and when I found out how babies came into the world, let alone into their mothers' tummies! And now we had to read out loud in front of our classmates (and remember – there were boys in our form!) about the yearnings of young Werther for Lotte, a young girl who was already as good as engaged and later married to a much older man and who therefore was not free to return the feelings of love to the tormented and ardent young Werther!
It was really too embarrassing indeed but at the same time most wonderful and exciting! This man Goethe! How daring of him to write so eloquently and

openly about his forbidden feelings and longings and also how divinely thrilling! I fell in love instantly with this passionate man Goethe, in particular since love seemed to have had an important role in almost everything he wrote.

 Goethe wrote "Werther" in 1774 when a work of this nature (it ended in the suicide of Werther due to his unrequited love!) had never been written before and therefore became an overnight and unprecedented success. Nearly two hundred years later Werther's sorrows and his love for Lotte still awakened the first stirrings of sexual awareness in many teenagers' hearts. We did not have pop music and pop stars to send us wild with longings. For us it was Goethe with his exciting writings and his even more shocking and dramatic private life! He had an association with a certain Frau von Stein for many years when he was living at Weimar and being Minister for Mining for the Saxon King! He also lived with his housekeeper, with whom he had a son, for many years before he finally married her and made an honest woman of her. Really, Goethe, you were quite a man!

I reckon I was very fortunate that German and German literature were subjects of huge interest to me right from the beginning for Germany has always produced a wealth of literary men, Goethe, Schiller, Lessing, Heinrich Heine, Rilke and too many more to mention here. No wonder Germany is known as the "Land of poets and philosophers". Their works fell on very fertile ground with me and kept my interest in school life very much alive and thriving.

Friedrich von Schiller was another writer and philosopher whose many works we studied extensively over several years. His plays and melodramas were less about love, more about revolutions and social unrest and wars. The Wallenstein Trilogy in particular was of huge interest to all of the class, even the boys, since these plays were set during The Thirty Years' War. "The Robbers" was another favourite, so were "Maria Stuart" and "William Tell". For a small village school at this austere time in our history we were well educated in literature for which I was always very grateful as it stimulated my interest in books for the remainder of my life.

Chapter Forty-Three

I believe it was after this year's summer holidays that, for a short while, our class had to go and join the same years' students in the neighbouring village of Neu Kaliss. Perhaps lovely Herr Schroeder was ill, who was still our head teacher, or there was some other important reason why we had to return to the other school for a few weeks. Luckily, it was not winter this time, so that the doubly long walk there was not that difficult, except when rain was pelting down.

Earlier during the summer weeks Ingetrud's brother and father finally succeeded in repairing an old motorcycle after months of dedicated tinkering in their garage. I think Horst was about 17 or 18 years of age, just the perfect age for a young man to be racing around the village on his bike to the envy of many other young boys. Of course, it was really his father's bike but they shared it equally and both men looked very proud when they set off on their noisy monstrosity down the sandy road, leaving a huge cloud of dust behind them.
One day, I had just started to set off for school, Horst came out of the yard with his bike and asked me whether he could give me a lift! Me? Sitting on this huge monster? No way, I had enjoyed watching the two men fiddle around with their old banger and the bike from time to time, especially when I was bored. But that did not mean I was really that interested in anything motorized, let alone being driven on any such monster.

"Nein, danke, Horst. Da kriegst Du mich so schnell nicht rauf!" (No, thank you, Horst. You won't get me onto THAT thing in a hurry).

To my surprise he looked really disappointed and I realized he was so proud of his achievement that I started, all of a sudden, to feel sorry for him and for having hurt his feelings. So when he encouraged me once more with: "Nun, sei doch kein Feigling!" (Don't be such a coward),

I gave in and, with difficulty, climbed onto the back seat, feeling terrified! I wore my satchel still on my back, leaving both arms free.

"Put your arms around my waist and hold on tight. I won't be going very fast. No need to be frightened".

I had never held onto a boy like that before and really did not want to do it, but there was no other way for me to feel safe. So that's what I had to do and off we went. To my utter delight we overtook one or two of my classmates on our way. To be fair, I felt as proud as punch knowing they would all be green with envy, especially the boys! It was actually rather a thrilling experience, probably similar to a first flight by aeroplane these days. Unfortunately, soon thereafter, our class had to return to our old school and Horst could no longer pretend he wanted to help me with my "long" walk so that this one exciting trip remained the only one.

Papa told me he, too, had owned a motorcycle when he was dating our mother. Like me, Mutti did not want to share the bike rides with Papa at first but once she had overcome her fear she soon began to enjoy her back seat rides most thoroughly. Like riding a bicycle, you experience a tremendous feeling of freedom and lightness and Mutti became an ardent "motorcycle bride", eventually learning to ride the machine herself when they were married and lived in Insterburg. Papa said he was so proud of her as she seemed to be the only woman in the town to ride a bike – skirting corners at a perilous speed! I have always found that hard to believe but Papa was adamant. We knew Mutti as such a timid woman. No one could have called her a daredevil girl although she was not to be beaten when she had set her mind on something – in her quiet but stubborn way she persisted, regardless what the demands made on her were.

Determining though to ride a monstrous motoring machine? Was that really our mother's style? Papa insisted that it was. She was only 18 when they married, a raring teenager, which may explain her daring exploits. Put any teenager behind a steering wheel today and they, too, believe they could become a racing driver in no time at all. They usually speed as though they own the road. It seems Mutti and Papa were not very different from the young of today.

Apart from the motorbike ride, I never will forget another exciting experience I made that late summer/early autumn of 1952. I went to the cinema! Well, not a special cinema as such. The local pub had an attractive dance hall at the back of the building which, once a week, was converted into a cinema. A large screen covered the entire back wall of the hall, giving the impression of a real cinema.

For the times and considering this was only a village pub, this was a rather progressive move which improved the cultural life of the village enormously.

Was this my first film I ever saw? May be not but it certainly was the only one I remember so well to this very day. The film had been made in Sweden and the German title was: "Sie tanzte nur einen Sommer" (English title: One Summer of Happiness).

I must have deserved getting the money to go and see this film. Although Papa was back in work, money for luxuries was still in short supply. In those days, no child got pocket money, not even the children of the well-to-do. Pocket money was an invention of much later years. I assume my parents considered me deserving of a special treat. They themselves did not go to see the film. I was all by myself – fortunately!

I remember getting out of the pub feeling dazed, shaken to the bone, thrilled and confused all at the same time. I was extremely glad to have been on my own as I would have been too embarrassed to have to discuss what I had just witnessed with anyone else. This way I had time to collect myself before meeting up with my parents and brother and having to reply to possible questions about the film.

By now you may believe I had seen extreme violence, suspense, murder even! What I had seen, and for the first time in my life, was NUDITY! We wrote the year 1952, not 2012! Nudity of adults was a subject of total taboo. To see, all of a sudden, nudity of a very young couple in love on the screen was considered to be immoral by the standards of most adults. For a young girl of only 13 ½ years of age with a very sheltered upbringing, this was a shock to the system, a thrilling shock, but a shock nonetheless.

The story is of a young couple, he just 19, having completed his baccalaureate, and she a beautiful but shy country girl, aged only 17! They fall ecstatically in love and spend the remainder of the summer together. The film portrays the new age of free love against old traditions of strict Lutheran values embedded in the minds and hearts of Swedish country folk. Kerstin, the girl, in particular, suffers a great deal of abuse from old spiteful village women. But their love survives. The following summer Goeran, her lover, returns from town. While on a trip on his motorbike, they have an accident and Kerstin dies on the spot. A tragic ending to a sensational film, which became such a huge success with the film viewing public due to the display of nudity, which had never been seen on screen before.

The film received The Golden Bear at the International Film Festival in Berlin in the spring of 1952. Young Kerstin was played by a hauntingly beautiful girl called Ulla Jacobsson and the role of Goeran by Folke Sundquist, names embedded deeply in my memory as they had opened a new world of intimate love that I found exciting as well as rather scary. Did love of this kind always end up badly for the women involved? The film suggested it. After all, we still lived in a man's world. I had experienced sex education with a bang and the confusion it caused occupied my mind for a long time afterwards.

The films shown in the village pub changed every week or fortnight and for months afterwards I looked at the advertising pictures shown in a display cabinet when I passed the pub on my way home from school. None looked even remotely interesting and were usually concocted in Russia full of propaganda of the Communist dream. I don't believe I ever went to see any of them, at least none that left an impression on me. "A Summer of Happiness" remained THE most impressionable film of my formative years and Ulla Jacobsson and Goeran Sundquest became my first adored pin-ups, if only in my mind since the era of idol worship was still a long way off and buying photographs or posters of your film star heroes was not yet part of the marketing game.

There was a boy at school, Hansl, whose parents were also refugees from somewhere in Eastern Europe. He had shown some interest in me for quite a while prior to this film. He kept throwing little paper squares across the class room with questions like:

"Would you spend our next break between lessons with me" or
"Can I carry your satchel for you on your way home?" or merely "I like you"!

I did not like *him*, however. He was good looking alright but in the way of a gypsy, dark and brooding. The type it was wiser to stay clear off. My instinct told me that and none of his notes ever got a reply from me. He, in turn, never gave up.

That autumn his little notes kept coming more frequently. Had *he* been to see the film as well? Sure he had, His eyes, darkest, deepest brown, stared ever more intensely at me, making me feel yet more uncomfortable. Could he not see I did not care for him? There was something dangerous about his gypsy good looks and the more he wanted to be closer friends with me, the less I wanted to know about him! Poor Hansl, I was not very nice to him. He had plenty of friends among the other boys in our class. Why could he not stick with them, for God's sake?

I'm sorry, but this part of my story is all about sex. Or so-called forbidden relationships. You may remember I was part of the church choir of the Lutheran church in the village across the river. Our pastor was a handsome man. That autumn a dreadful rumour spread through the village about him. Apparently he had started a relationship with one of the girls in the choir, who was only 15! She looked older and was well developed physically! The rumour also spread that the pastor had been involved with other young girls in the previous parish and that instead of sending him to prison, the church elders had decided to send him from his last parish in West Germany to our parish in the East, as that would be punishment enough for him. Clearly, it wasn't. His behaviour caused a furore among the inhabitants of both villages. He had a wife and children and many villagers felt very sorry for them. Not in the least sorry for *him* – nor for the girl, for that matter. I don't know why he continued to stay in his post, but stay he did. I had started preparation classes for my confirmation the following spring; classes which were part of my school curriculum and had to be attended. But I could and did stop my membership of the choir. His hypocritical behaviour had been too disappointing for me. I had quite admired him before. Now my respect was gone.

The forthcoming confirmation of all our class next spring was an event we were all looking forward to. In those days it was not a question of choosing to be confirmed as it is now. Then, confirmation was automatic and a most important event in a young person's life. Once you were confirmed you were considered to have left childhood behind and should be addressed by strangers with the polite form of "Herr and Fraeulein" and of "Sie" and not

"Du". It was the pass marker into adulthood. The religious angle hardly interested us. It was the social aspect we were all hungering for.

Werner had been confirmed a year earlier when Papa was imprisoned. As usual our mother had managed to kit him out splendidly. Miraculously Mutti had managed to get some cloth so that Trautl, the wonderful seamstress, could make Werner's first suit with long trousers! He wore a white shirt this time (a sign things were getting just a little bit better) with a black bow tie and looked really handsome and grown-up. His hair was long and swept back in an adult style. Of course, I was prejudiced, but I thought he looked like a mini film star of the thirties! We were all very proud of him. No doubt about it: he was going to be a handsome man.

Now it was my turn and time for Mutti to start worrying how on earth she would find some suitable fabric for a black dress for me. A black dress with no more than a white collar was the standard requirement in those days whether it was possible to find a fabric shop somewhere which stored some suitable fabric or not. And that was the big problem. Mutti had tried to buy or order a fabric from the village textile shop. Either she could not afford the price or the shop could not acquire a suitable fabric since we still lived in the Neanderthal age for anything factory made, Mutti resorted to another source of supply. She had been able to find out the address of one of her best friends from the Insterburg days (the one who had dressed up as Father Christmas!) who was now living in the United States of America!
She wrote to her, explaining how badly we needed some fabric for my confirmation gown. Could she possibly help?

She could help! Perhaps Mutti thought that anyone living in the USA was as rich as Croesus merely because The States symbolized the richest and most desirable country to be living in, a sort of worldly paradise, where everyone was really well off and could afford anything. The lady was clearly a good friend and it was my good fortune to be confirmed in a dress made of taffeta from America! No one in my or the neighbouring village could claim such a fame as my link to the top country of The Golden West (Der goldene Westen).
All the other girls were equally well turned out. Heaven knows how their parents had managed to dress their daughters appropriately for their special

day. I did not really care about it much at the time. All I cared about was knowing I looked in no way like a poor refugee girl and that I could more than match the outfits of the other girls. Only my hair style was a bit boring. Like a lot of girls I wore plaits and Mutti would wind them around my head in the old fashioned way of the Germanic custom of old. So I looked a bit prim and proper but for that my dress shone like silk when the sunshine touched it – nobody else could lay any claim to that!

However, I am progressing too far ahead. The fabric arrived in October and the excitement of opening a parcel, the first anyone of us had ever received since arriving here from Prussia, made my heart beat furiously. We were so excited about the parcel that Mutti had asked her sister and her daughters over to watch me open it. An American fabric!
What would it be? As if it would have had The Stars and Stripes printed all over it! Mutti's friend had sent 3 whole metres of taffeta, making it easy for Trautl to sew any shape of dress I wanted. I felt in heaven and could not wait for spring 1953 to arrive. I felt certain to outshine any of the other girls. In all these years at Heiddorf I had never had a new dress made up for me in a brand new material straight from a shop. Mutti always made sure we were neatly dressed and looking as respectable as we could , but all our dresses, Mutti's as well as mine, were made up of old material from second hand dresses, often given to us by Ingetrud's mother. Ingetrud and her older sister were quite a bit taller than me so that Trautl could easily use their clothes for making mine. Sometimes she just made a dress smaller, but often she had to use up materials from various items to create something new. It is amazing what one can do when one has to! There is a saying in Germany: "Not macht erfinderisch". The English translation, I believe, is: "Necessity is the mother of invention".

At last, on the threshold to young adulthood, I was going to have my very first grown up dress made up of one piece of cloth from America; not of several different types of fabric given to us by some kind neighbour. No wonder I could not wait for spring time to arrive!

Chapter Forty-Four

Just as when I was trying to remember other Christmas seasons, I cannot recall anything about the Christmas of 1952. Sadly it must have been another one of those unspectacular holidays of old. For mother and father it would have been a holiday, not having to go to work and enjoying their time with us two, playing cards or other games. Perhaps we might have had our aunt and cousins over to play games with us, but frankly my memory bank is completely blank when it comes to this yearly festival. I may have gone to church, my parents did not. But since I had left the church choir earlier that year, I may not have gone to church either. In later years we did celebrate Christmas like other people, with a tree and presents and a very special meal on Christmas Eve. Of course, we still had rabbits which were always eaten over Christmas, but sadly I do not actually see ourselves sitting at a festive table enjoying our casserole of rabbit. However, there were other events that winter which I can recall very well.

Let's start with my evenings at Ingetrud's house. In the winter I went across to them quite often. Since, apart from radios, there was no other entertainment, we had to entertain ourselves. For us girls this meant sewing, knitting or crocheting, the last two I enjoyed particularly. The daughter of black Johanna had presented her with her first grandson not very long after her wedding – so that's why the wedding came upon us so unexpectedly quickly!. Since I loved knitting and told Johanna about it on the many occasions when I watched her spinning the wool from her own sheep, she had asked me to knit a jumper for little junior. The main part of the jumper was in plain natural colour, but across the chest I was knitting a Norwegian pattern of elks in the wool of a dark brown sheep. A very exciting project for me. Whenever I went to spend the evenings with the Riek family, I took my knitting along. Usually we sat around their large dining table which stood in the centre of their sitting room! The men, Ingetrud's father and brother, were lounging around on the sofa or sitting in an armchair reading the paper and, in the case of the father, smoking a pipe. We girls chatted and giggled, as women folk do, while we were all working at something.

Suddenly, during a moment of silence, Ingetrud burst out loud for everyone to hear:

"Brigitte, look at Horst! I think he is in love with you! He's been staring at you all evening, without interruption!"

I had been concentrating on my knitting pattern exceptionally earnestly as I was working on the Norwegian pattern and had to count the stitches very carefully. In fact, I had hardly listened to the conversation around the table. When Ingetrud came out with this totally unexpected observation, I wished I could have sunk deep into the earth and disappear from view forever. How could she say something so embarrassing?! Obviously, my first reaction was to do precisely what I did not want to do, namely look across to Horst lying on the sofa. A split second was enough to notice that he was indeed still looking at me with his brooding brown eyes and smiling ever so gently, unlike me, not in the least bit embarrassed. Ingetrud had not been wrong, he really was caressing me with his eyes!

~~~~~~~"Oh, my God, what am I going to do?"

I could feel my blood rushing into my face and my mouth drying up. My knitting fell onto my lap and then onto the floor where it was left as I stumbled off the chair and out of the room, gushing wildly: "I have forgotten something at home. I'll be back in a minute" ; all the while I made for the door hearing everyone else in the room laughing and teasing me:

"Don't forget to come back. You've left your knitting behind!"

Of course, I did not go home. All I had wanted was to escape the scene of this embarrassment. What had got into Horst? I wasn't a pretty girl at all – at least not in MY opinion! And I wasn't even fourteen yet and looked no more than 11 or 12! Not a bit ready yet for "this sort of thing"! I was leaning against a wall in the courtyard trying to cool down my hot head and desperately searching for an answer to this tricky situation. It was winter and very cold outside and I started to feel it. I simply had to calm down, pretend I had the situation well under control and return to the sitting room as if nothing had happened. Yet I did not know how to pluck up the courage to do just that.

Eventually, I had no other choice but to make my way back as I was starting to feel very cold indeed. I had run outside through the hall and the kitchen and out of the back door. That was the way all family members entered as well as exited the house. There was a door at the front of the house, but no one ever used it and therefore it would be locked. I had to return the way I got out. Up the stairs and through a small back entrance hall which led into the kitchen. As I stood in the door to the pitch black kitchen I was overcome by a strange feeling of somebody's presence in the room. It was too dark to see anyone, yet I sensed a presence. I tried to feel for a light switch but to no avail.

"Is anybody there?" I stupidly asked knowing very well how pointless this question was. It did not stop me from repeating it though. Was my imagination playing havoc with my nerves? That must be it! But why was it so quiet in the sitting room? Normally we made a lot of noise with our banter and giggles. I did not really want to cross the room and walk towards the door in the right hand corner which led to the inner hall and back to the sitting room where everyone was waiting for me.
This fear was ridiculous. There was no burglar here, just the family to whom I almost belonged.
" Stop it and walk to the door!" my mind demanded.

My legs felt leaden. I was starting to feel hot again with fright but slowly, very slowly I inched my way forward with hands outstretched in front of me, since the dark was so solid, nothing was visible, none of the furniture, nor the door. As I got close to where the door should be, someone lounged forward, grabbing me and pulling me towards him. It was HIM – Horst, the lovely quiet brother whom, up to this moment, I had always rather liked. How could he do this to me, scare me to bits until I nearly died with fright. My legs and arms fought him as hard as I could, finally disentangling myself and falling down to the floor when the door to the sitting room opened and Herr Riek's voice said something to make light of the situation and to invite us back in, trying to turn the incident into a joke. I returned to the table but try as hard as I wanted to, my knitting needles felt like iron rods in my hands. There was nothing to it – I had to excuse myself and return home. Horst's clumsy way of attempting to embrace me would have been quite shocking to me, had the two of us been alone. But having the entire family as witnesses to this unexpected development was more than I could cope with.

Horst was a handsome young man; brother of my best friend and therefore my friend too. Anything else had never entered my innocent mind. Had he handled it differently, more gently, just between the two of us, being embraced and possibly kissed by him, might have been rather thrilling. We might even have become girl-friend and boy-friend. Now he had spoiled everything and I feared it might even spoil my friendship with Ingetrud and the rest of the family. I could not have been more upset. My parents wanted to know what had happened when they saw my distressed state. But I would not tell them. Instead went straight for my bed in our little separate bedroom, pulling the eiderdown deep over my head and hoping that Werner would stay away long enough for me to recover. Love was going to be a complicated matter, one I was obviously not ready for yet. Despite – or may be – because of the film I had seen not so long ago!

Horst's behaviour had altered the dynamics of our relationship and weeks went by before I was able to pluck up courage to enter their family circle once more as if nothing had happened to disturb my equilibrium. By spring time I felt comfortable enough to hop across as I had done before, yet making sure I could avoid Horst as often as possible. In fairness, he behaved very well afterwards, perhaps he, too, had seen the film which had inspired his imagination to go wild. He was eighteen, after all!

Chapter Forty-Five

The other event occupying me – and to some degree our entire family – was connected with school. To win over the young generation to love and appreciate living in "The Worker's Paradise", the government chose a few schools every year to be given a short holiday. This year it was the turn of our little village school, but only one or two classes were allowed to participate. The dice fell in our direction and everyone in my form went wild with excitement, boys and girls alike. Holidays were unheard of in those post war years. Now we were given the opportunity of two weeks' skiing in Oberhof, *the* premier resort in the Thuringia Mountains. Who had ever heard of such good fortune?

Our teachers were to come with us, all of them, since formal classes had to continue while we were there. The holiday part was going to be after lessons and during the weekend. A bit of a disappointment that, but still, we were excited. I had never travelled in my life before; other than languishing on that train fleeing from Prussia. Experiencing the snowy mountains of Thuringia sounded simply wonderful. Naturally, we would all learn to ski brilliantly and I had no doubt that I would simply love it.

Shortly after the announcement Herr Schroeder informed us that going on this trip depended on every pupil being a Young Pioneer. Those who had not yet joined the organization were advised to do so as soon as possible since otherwise the trip would be called off and another, more deserving, school would be chosen instead. Of course, it had all sounded too good to be true. How stupid of me to believe we were going to get something for nothing. You could sense the mood of the class sinking instantly from euphoria into gloom and bewilderment, for most of us wanted nothing to do with the Young Pioneers. It was meant to be an organisation similar to the Brownies in England. In reality, it was anything but. Yes, they may have had a bit of fun during their meetings, most of the time, however, they had to learn socialist songs expounding the glories of communism and the Worker's Paradise. Basically, it was a sneaky way to catch pupils at a young age, indoctrinate them early and regularly and turn them slowly but surely into zombie followers of the communist cause. I believe Hitler had tried to do the same by enticing the young boys to join the Hitler-Jugend (Hitler Youth). Up to this stage, most of us had succeeded in staying clear of them – now they had a way of catching us, dangling the holiday in front of us and knowing full well, how tempting it would be to give in and sign up, just to go on this dream journey. They, the Communist Party officials, had calculated right – everyone joined, bar one: ME! If they thought they could "buy" me with their rotten holiday, they had a thing or two coming!

There was no way I was EVER attaching myself to anything connected to their hated party line. Let the rest of the class go on their trip. I would not be bought, not even if they promised me heaven on earth. My father and mother had not gone through all their suffering so that their daughter would betray them for a mere trip into the mountains. They had done their devious calculations without me and my conscience. Thank you, "comrades" – I would rather not!

Naturally, my stubborn fighting spirit did not endear me to either the school or the party officials in the village. Remember? They had an eye on our family already due to Papa's activities and his anti-communist stance. Of course, father had been shrewd enough not to shout his views about generally, but from his history they knew he was a dodgy case. All they needed was visible proof of his anti-government stance and the handcuffs would be on his wrists again. Herr Schroeder tried to explain to me as delicately yet openly as he dared how important it was to use my head and ignore my heart. After all, I would not have to attend all future meetings of the Young Pioneers, if I did not want to. For now, give yourself a push and think of your classmates who would lose this golden opportunity of enjoying themselves in the snow – a once in a lifetime chance I was going to deprive them of with my stubbornness. I knew, after this conversation, I was making life very difficult for myself as well as for the school and my form. "Sleep over it for another night. You are a bright girl, Brigitte. I'm sure you will see sense in the morning" said darling Herr Schroeder. What a mess I had got myself into!

That same evening, there was a knock at our door. We had just finished our supper and were starting to relax. The person standing in the door was the village mayor!

We were quite startled about this "high" visit, deep down however, not altogether surprised. At least not myself. My fighting spirit at school against joining the Young Pioneers had come to his attention. Perhaps dear Herr Schroeder had informed him and asked his help to persuade my family to give up this ridiculously dangerous attitude. Indeed, the mayor pointed out that the party had been watching our family for some time. If they got the slightest hint of my refusal to comply with their wishes, it would have disastrous consequences for my family.

"I'm sure I don't need to say anything more, do I, Herr Mallon"?

He did not say this threateningly, but with a warm tone of voice and an expression in his face of total empathy and understanding. After all, he knew about my father's suffering in Russia. He was mayor not out of political conviction but for love of his village. He was a kind and popular man and we understood at once what he was trying to tell us.

Papa was once more in danger and this time entirely due to my inflexible obstinacy. Both of us were patriotic by nature, yet not about the kind of Germany we lived in but the one we dreamed about and wanted to help create even though we were only two unimportant fighters among the "Fussvolk" (the foot-soldiers) of its people.

The mayor's eyes had looked at all of us while he spoke. I cannot remember anymore whether he actually said the words "I'm taking a personal risk by coming to see you" or whether his eyes had expressed this warning. No matter, we understood the situation my behaviour had created.

The die was cast. The next day I returned home from school with a brand new pale blue Young Pioneer scarf around my neck, something I had been reminded to wear with pride! The drama had come to an ignominious end for my inner resolve while at the same time a most satisfactory one for everyone else concerned. It was impossible to be yourself in a Communist ruled state, never mind how deep your resolve. I never forgot the danger I had created for us all. In future, what my heart felt would stay just there. My lips would remain sealed, however sickening to keep the pretence. Yes, they had enrolled yet another Young Pioneer, but how aware were they of having sown the seeds of deviousness at the same time in yet another of their captives?

Chapter Forty-Six

The due date for our adventure was fixed for end of February 1953 returning two weeks later. Now Trautl had to get busy again with her sewing machine producing trousers and jackets warm enough and suitable for use on skis! Also a warm coat. Somehow Mutti managed to organize the fabric needed. Either she or I myself got some wool to knit a warm jumper for me. I had completed the jumper for Black Johanna's grandson, now I could knit one for myself! The textile shop in the village must have produced the wool; three different colours which I worked into stripes. The excitement of this new colourful creation soon made me forget the embarrassment over Horst's behaviour and I resumed the cosy evenings at Ingetrud's house, knitting away more furiously than ever to get my jumper finished as soon as possible. Best of all before Christmas in order to get as much wear out of it as I could. Who knows whether the jumper would still fit me next winter? For I had started to grow tiny breasts! Later than some of my other girlfriends at school which was a bit lucky. At least it meant that by the time my body started to develop properly the boys in the class were used to watching this process with the other girls and did not bother to tease me about it, I hoped.

Because of the preparation classes for the confirmation and the many fittings for all the clothes Trautl had to produce for me, the winter of 1953 was a much busier season than any of the previous winters. My jumper needed knitting fairly promptly and I had to put in a lot of extra study time for the important final exams in early summer.

We had regular oral as well as written tests throughout our school year in all the subjects we were taught. These exams did not really count for much, except that they gave us and our teachers a better idea of how well we had taken in what our poor teachers had tried to cram into us. The only truly important exam was the one at the end of the school year as our progress was charted on these exams alone. If a student did not perform well enough during this exam, he or she might not be allowed to move on to the next form – a huge blot on your future career path. But also a shameful situation to find yourself in with your new – a whole year younger – classmates!

I was now in form 7, 7b in fact, which tells you that we had two forms for pupils of my age group, but I did not make friends with anyone from the other form as this was in the adjoining village school. Next year would be my last school year here. I was hoping to go to " Hochschule" (High School) after completion of my basic schooling. I knew there was still plenty of time for achieving this goal, on the other hand you cannot prepare for it early enough, as there were only a certain number of pupils eligible for this advanced education, which ended with the baccalaureate, the German equivalent of A levels in England. And, like in England, the grades of your baccalaureate had to be very good in order to get a place at university. There was no doubt in my mind that I wanted to study. No one in my family had ever been to university but that did not stop me dreaming about it and working towards this goal.

So far I have told you only negative impressions of life under communism, how poor and backward our existence was in comparison to stories we heard about life in the Western part of our country.

In fairness to the DDR one aspect of their ideology deserves praise: their educational system was excellent. The Ministry of Education decided the annual curriculum, which was taught in every school in the country, regardless of where the school was or how big or small it was. All children had to attend basic school for the first 8 years of their academic life. Thereafter the cleverest were chosen to attend High School, ending with the baccalaureate, followed by university for those students who passed the entrance examination. Children from all walks of life had equal opportunities – at least on paper! Often equality stopped if you were considered to be unsuitable for the higher education. And unsuitable were often those whose parents did not fit in with our new proletarian society; i.e. if their parents were considered to be part of the bourgeoisie!

During those early post war years there were still some factory owners or substantial land owning farmers living and working as they had done prior to the end of the war. Their children were excluded from the universities, even if pupils were academically brilliant. My maternal cousins in Saxony were excluded from higher education because their father had been an officer during the war. It did not matter that our grandfather was a station master and therefore suitably working class. At the time I was not aware of the social distinction being made for the choice of university entrance. Higher education and a university degree would certainly compensate me for the early years of feeling a lesser person due to our refugee status. This dream spurred me on no end and I had visions of becoming a doctor of medicine since I have always been keen to be of help to people. I could not think of a better way of helping people than to restore their health.

Fired up by my ambition I was happy to spend almost all of my spare time revising. For me delving into my school books was the fun part of my childhood! The communists definitely knew how to instil ambition into their young citizens. One example was a medal I had received the previous summer for "Good knowledge" which I wore to school with enormous pride. I cannot remember how many pupils were eligible for such an award every year, but certainly never more than three, possibly even fewer, from each form. Despite my intense dislike of our socialist state, I was thrilled to have received this award as it gave me a certain status in the class room and a recognition of my worth in the small world of our village community.

I don't recall whether my father congratulated me on receiving my medal or whether he made his usual comment: "I expect that of my daughter!"

Papa had been a very intelligent boy at his village school. As you may recall, his ambitions of going to university and becoming a forester, spending his life in the beautiful Rominten Heath, were not fulfilled. Father told us he had spent his entire childhood in the wilds of this most beautiful heath and woodland around the Goldap lake. East Prussia and especially the area called Masuren (Masurskie as the Poles call it today) is a slightly hilly landscape of a great many mixed woodlands interspersed by (some say) almost two thousand lakes and rivers and their tributaries, and apparently most beautiful. It has a very diverse and plentiful wild life, not often found in other areas of Europe to the same extent anymore, like for instance, the European bison. The most unusual animal of the Prussian forests was and to this very day is the elk. Papa talked a great deal to us in very nostalgic tones about this strange animal as well as the magnificent stags and herds of deer which were hunted daily by the rich landowning farmers (the Junkers) and their aristocratic friends in the days of old.

During the Nazi era in the Thirties, it was Hitler and particularly Goering, his deputy, who also fell in love with the Rominten Heath. As Master of the German Woods he spent a great deal of time in the area, stalking deer with prominent guests and giving extravagant shooting parties in his hunting lodges. Since this romantic and fascinating woodland heath was very close to my grandparents' house, Papa and his brothers spent a great deal of time in the area closest to Goldap, steadily deepening the love for the forest, most greatly in our father. To him it was inconceivable not to spend the rest of his life looking after the land and the wild life it sustained. Sadly, it wasn't to be.

Indeed, fate had been very unkind to my poor father. Therefore, seeing me work so enthusiastically at my education, even though I was nowhere near as clever at mathematics as he was, made him expect me to succeed where circumstances had intervened for him. If I could fulfil my dreams, then he might feel somewhat compensated for his own shattered expectations. Papa may not have spoken the actual words on the occasion of receiving my medal. Even if he had, I knew, deep inside, he was satisfied with my level of input. Did he think that praise would slacken my efforts? Werner might have done so, not me. I possessed a natural zest for improving myself which never quite diminished with the passing years. I have never been ferociously ambitious, wanting to be at the top of the form come rain, come shine.

No, there were a few others cleverer than me; I was spurred on by an inner enjoyment of expanding my mind. In later life I often got nowhere, pursuing interests, attempting to learn more languages or doing different jobs. It was the challenge of acquiring more knowledge or learning a new skill, which powered me on. Especially during my school years in Eastern Germany as there was nothing else to stimulate my mind: no television or radio, no library or travel – until soon we would be travelling to snowy Thuringia!

In this way the weeks flew by. The 2nd of February saw in my 14th birthday, but my memory draws a blank on the day itself. Presumably I was rather pleased just having reached that significant milestone. Officially I could now be called "Fraeulein". In reality this would not happen for ages, since I still looked more like 11 or 12!

Chapter Forty-Seven

My confirmation was to take place on March 29th. The skiing holiday was coming up towards the end of February; things were heating up! We talked of nothing else at school. Everyone was on cloud nine! When the day of our departure arrived, I felt extremely excited as well as a little subdued. I had to leave my parents and brother behind. Saying good-bye to Mutti was particularly sad. I think a lot of us girls had tears in our eyes despite the thrill of this wonderful adventure. None of us had been separated from our families ever before and here we were, starting our first trip into the "tiefe, weite Welt" (the deep, wide world).

Our mood lifted once we were on our way; more so once we arrived at Thuringia, which was covered in deep snow, giving a magical look to the wood covered hills, a landscape so different from our flat fields and pine woods. The countryside at least held great promise. When we arrived at our final destination, we had an even better surprise: we stopped at two very large and attractive timbered buildings. The one we were led into had "Haus der Jungen Pioniere" written above the entrance in large capital letters (House of the Young Pioneers). We entered a large reception area which appeared rather grand to my country bumpkin eyes. We must have looked like a bunch of chickens looking around us in bewilderment, but it did not take long and big grins were covering our faces.

Apparently, before the war, this building had been one of the luxury hotels of Oberhof, a well known tourist destination for winter sports in Northern Germany. Our "people's government" had confiscated hotels like this one for the use of their young disciples . Private enterprise did not fit in with their communist ideology, not even in their best known winter resort. I felt sorry for the people who had once owned this hotel. On the other hand, how lucky for us to be in a place of such comfort and style! Mutti and Papa, I decided, will not believe their eyes when they read my first letter to them! Clearly, it had not been such a bad idea after all to have thrown my principles overboard and joined the Young Pioneers!

By Western standards our home for the next two weeks may not have been hugely luxurious, yet for us youngsters, who had only known times of hardship and deprivation, this was a rather grand place. Everyone had to share a room with two or three other girls (or boys), adding huge fun to the whole experience. However, if we thought the entire holiday was going to be spent with the minimum of lessons and the maximum of skiing and winter sport adventure time, we soon learned otherwise! The morning call was quite early, followed by assembly in the reception area. At our school at home we never had assembly, so this was something new – but not exciting!

The teachers and the Director of the hostel divided us into small groups and told us that this was precisely how we had to assemble every morning. Then we had to sing one or two socialist songs praising our wonderful leadership and that of our dear friends in the Soviet Union. I imagine it was all similar to the procedures followed by the Hitler Youth, only now we had to pretend to love and admire another hero: Joseph Stalin! This torture being over, we had breakfast followed by lessons, just like at home. Same study plan, same length of time. The only difference was the surroundings. Our "class room" was a beautiful large room, full of light; small tables for four, placed in groups around the room. Somehow, "school" was more fun in this lovely setting. Fortunately, I liked the three girls with whom I was sharing my room and my work table. I still remember their faces very well, but, sadly, no longer their names!

In the afternoons we had our "play-time" outside in the snow. The back of the former hotel looked out onto a large lawn sloping towards a hillside which turned out to be our nursery run. This was most convenient, disappointingly though we could not ski very often as they had only a few pairs of skis and boots available for a large number of boys and girls!¬ This meant, we only had skiing lessons a few times during the entire holiday; the rest of the time we used a sledge or just messed around in the snow or we were taken on outings with the whole class and our form teacher, Herr Schroeder.

Needless to say, there was no lift for our nursery slope; it was much too low for that luxury. Besides, the actual pleasure ski area was in another part of the resort where the correct facilities were available. Oberhof had even a "Sprungschanze" (a ski jump), the only one in the DDR for their competition athletes. Our youth camp was situated at the outskirts of Oberhof and all the area around it was part of the property. Simple though the skiing sessions were, we had tremendous fun, particularly when it was our turn to click our boots into the doddery old skis for fun on the "Idiotenhuegel" (the idiots' hill). I took to the sport like a duck to water and never forgot the moments of sheer bliss, sailing down the little hill without knowing how to stop. Stem Christies weren't necessary when you had endless meadows at the foot of the hill to run along until you came to a natural halt. More often than not we fell onto our bottoms long before we were even down the hill anyway. No need to teach us more than how to get up the hill with our skis on –by sidestepping. Who cared? We were semi-professionals from the start! We did not need ski instructors to show us how to enjoy ourselves – we had fun, fun, fun on our half-hour sessions on the hill, with instructors or without. I could not help noticing that Hansl, my gypsy lookalike admirer and classmate, always seemed to be near where I was floating down the hill. Was he hoping to rescue (and touch me!) after a possible fall on my bum? As far as I remember I never granted him that favour, although I must have fallen often enough.

Short though our skiing exploits were, they had left me with wonderful memories and the certainty that this was a sport I would really love to learn properly one day. More than ten years later my husband took me on our first skiing trip to Zermatt in Switzerland where I did indeed learn the tricks of the sport fairly easily, ensuring many more wonderful holidays in the snow with him and later on with our two daughters; indeed they were the best ones of my entire life.

Despite the lack of ski equipment or instructors, these two weeks were the most exhilarating experience and they also bonded us still further as a form team. When you sleep several to a room with your classmates, you have so much more fun with them, getting to know about everybody's little foibles and habits which make for excellent excuses for teasing in a harmless but amusing manner. I do not recall any upsets during the entire time but loads of laughter and congeniality.

The only blot in the day were those annoying assemblies when you had to sing abominable socialist songs in praise of our soviet friends or our beloved leaders. You really wanted to throw up with disgust. Instead you had to sing these propaganda songs with a cheerful expression on your face and joyful smiles! I found this really hard to swallow, all the while also knowing: there was a pretty good breakfast waiting at the end of this purgatory, school lessons and fun in the snow after a late lunch. There is a price to pay for everything in life; our price was assemblies!

Chapter Forty-Eight

On the 6th of March – I shall never forget that morning – there was a shift in the routine of our assembly.

We lined up in our usual groups and on the precise area allotted to us and were expecting the usual artificially upbeat address from the lady teacher who led the assembly every morning. She stood at the head of the almost completed semi-circle of pupils on a podium high enough for everyone to see her. Like every morning, she was surrounded by our teachers and other men whose functions were unclear to me. In contrast to their usual fairly friendly and upbeat postures, they all had very stern, unmoving expressions on their faces which struck me as odd, but I could not imagine why this was so. The lady on the podium asked for silence in an ominous sort of way and the room fell silent almost at once.

"Good morning, boys and girls! With the greatest of sadness I have to inform you today of the death of our most beloved father and friend, Joseph Vissarionovich (and then she paused for a short moment) Stalin."

Before she had completed his name, after that split second of silent expectancy, my heartbeat began to accelerate like the beat of a drum. Would she say "Stalin?" Could this really be? The pause in her announcement had only been a brief one, but I was surprised how many thoughts filled my mind in those few seconds of silent expectancy. I felt as tense as a balloon about to burst.

"Please, please, say it!"

And when she did I almost jumped into the air with joy. This was unbelievable, totally unexpected, the best news imaginable! The word "Hurra" (hoorah) was already on my lips but the deathly silence all around me must have been the warning for me to come to my senses.

"What on earth was I trying to do? Commit suicide and destroy my family?" my thoughts warned me.

Half-way through exploding with joy, something or someone had stopped me in my tracks. A guardian angel? Yes, it must have been, for I had followed my gut feelings and if you react to your instinct you don't have time to switch on your common sense. You follow that instinctive command and act accordingly. Miraculously, I did not follow this pattern. Something or someone had stopped me and all of my body and soul turned dead like a block of stone. Deep inside that frozen statue my heart still raced like a revved up motor; this time in the relief that I had been rescued from danger. I remember nothing more of that auspicious assembly. The realization of how close I had come to destroying my future and that of my family once again shook me to the core and deadened my senses to everything else that was said or done. Never to my dying day though will I forget the ecstasy pulsing through my body while outwardly I hoped I looked as cool as a block of white marble.

The lady on the podium droned on and on about the sad loss of our dearest and most beloved friend to whom we owed so much. Her words fell on deaf ears as far as I was concerned. For me the hated Stalin's death was unadulterated joy, more so as it had come out of the blue. No one had known of any illness he might have had. In later years some newspapers and historians of the Soviet era speculated he might have been poisoned which would not be surprising. The last thing on which a dictatorship is built is truth, leaving the ordinary man in the street totally bewildered and confused about the level of lies being spread about. One thing was certain though, Stalin was dead. No one would dare to invent such a claim. How he suffered his demise was of no concern to me.

Did we continue our day as normal, having breakfast, then lessons followed by lunch-time and fun in the snow? I was in the grip of such excitement over the "so very sad news"; that the intensity of it has wiped out all other memory – not only of that particular day, no, the entire rest of our holiday. Surely, the removal of this hated figure would result in an enormous improvement of all our lives, not just in the Soviet Union but also here in the DDR! In an instant my imagination went into overdrive. Now everything would change! Perhaps life here would become so different and enjoyable we might ask ourselves, at some point in the near future, why we ever considered fleeing to the "Golden West". Everything would come good now: I would go to high school next year, then university, followed by a wonderful medical career and untold happiness and riches!

Wasn't it wonderful, how the death of one single man could change the lives of millions? On and on I fantasized in the brief minutes after the announcement of the exciting new development. I remember distinctly that suddenly I no longer wanted to stay on there but was bursting to be home to discuss this wonderful event with my father and mother. Here I could not allow my true feelings to be seen or heard by anyone, not even my girl friends with who I shared my room. I could not be sure they would keep the secret. Better not trust anyone, except my nearest and dearest at home.

Chapter Forty-Nine

As I have told you earlier, the effect of Stalin's death on me was so powerful nothing else remains in my memory of the rest of our stay at Oberhof nor of our journey home.

Soon, however, the final preparations for my confirmation filled my mind with other excitement, and particularly the thrill of the dress! Looking at the professional photograph taken of me on the day, it looked a pretty ordinary dress, nothing to rave about, yet I felt so proud of it at the time. It may have looked a modest design, but none of the other girls wore dresses made of taffeta from the United States of America! That, at least, made my dress totally unique and special!

Mutti had started saving butter and sugar straight after Christmas to ensure she had plenty of ingredients for a Streuselkuchen (remember my 6th birthday surprise?) as well as Schillerlocken (home-made puff pastry horns filled with vanilla cream or butter cream), a special treat we all had looked forward to for ages. Naturally, Mutti had to invite Trautl and her family as well as her sister Ella and her 4 children, which meant there would not be much cake left over, worse luck! And, of course, there wasn't. Aunt Ella was not as good a housekeeper as our mother and I don't think she was such a good cook either, so my cousins tucked in mightily and the Schillerlocken especially were gone in a flash.

Traditionally, every guest as well as your parents gives you a really important present to mark this special occasion in a young person's life. However, I did not really expect my parents to come up with anything other than the splendid dress and the wonderful spread of cakes for afternoon coffee with our guests. I also did not expect any present from aunt Ella and her husband. They never had two pennies to rub together and her husband hardly ever did any work. Therefore, I wish to this day she would have just shaken hands with me, congratulating me on this milestone in my life and wishing me well. Unfortunately she did neither but greeted me with the harsh words:
"You have to imagine a present from us!"

A slap in my face could not have been more hurtful. It was such a tactless way of saying how sorry she was they were unable to give me a present. I nearly burst into tears but Papa saw and heard what had been said and he quickly said something to distract me to save the afternoon. I had helped Mutti with the baking the day before and could not wait to tuck into the treats on the table. Half-way through the Kaffeestunde (the tea party), Papa rose from the table and asked everyone for a moment's attention. He then made a short speech in my honour and asked me to come to him as he had something to present to me! In his hands was a small box and in it was a wrist watch embedded on a cushion of dark pink imitation velvet! Now I really did burst into tears, but these were tears of joy, of course! How on earth did my parents manage to save so much money to spoil me with such a wonderful present?
I flung my arms around my father and saw that he, too, had tears in his eyes. Mutti, too, got a huge hug from me and then I had to go around the table and show everyone my fabulous watch which Papa had put on my left wrist. He had also explained how to set the time by winding it up until it started ticking. I could see the envy in my cousins' eyes, making my present even more valuable to me.

When everyone had calmed down and was concentrating again on the cakes in front of them, I seized the moment to slip away and run outside where I could be alone with the joy of my new precious possession. Dear, dear Papa, he was always working so hard for us, usually denying himself in order to be able to give to his beloved family. At this moment I loved him more than ever. So, yes, he did not praise me ever for my work at school, but look what he has done for me now! Tomorrow I would go to school wearing my new status symbol like all the other girls would, since the gift of a watch was probably the most traditional present parents gave their child on this auspicious occasion. Just for once I was my class mates' equal – Papa and Mutti had seen to that!

I felt truly touched and deeply thankful and could not stop looking at my lovely watch on my arm. I glanced at it from all angles, bending my arm this way and that; my lovely watch looked the same from all angles – a dream in silvery metal and pink. As much as I admired it, merely looking at it was not enough. I undid the strap and took my watch in both my hands, weighing it and touching it lovingly. What joy this day had brought me, elevated to young adulthood and owner of my very own wristwatch, an enormous luxury in those Socialist Republic days. I was about to put the watch back on my arm when something spurred me on to give it another caress and to see that it would really work the way Papa had shown me. I decided to check on winding it up a little more; to make sure it really was in good working order and would respond to my every command so to speak. I started off winding the little screw very gently. Nothing happened. So I tried a second time, but somewhat harder and then it happened: an ominous cracking sound - I had the winding screw in my hand! Broken!! My beautiful, brand new watch was broken – and by my own hands!
A watch it had taken my father to save up for ages. How could such a cruel thing happen to me!?

I wanted to die, sink instantly into the earth, never to be seen again and never having to confront my parents with this terrible confession. I felt sick with shock. Tears were streaming down my horror struck face and onto my precious taffeta dress. I had no handkerchief, had to wipe the tears away with my hands. I decided under no circumstances was anyone allowed to see me like this. I ran to a hiding place near the outside lavatory, shaking all over my body and crying, crying, crying. How could a day end so horribly when it had started off so happily and full of expectation and excitement!?

I realized the family must be wondering what had happened to me and where I was. As a result I tried really hard to stop crying and to calm myself down. My eyes must have been very read and blotchy. I could not possibly walk back indoors looking like that. Everyone would instantly realize something dreadful had happened to me. There was no way I could admit to my parents I had destroyed their marvellous gift, though it had happened unintentionally. I remember that anger eventually helped me: anger with this hateful country where nothing worked, nothing was any good, where even factory new products did not last longer than two seconds. Had we lived in the West this would never have happened. The quality of everything over there was so much better. Everyone knew that even if they had only heard about it. By comparison, all products here were very shoddy. It did not matter whether factories had work quotas or not, neither volume nor quality of their products were up to anything. What can you expect from a Soviet led government? The Russians had been backward before the war and they are still backward now. And what makes it worse: we have to dance to their tune! I hate them, all of them! They have ruined my much looked forward to confirmation day and they will ruin my entire life! Spitting out these hateful thoughts did me a power of good. Slowly the venom of these ideas helped me to stop sobbing and I went into the laundry room to cool my eyes down with cold water in the hope it would deceive everyone inside of the agony I had just been living through.

I cannot recall how long it took me to gather up courage to face my parents and my brother, who was usually pretty good at spotting when something was amiss. To my utter amazement, no one noticed anything. The watch was in its rightful place on my arm, if minus the winder. For quite a while afterwards my parents were unaware that the watch was broken. When someone asked me the time I would make it up but it was stressful trying to keep up the pretence. Therefore, a few weeks later, I confessed. Not the truth, mind you! Not that I broke my precious gift the very first day of its life with me.

How could I possibly do this to my father? No, no: instead I lied I had noticed in geography class that my watch had stopped; I began winding it up and, suddenly, to my undying horror, I had the winder in my hand! Previously, when I had to wind it up, it always had worked perfectly and by now I had become quite practised in this delicate task. Therefore it wasn't my fault at all it had broken. I knew how to wind up a watch! It was just another sign everything which was manufactured under this rotten system was complete crap, not worth having!

They say time is a good healer. I can confirm this to be true. Somehow, over time, I had got used to the tragedy of my broken watch. Consequently, the confession was nowhere near as traumatic for me as it would have been on the day of my confirmation. Yet the memory and the guilt of this experience is as tormenting today as it was then. "If you can still hear me, Papa, from wherever you now live in God's realm, please believe me, I am and I was so very, very sorry!¬"

Clearly, shopping in the People's Paradise was not quite the same joy and satisfaction as shopping had been in Riga in the old days.

Chapter Fifty

The big day of my young life had passed and life continued in the old routine. There was only one more term left before the important end of school year examinations. I buckled down to my revision work of what we had been taught in the past months in the hope of ending the year once more with really good marks. I did not see as much of Ingetrud and her family as I spent most evenings bent over my books instead. This applied to Ingetrud as well since she was still at high school and found the last term just as demanding. If, however, the weather turned exceptionally warm in May we would find time to run to the river beach for a swim in the early evening sun.

There was also no significant change in the wider world around us. Stalin's death, secretly welcomed by so many, had impacted our day to day life in no way whatsoever. If I had thought, on the morning of the 6th of March, 1953, that soon we would see light at the end of the tunnel and the yoke of Soviet rule would now be eased, I had been mistaken. I never quite understood the way the Russian Communist Party functioned at the top level. There seemed so many grim looking party chiefs clambering for power and positions in the Soviet corridors of power. Stalin's successor was made premier very shortly after his death – a man called Georgi Malenkov. The Soviet grip on our government which was ruled, as I understood it then, by Walter Ulbricht who had been made First Secretary of the SED (Socialist Unity Party of Germany) several years earlier, remained as strong as ever. To us it seemed our leaders in Berlin were more communist and ardent in their pursuit of the Leninist/Stalinist ideology than other leaders of communist countries, such as Poland, Czechoslovakia, Hungary or even the Soviet Union itself!

Thus, over the past few years, I had begun to hate Walter Ulbricht almost more than Stalin himself. I hated his ugly bespectacled face with his goaty beard, hated even more his unattractive voice and dialect. We had to endure seeing and hearing him every time we went to the cinema (which, luckily, was not very often) as the Newsreel always preceded the main feature film. I remember vividly thinking that those people who had opposed Hitler during the Nazi dictatorship must have felt the same inner venom boiling up inside them when they had to listen to his raving lunatic speeches. Why, oh why did Germany have to suffer such terrible leaders? I was much too young to know what a true democracy meant, but my inner feelings told me very well, the system we lived under was against human nature, which longed for freedom of thought and expression. Perhaps my passionate revulsion of life under communism was unusual for a young girl my age. But then, most of my classmates had not experienced what our family had. Consequently they lacked the passionate dislike of our political system which occupied a great deal of my mind and my time. Only, I could not express myself for fear of reprisals. Perhaps there were far more who thought likewise, but, like me, they had to keep it to themselves.

Spring came and went and it was now June 1953. The shortage of goods in the shops was as bad as ever. Stalin's death had brought no visible change. We were still rushing to the HO shop as soon as one could see a queue outside; a sign that some sort of delivery had been made. As of old, people queued for whatever it was that had been delivered – we needed everything and were ready to buy whatever was filling the shelves: margarine, flour, sugar or salt. You bought it since you could not be certain when the next opportunity for any purchases would arrive. To quote Glenn E. Curtis's book once more:

"In June 1953, hoping to pacify workers with an improved standard of living, the SED announced the New Course. The New Course in East Germany was based on the economic policy initiated by Georgi Malenkov in the Soviet Union. Malenkov's policy, which aimed at improvement in the standard of living, stressed a shift in investment toward light industry and trade and a greater availability of consumer goods. The SED, in addition to shifting emphasis from heavy industry to consumer goods, initiated a program for alleviating economic hardships. This led to a reduction of delivery quotas and taxes, the availability of state loans to private business, and an increase in the allocation of production material.
The New Course did not, however, alleviate the burden of the East German workers. High production quotas and spiralling work norms remained in effect".

At least it was summer and everything feels better in warm sunshine. Mutti had sown her carrot seeds and had planted her potatoes in our allotment. Papa still had his above ground job in the mine and Werner was working and living in Wismar on the Baltic coast, where he was learning to be a bricklayer! The only type of work he was able to get. He was going to be 16 in July and it must have been so hard for him to be separated from us. Together with lots of other youngsters he lived a military-style existence in a youth camp where he was exposed to a similar indoctrination as we had been exposed to in Oberhof.

Werner was a sensitive boy, not the kind you would expect on a building site. I often wondered how he was coping among the muscled men in charge of the young apprentices. He would come home from time to time on very short recuperative holidays when Mutti's love and cooking would resuscitate his physical and emotional spirits. No one had a choice in what they could do and where. You had to follow the work and learn a trade. He was lucky to have been given the chance of an apprenticeship rather than labouring in the fields. One day, perhaps, we could flee from this part of Germany which had never felt like a proper homeland to any of us and start a different life altogether; a life of promise and freedom. Of course we realized that over there, in the

West, we would have to start all over again with nothing but the clothes on our backs – just as we had done eight years earlier after our arrival from Prussia. This time would be different. We had our father with us and we would live in a free land. No one can imagine what lack of freedom means if one has not actually experienced it. None of us felt attached to the few material things we had been able to acquire during these eight years here. In exchange for freedom, they meant nothing.

But the opportunity for such a daring move would not easily arrive, never mind how hard we all wished for it. One day it would come. We knew it deep inside, it was just a question of time. Meanwhile we had to do what each of us could to keep body and soul together. All the while staying hopeful.

Chapter Fifty-One

I cannot remember what kind of weekday June 16th was, nor how I first heard about the riots and demonstrations of construction workers in Berlin. Apparently these totally spontaneous strikes were a result of yet another increase in production quotas demanded by the SED (Sozialistische Einheitspartei Deutschland) – the Social Unity Party of Germany led by the despised and hated Walter Ulbricht. These newly imposed quotas acted as an explosive element in a highly dissatisfied work force in Berlin. Their instantaneous outcry in the streets of Berlin were a shocking surprise to the government but wonderful news to the rest of the population.

My father came home from work in a state of extreme excitement. The workers in the mine had heard about this on the radio and the news spread like a wildfire among their colleagues. My father's pent up frustration and hatred of the communist system released itself with the powerful force of a canon and could not be stopped any longer. Without considering the consequences he went from person to person and tried to persuade them to take up arms, so to speak, and join in the demonstrations started in Berlin.

"We must use our faith and believe that everyone in every factory all over our country will follow these men. I'm sure we are not the only ones having listened to the radio reports. So, come on! They need our support if they are to have any success. Show courage. What are you waiting for?" he addressed his colleagues with his usual passion.

Papa showed no fear. Once again he was in his element, showing the courage of his Huguenot ancestors, who had left Southern France to escape the persecution of the Catholic Church and settled on the vastly different shores of Prussia by invitation of Frederick William, Elector of Brandenburg and Duke of Prussia, the grandfather of Frederick the Great. My father's passion and courage were the two most outstanding features of his character, along with his devotion to his beloved wife and family and to hard work and discipline. Admirable though these qualities were, they had also got him into a great many problems as I have told you earlier, yet I could not help admiring him. We discussed this unexpected and amazing event all evening. Papa felt he had not had much success persuading his colleagues to join forces with the Berliner heroes, but he hoped that sleeping on the events might change his "Kumpels'" (comrades) minds. The word "mind power" may not have been coined yet in those days, but it was what Papa had required of his work mates.

Some said, after the fall of the Berlin Wall and with it the East German government, that mind power must have played a role in the totally unexpected turn of events. Today we all know what a powerful tool it can be.

So Papa went to work ever hopeful. Mutti had spent an anxious night, but not Papa. He always slept through every disaster, sleeping the sleep of the just. Not so poor Mutti. She was extremely concerned for his safety and had pleaded with him earnestly not to start agitating all over again, but to keep his head down and hope for the best. To our utter surprise that was precisely what our father did. In the end he always listened to our anxious unadventurous mother. Her love and approval of him almost always won the day. But I think another reason he managed to restrain himself was the lack of support he got from his colleagues; all of whom feared for their loss of livelihood or worse, for their loss of freedom.

By the morning of the 17th June the strikes and demos had turned into a fully blown uprising of hundreds of people; not only against the new work quotas but against the republic in general, demanding free elections and the death of communism! We could not believe what we heard secretly on western radio stations or from friends and neighbours. However, by the next day the government had collected their shocked nerves and had approached the Soviet armed forces in Berlin and their own People's Police to squash the riots by all possible means. Tanks appeared in the streets and by evening the very first revolt against any Communist dictatorship, not just our own, was over. As suddenly as it had started, it had died an ignominious death, together with approximately 500 participants.

You cannot smash tanks with stones and sticks alone or with the anger of many hungry and despairing people.

That evening, after Papa's return from the mine, the atmosphere in our home was full of gloom and disappointment. The management of the mine had warned their work force not be foolish and follow the lead of those "enemies of the State" skirmishing in the streets of Berlin. Every worker stayed silent and remained focused on their work, like the good robots they had become. We feared we might not see our father back home that night, but our fear had been unfounded, or so it seemed.

A deep silence fell over the land and our village; a silence of fear of possible reprisals for anyone who might have encouraged the riots in the capital, people like my father, for instance!

Chapter Fifty-Two

Somehow the days slipped by and nothing happened. I was able to concentrate once more on my forthcoming school tests for which I had worked so studiously for so long. The exams came and went and on my last day at school, I believe it was the 4th July 1953, I was presented with a really pleasing report as well as a prize for hard work and good conduct!

My prize was a book about a female veterinary surgeon, a subject I was not in the least bit interested in. Almost 50 years on, I still own this book, but have never read it and never will either! But I am cherishing it, since it is the only remnant I have, together with my last school report, of my childhood in Heiddorf. Another reason for valuing this book so much is the written dedication by my form teacher, our beloved Herr Schroeder.

"To the pupil, Brigitte Mallon, in appreciation of her good work and conduct. Signed: H. Schroeder, Form teacher. Heiddorf 4.7.53"

These are the marks in my school report:

Conduct:	Very Good
Diligence:	Very Good
Attention:	Very Good

Brigitte's diligence and achievements are praiseworthy.

Subjects:	
German, oral:	1
German, written	1
Mathematics:	1
History:	1
Social studies:	1
Biology:	2
Physics:	2
Chemistry:	2
Geography:	1
Russian:	1
Sport:	2
Music:	2
Drawing:	2
Needlework:	1

Rather splendid results, but to be fair and honest. I really did not like mathematics, nor the sciences. The only reason I got "very good" or "good" in these subjects was due to cramming in theoretical knowledge in a parrot fashion. I wasn't really naturally gifted in these subjects. However, I did deserve my very good marks in the other subjects and have continued an interest in all of them until the present day.

It must have been on the 5th or the 6th July, immediately after the end of my school year, that the everyday routine of our day was spectacularly broken by Papa's return from work around 3.00 to 3.30 pm. Mutti and I were working on our small allotment close to a country path leading towards the woodlands as well as the main road to the village where our father's workplace was.
From the allotment it was easy to see anyone coming down the path from that direction. We could spot Papa on our bicycle from quite afar. He held the steering wheel by one hand; the other hand covered his face most of the time which seemed extremely odd, just as it was very odd for him to come home this early. Normally he would not return until about 5.30pm.
As he got closer he called out towards us:

"Come home! Very, very quickly! Leave everything as it is and come straight home! And hurry!"

We could now see that his right hand covered his right eye from time to time, although this was not strictly necessary since he had some padding strapped over it.

"Hugo! What has happened?"

Mutti shouted anxiously, her face turning as white as a sheet and her chestnut brown eyes staring in horror from Papa to me and back again. But father only waved us on furiously to follow him home, which we did, running after him as fast as our legs could carry us.

Father would not answer any questions while we were still outside, but once indoors the events of the day at the mine flowed out of him like a torrent. He had an uneventful morning's work. Soon after lunch he was required to solder something together and, not having had any protective glasses for this dangerous job, he got an iron splinter into his right eye and had to be taken to the work's surgery. The doctor there was just a General Practitioner, not an eye specialist. Therefore, Papa was given a referral document to the Charite Hospital in Berlin, which was the largest hospital in the DDR and had the best eye clinic in the land. The mine's work doctor bandaged his eye and asked Papa to go home at once and take the very next train to Berlin as otherwise he feared Papa might lose the sight of his eye.

"You have absolutely no time to lose, Herr Mallon. Tomorrow could be too late!"

As Papa left the surgery and walked along a narrow corridor towards the exit, the doctor's assistant came towards him. As she got level with him she whispered, without looking at him:

"And when you are in Berlin, Herr Mallon, don't come back!"

These whispered words of warning changed our lives. Papa understood their meaning at once. Three weeks had passed since the 16th June and Papa's attempts to persuade his work colleagues to lay down tools and join the rioters in Berlin. Since then, all had seemed quiet on the work front but he had noticed and heard that some of the workers had been interviewed by party members; no arrests had so far been made. Someone must have denounced Papa which had come to the doctor's attention. It was a miracle the police had not come for him yet; an even greater miracle that he had this accident on the very day when news of his imminent arrest had reached the doctor's ears. I believe such coincidences aren't chance – they have been arranged by angels. And that the doctor and his assistant were courageous enough to give my father the veiled warning was another gift from heaven.

We knew the next train to Ludwigslust for the connecting train to Berlin would leave Neu Kaliss station in just over an hour's time. There was no further train that day. So decisions had to be made at the speed of lightning. This was the opportunity we had waited and prepared for over a long period of time. Now all that was needed was putting it into action. The doctor had signed Papa off work for several days giving us a good chance to successfully execute our escape. The greatest difficulty was Werner's absence. We had to get him back home as soon as possible as there was, of course, no question of leaving him behind. He had been instructed, before starting his apprenticeship, that if he received a telegram from our parents asking him to request compassionate leave for his grandmother's funeral, it was a sign to return home at all cost. This telegram was sent off that same afternoon. Our parents decided I should travel with Papa and that Mutti should follow as soon as Werner had arrived home.

One minute I had been working with Mutti on the allotment, the next minute we had all reached the eye of the storm and I was looking for my blue Young Pioneer's neck scarf and my badge for "Good Knowledge". Wearing both of them would make me appear to be a good young communist school girl – and, hopefully, make me safe from suspicious looks by controlling police. Papa had only enough time to have a quick wash and change into his best clothes and then we had to say good bye to our mother. Because everything had to be dealt with under such pressure, even the parting from our mother was not as traumatic as it might have been otherwise.

The fear and the tears followed later. For it was not until Papa and I had safely arrived at West Berlin and the house of my uncle Fritz that I began to be fully aware of the possibility, that we might never see Mutti or Werner again. We tried hard to eliminate these thoughts from our minds and hearts, but in vain. The threat was too monumental to be ignored. Mutti had told our father she would first travel to Bischofswerda in Saxony to say her final farewell to her old mother and her sister Erna before getting off the train in West Berlin on her "return" journey to Neu Kaliss.

This meant we had to wait for several days before we would know whether she and Werner had indeed been successful in their attempt to join us. Had the police become suspicious of them while on the train, we most certainly would never have been united again! They must have been petrified to their bones in the train back from Bischofswerda and – according to their train tickets – on their journey home to Heiddorf. For had they bought a return ticket to Berlin only, the police would most certainly have questioned and probably detained them. Since so many, many thousands of residents of the DDR fled their country daily by this route, the police were extra vigilant in examining every face on that train. Back then these trains still stopped in the western part of Berlin, where they had no control over who got off. They knew very well that most travellers would probably step off onto a western (thus FREE) platform, but if travellers had a valid ticket and did not look especially suspicious, they could not stop them getting off the train when the train stopped at stations anywhere inside the western zones. Often people were forced off the train while it passed through East German areas if passengers looked a little nervous, or otherwise suspicious – never to be seen again!

They did not necessarily end up in prison, but they would be intensely questioned until they were either found innocent or not. Trying to stem the flow of refugees in this way was a fruitless task. All they could do to these hapless passengers was to make their journey very unpleasant and inconvenient. If they had attempted to flee they would simply take the next train and try the same again. However, some were actually forced to return to their home address.

In the case of my mother and brother, this would have been a tragic disaster. By the time they would have arrived back home under this kind of threat the local police would have been waiting for them by their front door. By that time my father's leave from the mine would have expired and it would have been evident my father and I had remained in Berlin while Mutti and Werner had attempted to join us.

This eventuality did not bear thinking about, yet we could not erase it from our thoughts for one minute.

After three years of hoping and yearning to find ourselves in the free part of Berlin, only half of our family could breathe in this pure and wonderful air. Would the other half manage to deceive the searching police and come through to join us? We had never thought that our flight to freedom would have to be attempted in this traumatic way. To see Papa's sad and inward looking face during the entire journey to Berlin made my heart ache for him. After almost ten years of separation from his beloved wife during the war and his captivity in Russia, he stood the possibility once more of losing her and his son. I think that was the reason he had insisted that I come with him. If he could not be reunited with our mother, then, at least, he had one of us with him to sustain him. What a terrible turmoil he must have suffered before he knew he had his beloved family with him once more!

To cheer Papa on our fateful journey, I did what I have always done – I chatted away as cheerfully as I could. If there was no response, I continued to put on a smiling face for him whenever he did look at me and I tried to be brave, very brave. Naturally, I, too, feared for my mother and brother. After all, we knew our mother's timid nature. In that sense she was the complete opposite to our father, who had the courage of a lion and the persistence of a tiger.

I just prayed that all would go according to plan. If the police were to question mother …….. well, I did not want to go there. She would try to give the appearance of calm, all the while growing ever more fearful and nervous the longer she was questioned in front of the other passengers, then her nerves would most likely give in. That is just the way she was. So we needed luck, a lot of luck and hope in our hearts.

After several days of intense waiting, Mutti and Werner stepped off their train in Berlin, having successfully escaped police control. The joy of seeing her and my brother again was so overwhelming that all the worrying times vanished like a puff of smoke. The shackles of life in the DDR were behind us. I felt like extra wings were growing all over my body, not only near my shoulder blades!

Now our minds could fly, our hands could work and keep the proceeds of this work to buy sufficient good food and grow in well-being and happiness. If you have not experienced life in the post-war years on the eastern side of our broken land, having lost your homeland in the Eastern parts of the old Germany as well, you cannot possibly empathize with our feelings at that moment of reunion in the free world. Once again we had lost everything, except the clothes we stood in, but we felt we had gained the world – we were FREE! Now everything would improve, we could flourish. Thanks be to God – and to Uncle Fritz and his wife Tina, who gave us shelter in return for work during the first few weeks in this new world. All was well.

During the years of hoping and planning to bring this change about, it often seemed impossible to achieve. In the end, once we were reunited, it felt incredibly easy as if there had been no danger attached to any of it, as if life "back there" had merely been an allusion. As if every part of our previous existence had been a necessary preparation for this very moment – the true beginning of our lives as a family, the inevitable reward for our past privations and courage. I felt giddy with joy and excitement for the years to come; a wondrous life lay just around the corner. Fate and our father's immense courage had finally set us free.

Although the Yalta and Potsdam Agreements had a most devastating effect on millions of Germans and particularly the surviving population of the Eastern parts I later learned to appreciate at least one of the agreements made at

Potsdam: The division of our capital city Berlin into four occupation zones – British, American, French and Russian. This would enable the Allied Forces to have a presence in Berlin, in exchange for which the Americans had been prepared to give up the conquered territories of Thuringia and Saxony to the Soviet Union. How fortunate this part of the Agreement had been for the future of Berlin but also for those hundreds of thousands of disillusioned citizens of the DDR who fled the barbarism of the Communist regime the way we did – by using the public trains connecting all four zones of the city and stepping off in one of the allied sectors to seek refuge! And how fortunate for our family, too!

By summer 1961 approximately 3.5 million defectors had crossed over into West Berlin, seriously damaging the economy of the DDR since most of the refugees were the young who had a long future of stifling misery in front of them. On August 13th 1961 the people of Berlin woke up to the construction activities of a steel concrete wall which finally reached a height of 3.60 meters. It was erected to divide East Berlin and the three western sectors as well as surrounding the outer borders of the Western zones with the Soviet Zone thus isolating the city and turning it into an enclave inside East Germany. Between 1961 and the fall of the communist Eastern government on 9th November 1989 crossing this wall or the Inner German border between the two Germanys was nearly impossible.

The Inner German border ran from the Baltic Sea to Czechoslovakia and was extremely heavily fortified with a mine strip and watchtowers on the Eastern side preventing any movement between the two republics. Once the remaining loophole in Berlin was closed by the erection of the infamous wall (ostensibly "protecting" the East German population from infiltration by the West German fascist elements!) the die was cast: East Germans were imprisoned until 1989, when the regime crumbled and Berlin youngsters famously started climbing the wall from both sides, ecstatically hacking away at the wall and taking pieces home as a memento. The jubilation over this historic event is hard to imagine. As it unfolded, TV cameras captured every moment and brought it to the homes of every German family, scenes of such incredible joy and wonder that no one, I believe, who ever watched them in amazement will not forget them for as long as they live.

The student son of one of my friends from England spent New Year's Eve of that year in Berlin celebrating the new found freedom. He, too, returned home with small pieces of the wall he had broken off himself. He gave one to me which I am still treasuring as if it were a huge uncut diamond! Priceless!

Chapter Fifty-Three

Tina had an unmarried older sister who owned rather a large house where we found shelter for the next few weeks. In return, Papa and I continued working in the delicatessen shop which was a huge help for our uncle. Well, not MY help was useful but Papa's. Uncle Fritz took an instant shine to me. I think he had already noted that he liked me when he came on his shopping sprees for "Black" Johanna's scrumptious sausages for sale to the high society of the Grunewald. He liked children and I believe he rather wished to have a little girl of his own - perhaps a girl like me. This may have been the reason he suggested that I too, should help in the shop. A lively, chatty girl would liven up the atmosphere. He gave me a white overall and showed me how to weigh out loose sugar into paper bags of one pound, 500 grams. "But make sure you don't actually make it 500, more like 495! I've got to make a profit, see?"

No, I didn't. He was charging a certain sum (including his profit) for 500 grams a bag. So why did I have to cheat people out of five grams? I did not like that idea at all, but orders were orders. Of course, I had completely forgotten that I had been guilty of precisely the same deed when I dipped into our mother's sugar bags years earlier! So, it seemed I had learned something from my misbehaviour at long last! We owed Uncle Fritz and Tina something in return for our lodgings and food. I could not make any fuss about this, but inwardly I was shocked. Honesty at any price was my life's motto nowadays. Not the best principle to follow if you are in business, it seemed. To be fair, my honesty had got me into trouble more often than not in the past. Perhaps it was not such a good philosophy after all? I realized I had to learn on the hoof! Yet I doubted that I could. My principles were already too deeply rooted. I had never been able to deny them – except when my thirst for sugar had got the better of principled me. There was a stubbornness in my character which had always gone into battle for my beliefs. Sometimes to my satisfaction and advantage but very often also to my disadvantage. We only need to remember how close I came to destroying my family's future over my refusal to join the Young Pioneers! In this case though, common sense prevailed and I measured 496/7 or 8 grams of sugar into their paper bags when uncle Fritz was not looking. A fair compromise, I thought.

For the first few days my job was quite interesting, a new world for me. As I could not do all that much beyond weighing out and clearing up untidy shelves etc. I sometimes had spare time when I was at a loss to know how else to occupy myself, especially if Uncle Fritz was not around. One afternoon I decided to go outside and watch the exciting new world go by. The fast moving tempo of the traffic, on the road as well as on the pavement, was so intriguing to watch after the solitude and stillness of our rural life. I stood there gaping at the carnival of movement, the elegantly dressed women, people riding bicycles alongside the flow of cars passing over the bridge. Naturally, I had never seen so much traffic ever before and was simply fascinated by, what seemed to me, a glitzy city life. I stood there leaning against the frame of the shop door spellbound and totally absorbed when my uncle's voice catapulted me out of my reverie :

"What are you doing out there still wearing your overall? What do you think the competition is going to think?"

"The competition? What is the competition, Onkel Fritz?" I uttered in confusion.

Had I done something terribly wrong? Clearly I wasn't a stupid girl, but this word "competition" was new to me, never heard it before. I was quite upset, I remember, as I had wanted to please our uncle and now I had done something wrong without knowing what it was. Where I came from, no one "competed" in business against anyone else. There were no businesses other than one of each in our village. Communism was not interested in private enterprise and its growth anyway; in fact, it resented it. So Uncle Fritz had to explain to me that here in the West of Berlin stimulating business and enterprise for growth was most important. Everyone was aiming to be better and more successful than the other businesses in the area. Thus, if I stood outside the shop door wearing my assistant's overall ,"the competition" (in other words, the competing shopkeepers) would think our shop was not doing very well or else I would not have time to saunter outside, watching the world go by. My first important lesson about the new world I had entered: always pretend you are busy, even when you are not! The competition needs to be deceived or at least to be kept guessing about your state of affairs. Something else I would have problems with: deceit! Even a mild version like keeping people guessing. Oh dear, will I be able to come to terms with this new way of living and working in this free world – this "competitive" world? Tiny dents were starting to appear and assert themselves in the mental picture I had created in my mind about "The Golden West". I had better make some quick adjustments as Uncle Fritz had already pointed out so wisely. You did not need to go hungry here, but it was also no land of milk and honey, unless you were diligent – and you competed, not merely at school but also in your working life.

Mutti helped Tina's sister with the housework and cooking of meals. Werner probably did nothing at all. He certainly did not do anything connected with the shop. He blended into the background so much in those early days and weeks in Berlin that I find it hard to remember whether he was even there. But, of course, he was. Perhaps I approached my new life with more enthusiasm than he did. Therefore I only remember my own feelings about this new challenging chapter in our lives and no one else's.

After a few days of my "apprenticeship" among the bags of sugar and flour Uncle Fritz suggested I learn to deliver orders to the grander houses in the area – on his bicycle! I did not mind making deliveries, but on bicycle?! Oh dear, how would I manage? Me, the "Landpomeranze" (the country bumpkin) throwing myself into the buzz of Berlin's Kurfuerstendamm as if I was born to it! I was petrified, but Uncle was not going to have any of it.

"Now you are here, you have to adapt! Or else you won't make any progress in life!"

Of course, he was right, yet I remained scared stiff and begged him to start off deliveries in the Grunewald, which seemed a more quiet area. He could see that this was wise. My first deliveries were therefore nearby and the parcels small which would not destabilize my bike with their weight. Soon I got the hang of it and was able to widen my field of activity! Sometimes, though, I did get myself into a pickle crossing over the roads, especially from the Kurfuerstendamm into its side streets with its grand buildings and smart shops which had started to spring up. There may still have been some signs of the devastation the war had left behind but to me this magnificent avenue appeared as if the war had not touched it at all. In retrospect I am quite certain there must have been considerable war damage still remaining, yet not to my overwhelmed country eyes. The trees along the avenue had only been replanted a few years earlier and were still hugely overpowered by the buildings framing the avenue.

Uncle Fritz told us all the established old trees had been plundered and bits sewn off towards the end of the war and immediately thereafter, because the population of the city was without any gas or electricity supply and everyone had to scrounge for anything which would burn, furniture, wooden toys, sheds, even their beloved trees! Just anything for a fire which would keep them warm for a while or provide heat for a meal. It made me realize how lucky we had been to have lived in the country near woods where I was able to collect pine cones and twigs and small branches for our stove cum cooker. Collecting such heating material had become my daily duty during the warmer months of the year, while Werner played football, but it also became something really enjoyable. The peace of the forests made me feel the world was still whole and beautiful. This peace in nature created peace and joy in my heart that no one could take away. The poor city dwellers here never had this compensation for all the hardship they had to endure day after day, month after month. I began to see another side to life in a city, away from the glamour of cars and shops and began to appreciate how fortunate we had actually been to have landed in Heiddorf after our flight from Prussia. If only Heiddorf had not been beyond the river Elbe and thus in the Soviet occupied part of Germany, we might never have wanted to leave it!

These reflections soon led me to realize, too, that I might never see my friends again whom I had left behind: Ingetrud, Benita, Gerda, my class mates. A kind of homesickness took a hold of me, especially at night after my perilous bike expeditions. Then, for a while, I was not so sure the exchange was such a good one after all. Yes, here we were free, but without friends and our struggle for recognition and respect would have to start all over again. These were days of mixed feelings: on the one hand we had left the constricts of virtual imprisonment under communism behind us and were able "in freier Luft den Atem leicht zu heben , oh welche Lust!" (to freely breathe again, oh what joy!) as the Prisoners' Chorus sang in Beethoven's sole opera "Fidelio" . On the other hand the gain of freedom had brought the loss of friends and a familiar, if difficult, way of life.

Chapter Fifty-Four

Every day hundreds of refugees had stepped off those trains connecting all four sectors of the city to seek asylum . All of them had to enter large refugee camps until the authorities had found places for them in West Germany. Berlin, being an enclave inside East Germany, could not possibly cope with the enormous influx. Papa had also registered us with such a camp, stating he had a brother in Essen; consequently that was the city he wanted to settle in. Fortunately, at least this time around, we did not have to live inside the camp. In a way it was fair that Uncle Fritz helped us. We, too, had helped him years earlier by introducing him to our dear Black Johanna and her wonderful sausages for his top drawer customers. However, after two or three weeks we were getting anxious to move on, yet there was no sign of us being flown out of Berlin. That's when our father's fighting spirit set in once more. He either rang or went to see the officer in charge as often as he could to make a nuisance of himself in order to speed up the next step of our journey. Despite his efforts, it took about four weeks before we were at last able to leave Berlin - for a refugee camp outside Hamburg!

Unlike during our arrival at Heiddorf in January 1945, we now had to live like proper refugees in a camp; cheek by jowl with masses of other people in a hall, having almost no privacy and certainly no peace! Sleeping was not easy, nor was it any fun sitting around in our tiny allotted living space with absolutely nothing to do all day, except to queue up for our bowl of soup at lunch time and our evening meal . Naturally, father could not put up with these conditions. Within a very short time indeed he had found a proper job in a machine manufacturing factory. He was in heaven! His boss had taken impressively to my father's skills and work ethic which were indeed beyond reproach. Unsurprisingly, it did not take long and his new boss asked him whether he would like to stay on for good. The factory owner did not have a son and heir and had been looking out for someone suitable to train as his successor for some time. His intention was to hand over the directorship of the factory on his retirement to our father.

Meanwhile they had plenty of time to teach Papa everything he still needed to learn but the factory owner had complete confidence in his abilities and eventual success. You can imagine how happy and enthusiastic our father was about this good stroke of fortune. He had liked his boss and his work place from the very beginning and could hardly believe his luck. So many years of struggle and strife and here was Fortuna smiling on him within a very short time of our arrival in Bergedorf near Hamburg, inside the "Golden West"! Life here was golden indeed and Papa could not wait to tell his wife and children about the wonderful about-turn of his life!

He had not counted on our timid but determined mother though! She was not having any of it! Papa had been a Civil Servant in Prussia and still had an entitlement for employment by the Post Office as a civil servant again. "Think of the good pension you will get! And here you have nothing but, perhaps empty promises. "It is too risky, Hugo. In the Civil Service you will have security for life!" Mother's father had been a station master all his life – a very respectable position in the large village of Peitschendorf in Masuren and a job for life! This was the world she had grown up in and this is what she had wanted for herself also. I knew Papa would cave in; he loved our mother immeasurably and could never do anything against her will.

Werner and I had loved the idea of staying on in Bergedorf. The thriving port of Hamburg was just around the corner and with it the excitement of a large Hanseatic City with lots of good schools, work opportunities and entertainment. We were really devastated and quite cross with our mother about her insistence on rejecting this fantastic opportunity. Who wants to go and live in the "Ruhrpot", the industrial area of Germany? Here it was green and pleasant, similar to our "home" in Heiddorf, only better, bigger and in the

West! We could not understand our parents' decision, but we were only the children and had to follow their lead.

Once the decision had been made to abandon Papa's dream, he went daily, sometimes twice daily, to the offices of the person in charge of the camp to ask when we would be released and allowed to go to Essen. He knew the more often he went there the more tired they would get of seeing him and would want to get him out of their hair. He had calculated correctly. After a week of pestering them we were given permission to leave the camp and move on to the next one – in our chosen destination of Essen. Once again our living quarters were in a large hall, together with a great many other families. As in Bergedorf we had no room of our own, back to a small space divided from the other families by simple room dividers. We slept on mattresses, no proper beds. Since we had almost no luggage we did not mind not having any other furniture. Meals were given to us in an adjoining dining room; no choice of food, of course. You were cattle and had to eat what you were given. Since we had very little money, we had no other chance of buying what we felt like eating. It was not exactly the start of our new life that we had envisaged, but we knew there would be an end to it some time, so we buckled down to our lot.

By this time it was the end of August or even early September. The new school year was about to begin. All the children of our camp had to go to the local school in Essen-Katernberg, this being one of the worst and poorest suburbs of the city.

In 1953 the city of Essen was synonymous with coal mining. Essen was the heart of the coal mining industry. Practically every man in the suburb of Katernberg was a miner. The buildings were covered with soot. Wherever you looked was ugliness and poverty, poor looking shops, bad roads, tasteless grub; above all else, miserable people. There was nothing redeeming about our situation, except that we had hope. Living on hope seemed to be what our life was all about – not for the first time either!

Sometime in early September my last year of basic schooling began. Since we lived temporarily in the suburb of Katernberg I had no choice of where I wanted to spend this important last year. I had already been informed I could no longer dream of entering any higher school education. In West Germany pupils were selected at the age of 11 for higher education. I had missed the selection process by three years! No one in the new government had expected a flood of hundreds of thousands of refugees entering West Germany. Therefore the Education Authorities were totally unprepared to accommodate the constant flood of refugee children. The authorities had also recognized the often great flaws in the East German teaching of history, foreign languages and, to a smaller degree, even German literature and the sciences. For a start, according to the East German curriculum, almost everything was invented by Russians. Our entire education was based on communist ideology. I remember hardly anything of English history, except the period of Cromwell. His anti monarchist stance suited their political outlook to a tee. We were by no means uneducated, far from it. But many aspects of our teachings had been distorted and did not match the standard of education taught in the West German schools. A very few refugee children were selected for re-education at special schools, of which there were very, very few. If I am not mistaken you could count them on one hand.

This revelation was a heart-breaking blow. Without higher schooling, a baccalaureate and university degree were out of the question. History was repeating itself in our family. Like in the case of my father, my dream of going to university was shattered overnight. Not only that dream. In addition I had to accept spending my last year of basic schooling with the less gifted pupils since the cream of my year had already been separated from them three years earlier. My life in the free West did not have an auspicious start! The school building was as uninteresting and plain looking as all the other buildings in the vicinity: blackened red brick; plain classrooms with ink stained shabby desks. There was no sports field attached to the school; thus sport was not taught. Attending school had only one advantage: it took me away from the noise and near squalor of the camp. Hopefully, I would, some of the time, learn something new and fascinating. However, that dream, too, would be shattered!

Within a day or two of starting our lessons it became obvious I was ahead in almost all subjects by approximately one year! My hand went up constantly as soon as our teachers had asked a question. Remember how fastidiously I had worked during my last year at Heiddorf? Now all that information was being taught all over again and I had never any problems digging into my memory bank for the answers. The teachers soon learned to ignore my raised hand. They must have realized pretty soon that "smart ass" Brigitte from the East was outclassing their own students and that this would not go down well with them. How right they were! After only a few days of lessons the sneering and bullying from some of the uncouth boys turned into something much more aggressive: as a newcomer and still friendless I had to walk home all by myself at the end of the school day. Their opportunity to go on the attack! I was spat at and had bricks thrown at me. Fortunately I have forgotten what dreadful names they called me; some of them I had probably never heard of before! This was, after all, the roughest area of Essen where upper "high German" was out of fashion at the best of times. Having found a perfect prey for their venomous jealousy they indulged in their aggression with all the passion they could muster. By the time I had reached the camp their spit was sticking all over me and I was bleeding where their stones had done their damage.

My father was livid, went straight away to the school to complain to the headmaster who assured him that these attacks would now never happen again. But, of course, they did. From then onwards either my father or some other man from the camp came to collect me every day until the attacks stopped. But the harm was done. I hated the school, never made friends with anyone and felt thoroughly isolated and unhappy.

It was not until the middle of January 1954 that my father had succeeded in finding work and a home of our own in another, much better part of town with a considerably better school. They gave me a report for the four and a half months of schooling I had received at Katernberg which I still have. Oddly enough my teachers had given me "Very Good" for my conduct but only "Good" for homework and lesson participation. All other subjects received a "Good" as well. How the teachers were able to assess my true ability during this difficult time beats me since my enthusiasm throughout was at a very low ebb indeed.

My new school at Essen-Schwanenbusch was much more agreeable. Within a very short time I made friends with a lovely girl called Helga who became very protective of me and stayed friends with me for many years. Not only did we spend every free minute during breaks together; Helga also invited me home where I soon became part of the family. Both her parents as well as her grandmother were extremely kind and friendly, having also had a tremendous sense of humour. There was never a dull or sad moment in that house which soon helped to put the horrors of Katernberg somewhat behind me.

Because we were in our final year, this ended much sooner than was normal; in fact my final report from this school was dated the 31st March 1954! Having been much happier there from the start, my work input improved accordingly. It was soon noted that I ranked among the best in the form. This meant I was one of a few girls who the headmaster had put forward to sit an entrance exam for the local school of commerce in the centre of town. It was a privately funded school. However, every year they were given a grant by the local council for three subsidized places for which Helga, myself and three other girls had been shortlisted.

To our never ending joy both Helga and I were among the successful three candidates. In addition, because I was a refugee and my father had only just started to find employment I was given a full bursary! I was as proud as punch! All we had to pay for were my books. I even walked to school to save my parents paying for the tram. It was also good exercise and I had Helga for company. After the first year her parents moved to their own house in one of the leafier suburbs of Essen. Whereas my parents were only just starting to build a better life for ourselves, Helga's parents were typical of the hard working locals. Like my father, Helga's father was a civil servant but he had been able to start saving for a house of his own years earlier. As a result they were already on the upwards spiral after only 9 years since the end of the war. We would get there, too, one day – now that we had the same chances.

Helga's move away to the outskirts left me quite inconsolable for a while. She was the only good friend I had made so far and we had become really close. Instead of seeing her daily after school I now began to travel out to their new home nearly every weekend. The area was quite countrified and, like during the years in Heiddorf, we started to wander off to the nearby woods in search of mushrooms and other goodies such as wild raspberries or blackberries . It was almost like the old days in the East and I felt so happy to have found this lovely family where laughter echoed through the house from morning till night. Helga had a younger brother, Volker. Her grandparents lived next door, making it a lively and happy family set-up, much needed for a displaced young person like myself to build her optimism on.

Chapter Fifty-Five

The experiences of the past eight to nine years were beginning to show in their toll on my health. While still in Heiddorf I had started to have rather bad stomach pains. They varied in severity. Because there was no doctor's surgery nearby, nothing got done about it. While living through the Katernberg troubles these pains flared up badly again. By the time my parents had found our new home and also a local surgery, I was diagnosed with severe inflammation of the stomach, caused by extended periods of nervous tension, in fact, years of it. My new doctor was a lovely man., He did not believe in mollycoddling my poor stomach by feeding it porridge and blancmange.

"Eat as much dark bread as you want. Pickled gherkins and herrings, too. In fact, the sharper the fare, the better! I'll put you on my famous "Rollkur"(rolling cure) and you will be much better soon. And don't forget: Lots of laughter! That is the very best medicine of all! Come back in four weeks' time!"

Three times a day I had to drink a full glass of vile medicine on an empty stomach, lying flat on my tummy for 15 minutes, followed by another 15 minutes on one side, then rolling onto the back and finally onto the other side. Luckily this was during the summer break before Helga and I started the new term at the commercial school. After the prescribed four weeks I was indeed much better. My doctor's "Rollkur" and the love and laughter at Helga's home had fixed me up.

Our new home was a flat on the third floor of an old apartment block in the Saarbruecker Strasse, a pleasant area near the Wasserturm (water tower). It had two bedrooms, a sitting room and a kitchen and lavatory. No bathroom! There was a public bath nearby where we went to keep clean. My brother got the 2nd small bedroom. My bed was a pull-out bed in the sitting room. Belonging only to myself! Over time the glamour of my own bed faded as I could never go to sleep before the rest of the family did. Both my parents worked and saved incredibly hard. In our own ways, so did Werner and I. My poor brother had to work on a building site completing his apprenticeship as the world's best bricklayer! To his credit, Werner was not the complaining type. On the contrary, he knew he was cut out for better things. Only for now he had to play by the rules. He was blessed with a wonderful dry sense of humour which made him a popular figure on site. Furthermore he also had a brilliant talent for picking up local dialects within a remarkably short time. All of which made him very popular with his colleagues and at further education evening classes. He knew how to play the game in this new world much better than I did. No one had to protect him from spit or flying bricks! If he was asked where he came from, he was never from Prussia, always from Essen; giving his reply in perfect "Ruhrpot" slang. Papa tried to copy his shrewd son, but with less success. When in later years Werner moved to Cologne he became the proudest citizen of Cologne almost within days, having mastered the Rhineland dialect almost as fast! Of the four of us he was the one who adapted the fastest to his new surroundings and his new homeland. There was no doubt that, in time, he would manage to make a success of a professional life and leave his bricklaying days behind him, which indeed he did. There was a lot of optimism in all work places owing to an unparalleled growth of the economy, something we were not used to from our experience in the East. The economic upswing was credited to an exceptionally competent Minister of Economics, Ludwig Erhard. Under his inspired leadership the economy continued to grow at a rapid pace. By 1961 unemployment in West Germany was so low that foreign unskilled workers from Turkey, Italy and Greece were recruited to satisfy the demand for labour. Everyone worked exceptionally hard and therefore began to enjoy a modest prosperity, including our own family.

I was 15 ½ years old by the time my two year course at the commercial school began. We learned typing, shorthand, commercial English and German. My first English lesson began straight away with a short letter consisting of the following:

"Dear Sirs,

Thank you for your letter dated ……..

Yours faithfully."

Both Helga and I liked our time there very much. I became pretty competent at typing and shorthand but only because I really did put a lot of effort into my work. By the end of the two year term we were told that a certain professional insurance company for the mining industry needed four or five typists for their pool. The school head recommended that Helga and I as well as several other girls should be considered for interviews. And once again, to our amazement, we actually landed our first job there without any problems! Helga was not in the same department as myself which was probably for the best as it avoided competition between us! The weekends at home became ever more trying for me. I missed not having a room of my own where I could withdraw with a good book and avoid having to watch silly football on our black and white TV, the pride and joy of our father and one of the outward signs that our lifestyle was improving – thanks to my father's hard work. He was working in the main repair workshop for all the cars and busses the Essen post offices were using; not the best paid job in the world, but with a good pension waiting in the wings, so important to our mother!

Meanwhile, no one else in the family thought of pensions; we were all at the beginning of our run-of-the-mill careers, which would, hopefully, lead us to more flourishing times. Both Werner and I earned a young adult's pay; consequently we paid our mother a certain sum every month for our food and keep. This was the custom in every family in those days; a very good one, too. We learned from the outset to be responsible and not to take our parents for granted. It never occurred to us to complain, on the contrary, we were proud to be able to contribute a certain share to the family income. My parents, more than most, had had extremely difficult lives. Now it was time to lessen their burden. Father did not want mother to go out and work any more . He felt it was his duty to look after her as best as he could. In return we all enjoyed a warm and disciplined family set up. Meals were steaming on the table with dependable regularity, our clothes were washed and ironed and a loving ear was always ready to listen to our concerns.

By now Aunt Ella and her family had also succeeded in leaving Heiddorf and had settled near Cologne. A great many Sundays they came to see us, since mother knew better than many how to bake good cakes! Their visits were always most welcome for my parents, who, being generous by nature, loved their company. All of them shared a passion for football. The television blared for hours. The sitting room was full of cigarette smoke (from the visitors!), loud cheers when goals were scored, lots of coffee and cakes were consumed – I could bear none of it. As often as was seemly I escaped to Helga's family and their cheerful bantering and laughter.

Gradually I found other ways of amusing myself, going for long walks or to the cinema with a friend from work or, best of all, to the local Museum of Art, the Folkwang Museum, which was well known throughout Germany for possessing a great many Impressionist paintings as well as a comprehensive collection of artwork from other periods. I discovered art was much more my line of interest; art and colours! During the week, mainly on Saturdays, I would go to the centre of town to the bigger shops merely to look at the different types of wool in the haberdashery department, letting my fingers lovingly stroke the reams on the shelf; feeling their different textures and admiring the wealth of colours. Knitting was still very much in vogue and I, too, knitted the odd jumper or cardigan for myself. It was fun and saved me money, too. The museum was quite a bit further out, but I did not mind walking both ways. After all, there was all afternoon to kill. Besides, I never got tired of sitting and staring at the Renoirs, the Manets and Monets and Rodin's sculpture The Thinker. A huge favourite of mine!

My escapes did not go unnoticed, especially by my disliked Aunt Ella who could not remark often enough : "I think we are not good enough for Brigitte!"

She was right there! Was it my fault I was made of different stuff? My parents and Werner could not be persuaded to get interested in books or art either, but they were my family and all of them had good characters. They also did not smoke. My parents did not really mind me pursuing my own interests. When we were alone on a Sunday I usually stayed at home, too, joining in the football frenzy, happy to watch my father and brother growing really close in their support for the sport. The happiest smiles on father's face were those when their favourite team would score a decisive goal! Sometimes even I could enjoy myself with them. Ours was a simple life; most people's lives were in those days, despite the modest economic improvements.

Chapter Fifty-Six

In the summer of 1957 I had my first paid holiday. Four years had gone by since our flight from Heiddorf. Mutti had kept contact with those relations who were still there, mainly with Trautl who had made our clothes for so many years. She had fallen in love with a local man, married and had children. She was happy with her life and had no reason to consider escaping. Before Mutti and Werner followed us to Berlin, our mother had asked Trautl to keep safe those of our belongings which were of some little value, like new sheets and towels, in case we could somehow get them over to the West at a later stage.

Mutti could not attempt the sale of any of our belongings prior to her leaving as that might have looked rather suspicious to the many spying eyes lurking everywhere. Trautl and Mutti had kept up a good correspondence throughout these past four years. We came to the conclusion that it would be quite safe for me to visit Heiddorf, since I had been a child when our parents had fled the country. Other youngsters had been to visit with no harm having come to them. If I went over for at least a week during my holidays I could try to sell as many of our belongings as possible. We had acquired all essentials for daily life not to need those in the East anymore, but it would still be good to have the extra cash! The exchange rate was rather poor but a little extra money was better than none. So off I went rather bravely! If I had not missed my friends so much, especially Ingetrud and Benita, I might not have gone quite so happily. They were a very strong pull. In fact, I could not wait to see them all again, even my classmates and dear Black Johanna and her grandchildren, last but not least Horst and Herr and Frau Rieck.

It was not until my parents began to discuss this forthcoming trip that I began to admit to myself how much I had been missing my old childhood friends. Here, in the West, we enjoyed free speech and the possibilities of constantly improving our lives economically. Apart from the friendship I had formed

250

with Helga, none of the other connections I had made could compare to those bonds of our early struggles. As a family we had made certain gains but had also incurred certain losses. Perhaps I had felt this more acutely than my parents or even my brother. Firstly I had lost the chance of higher education but I had also lost so many irreplaceable friends. Now I could see them all again and take up where we had left off four long years ago. With these hopes in mind I set off reasonably happy although with some fear lingering which I was trying hard not to acknowledge. All went well. I had all the correct papers for border control and stepped off the train in Neu Kaliss full of expectant excitement. Trautl and her family gave me a very warm welcome and I was truly thrilled to be back "home". The first two days were busy negotiating a price for those sale items with the various people who had shown interest in the purchase of them. Four years on there was still a shortage of everything and this was therefore a good opportunity for them to acquire something they needed at a reasonable price. I got rid of everything!

These transactions completed, I was dying to meet up with my old friends and give them the surprise of their lives. My first pull was towards the house of Ingetrud's parents. I had been there before but no one had been at home. This time I heard plenty of chatter coming from the kitchen. The door was wide open. Ingetrud's parents, her sister and Horst were talking jokingly about something. It was just as I had imagined it, warm and lively. My knock startled everyone into silence.

"Brigitte?" asked Frau Rieck. I had forgotten that I had changed and grown up quite a bit. No wonder there was a question mark in the air. They had heard of my arrival but seemed nonetheless astonished to see me.

"Where is Ingetrud?"

I could not wait for our reunion. For some unknown reason we had had no contact during the past four years since our escape and my excitement of seeing my old friend again had escalated into near frenzy.

"Ingetrud is not here. She is in Berlin, working. Has been these past two years."

I was dumbfounded. The disappointment rushed through my body like a bitter medicine, took possession of every fibre. Slowly it began to dawn on me how much time had passed. Ingetrud was a few years older than I. Of course, her life had not stood still either. How could I have been so silly to expect her to be there like in the olden days. I should have realized time does not stand still, not even in the communist world of my childhood.

"Sorry to disappoint you, Brigitte. But look, here is Horst. He has just come to see us and is about to leave. You are lucky. You have just caught him in time!"

said Frau Rieck. My eyes followed her hand and came to rest on the uniformed body of a man smiling invitingly at me.

"Oh, my God! He has joined the police! The hated Volkspolizei (People's Police)! How could he have done such a thing?" it raced through my shocked mind. His eyes were as handsome as ever. Not just his eyes. Now I was old enough to register his extraordinary good looks and they were directed towards me with obvious pleasure. A pleasure I wanted to return but could not. Everything was turning out so horribly wrong.

"This uniform! How could he?"

My disappointment must have been written all over my face for everyone stopped talking, giving me much colder looks than I could have imagined in my dimmest dreams. I began to wish I had never come. My legs seemed to turn into jelly. My heart beat furiously to combat the energy draining from my body. All my expectations were shattered. Seeing Horst again and looking so gorgeous made me realize instantly that I had always rather liked him, much more than I had wanted to admit to myself. Now he stood next to me with his eyes caressing me the way he had done years earlier. Yet, now, I knew at once it was too late. The uniform made it too late and forever impossible. I would never be happy to return and his uniform made it unthinkable for him to follow me to the West. Why had I never written to any of them? And why, oh why had I not realized that my heart had become rather fonder of Horst than my head had allowed me to believe.

In this one instant I had lost two of the people I had loved. Although I asked Frau Rieck to give Ingetrud my address, I knew she would never write. Indeed, she never did. Worlds separated us now. No, not worlds – the universe! Everyone looked at me differently. The affection of old was gone.

By fleeing I had deserted them, not the hated system. But THEM! Unlike us, they had started to come to terms with the communist government, hence the hated uniform! It took only seconds to register the situation and I mumbled some excuses for having to leave; I was expected for supper or some such reason. I mumbled a quick

"Auf Wiedersehen". "Auf Wiedersehen, Brigitte".

We smiled politely but knew very well we would never see one another again. It was obvious, I no longer belonged.

Horst offered to see me out. I felt he wanted to use this moment to be alone with me. My turning up so unexpectedly after four years of absence had caused confusion in all our minds, especially in ours. We suddenly realized what we had missed and how irretrievable lost time is. He said something to that effect. He was stationed several kilometres away in one of the larger villages and his next few days off were not for some time. We did not even touch one another. Both of us knew how hopeless and how sad our situation was. I so wanted him to hug me and give me my first kiss. Since this would have made matters only worse, we smiled melancholically at one another before I quickly turned away ordering my legs to walk away as fast as they could, away from the scene of my first bitter heart break. No one followed me.

Chapter Fifty-Seven

From time to time I had received the odd letter from my friend Gerda. Therefore she had known of my arrival. We had met up briefly before my visit to the Rieck's house. Although she lived only a few steps further down the road I could not bear to nip in and see her as I was too upset. Instead we met the following day. Nothing much had changed around her house which was reassuring. Gerda had grown into a rather nice looking girl. I remember we still got on fine once we had overcome the initial moments of slight estrangement. At least I still had Gerda as a friend with whom I could spend some of my remaining holiday.

My other good friend, Benita, was also no longer at "Findenwirunshier". The fate of Benita's parents had taken a very tragic turn, even shortly before Papa and I took our fateful train to Berlin. One very early morning a number of police men stood outside their manor house, arresting both parents under the pretext that Benita's father was an enemy of the state.

One of his employees must have denounced him for having succeeded in getting an industrial leather belt for his machinery; an essential tool for the working of the mill. Since this kind of product was impossible to purchase in the East, it was sufficient proof to the Party Herr Markurth had somehow smuggled it in from the West where he had several relations. He was marked as a serious economic criminal and his wife was arrested for complicity! All three children were taken into custody until a family in Ludwigslust, who were close friends of Benita's parents, took them into their family home. No one was prepared for this horrendous turn of events. The entire village was in shock for a long time. I believe it was Gerda, who told me in her letters that both parents went on trial and were given a two year sentence for their "heinous" crime against the interests of the socialist people's republic. Gerda's letters then stopped and I had no idea of the address of the protective family in Ludwigslust. Until my adventurous trip back to Heiddorf that was all the news I had about my lovely Markurth family. I had hoped to find out more during my return.

Benita's mother, my fairy godmother of old, had been released after one year's internment. There was no amnesty for Benita's father. While in prison, their entire property was seized and confiscated and taken over by the State. Of course, this had been the intention of the authorities all along. Private ownership of any kind was a thorn in the eyes of the communists. "Findenwirunshier" was a particularly large and prosperous farm and industrial mill. Therefore a reason had to be found sooner or later to "legitimately" confiscate this flourishing enterprise. We all knew the family had been sitting on a time bomb. Only no one wanted to openly admit to it.

Having had such wonderful memories of the family and the days spent roaming the farm and the mill with Benita, her brothers and their friends, their property was among the first places I visited after my arrival. The large wrought iron gate to the farm yard and the villa with the lovely garden beyond was closed. There was no sign of any activity although an empty trailer was standing under my beloved massive walnut tree. The second smaller house which had stood empty before was now a kindergarten; at least one useful change. The two large building blocks constituting the mill lay derelict. It was a deeply depressing sight to see this wonderful place barren and unproductive. What a difference between the two new German States! One stagnating and backward with its people still short of most of life's essentials – it was now the summer of 1957! - while the other was experiencing an economic miracle ("Wirtschaftswunder"). It did not take long for me to feel the drabness of life here. We had not had the easiest start of our new life in the "Golden West". Comparing it with what we had left behind I now had no doubt at all that we had been most fortunate to have made a safe escape.

For lack of something better to do I spent the rest of my spare time getting in touch with a few of my old class mates. Luckily, a dance had been arranged for Saturday night at the Oak Tree Pub. It was to take place in the same hall behind the pub where, usually on a Saturday night, they used to show a film. Latterly, there were dances a few times a year, giving the young of the area a chance to mix with the opposite sex! I went to the dance with two of my former school friends who assured me this was a very popular and fun event where lots of our old friends would be meeting up. They were right. One of the keenest dancers on the floor was, you might guess it: Hansl with the gypsy good looks! He looked rather handsome in his grown-up suit, swinging a different girl in his arms with every dance. There was no doubt, he had the command of the dance floor and he knew it! His movements were very assured and I had to admit he cut a very fine figure in these ordinary surroundings. The way he scanned the dance floor for new prey made it evident that none of the girls he had danced with so far had met with his satisfaction!

When I saw how competently the young people on the floor were displaying their dance skills I began to feel sorry I came for I had never before danced in my life and was dreading to be asked, even by some farmer's boy, let alone by the gypsy king! Fortunately he was busy sussing out the keen girls near the dance floor whereas my friends and I were stuck in some far away corner of the hall where we were not so easily noticed. Until, of course, one of our former class mates, a boy called Siegfried, came to ask my friend Karin for a dance! As he got close to us, he looked at me while he was directing Karin to the floor and stopped his stride in astonishment:

"Brigitte? Is that you?"

"Well, who do you think it is, silly!" Karin exclaimed, grinning with delight. My anonymity was broken. One or two other boys came up towards us and it did not take long for Hansl to stand in front of me, giving me his most seductive smile and asking:

"Where on earth have YOU sprung from? I thought you were in the West!"

As if no one had ever returned for a visit! Perhaps no one had in Heiddorf, since my presence created quite a stir in the hall. Everyone wanted to dance with me! If only they knew how clumsy I would be! There was nothing to it, I had to refuse and explain I had just come for the fun of it and for the music. Still, Hansl would not give up. After all, as the king of the dance floor he had never been refused before.

"It's not as hard as you think it is. I'm quite good at this. I will show you. Come on, don't be a spoil sport! This is a special evening for all of us. Come along!"

So along I went, if reluctantly. When I tell you that he never came to ask me again you will understand that my first dance lesson was not exactly a raving success! His loss was somebody else's gain though – Siegfried had clearly taken an instant fancy to me when he had asked Karin for a dance. Once we had somehow struggled through our first dance, he came back for every other one. He was very patient and a good instructor. In contrast to Hansl he was rather shy as well as patient; making me feel quite a bit more comfortable and relaxed. Slowly my tension dissolved and after a few attempts I had mastered it sufficiently not to constantly trample on his feet.

During our school days, Siegfried had been a withdrawn and colourless boy, also a refugee; not outstanding in any particular way. Unlike the brash Hansl, he never sent love notes flying across the classroom. I did not even remember any conversations with him back then. Now his manner was still rather shy yet by no means diffident. I admired his courage to continue teaching me when, evidently, I was no dancing queen. .

By the end of the evening he plucked up courage and asked me whether he could meet up with me the following afternoon (a Sunday). I said yes, having nothing better to do after lunch-time with Trautl and her family. Like so many summers in the fifties, it was hot and sunny. The cornfields looked splendid, a beautiful shade of maize yellow. Not long and the wheat would be harvested. We walked through several fields, then alongside the river towards the forest where Papa and I had spent so many seasons, he digging out tree stumps, me getting him his lunch and picking mushrooms and raspberries and listening to the echo of his voice. I told Siegfried of these lovely memories and he told me how much everyone had missed me during the final year at school; my constant chatter and my cheeky remarks and laughter or my self- deprecating angry conversations I used to have with myself, totally absorbed in my own telling off and oblivious to my class mates who were raising their eyes to heaven and thinking: "Here she goes again!" Somehow I always managed to draw attention to myself without really meaning to. I remember well that I was always acting and fooling around with girls as well as the boys despite my deep seated shyness. Perhaps others saw me as a bit of a tomboy, lively and bright, always ready to burst into a smile. In short, I was popular. There was a definite gap in the class room without me, so Siegfried said. I had never given it a thought how the class would react to my absence. So it was rather flattering to hear that they had missed me.

We chatted very animatedly, telling one another about the four years we had spent apart. It was enjoyable hearing what I had missed since my sudden disappearance. Strange how people and situations can change over time. This boy had never interested me during the seven years we had spent together in the same classroom. Now he was entertaining me quite acceptably, which really did surprise me. However, my even bigger surprise was our saying good-bye! Before I knew it he had grabbed me by my shoulders, just as I was attempting to turn away from him, and planted a kiss on my unlooked for lips. Had I been too friendly and naïve, just like in the olden days? Obviously I had! His tongue was trying to mess around with my reluctant mouth. Why on earth had everyone been saying that kissing was such a sweet and wonderful thing? Disgusting was a more appropriate description for me. Why had I not seen this coming? I could have spared myself this unpleasant experience. I had agreed going for a walk with him again the following day, but now my mind was made up: "Get away! And fast!" I thought. He should be so lucky to have another such chance! Would it have felt like that with Horst? No, I did not want to believe that. But since I would never see Horst again I would never be able to have an answer to this question. O my God! Was young romance always as complicated and disappointing as this?

I walked home to Trautl as fast as it looked decent. At her home, in the company of her sweet little boys and her husband, life was normal and comforting. I hoped Trautl would not notice my inner turmoil. My return journey "home" was rapidly turning into a dramatic disappointment on several levels. Apart from the successful sale of our belongings, nothing had quite turned out as I had hoped – least of all my very first kiss! Who will be the one to kiss me again? And will he be the right one? Oh dear! I do hope so! But not for a while, not for quite a considerable while! I needed to get over this disturbing experience first.

Chapter Fifty-Eight

When Papa and I had left Heiddorf four years earlier, the enormity of our sudden escape with only minutes to spare and leaving Mutti and Werner behind had erased all superfluous emotions. We were both in a state of extreme shock but able to focus with total concentration on doing what was necessary. Like automatons, we did what had to be done, trying to avoid emotions which might otherwise overwhelm us. No one saw us off at the station and I do not remember looking back in anguish either.

My second departure from Heiddorf turned out to be quite similar. Trautl did come to wave me off, but I was just as glad to leave the place as I had been the first time around. The village of my childhood had moved on and so had I. The past cannot be recaptured. That was something I had learned, painful though this lesson was.

Back home in Essen life continued much as before – very ordinarily. I quite liked my job at the office and got on well with the other girls in the typing pool. Once every summer the company arranged for outings to special beauty spots in the countryside. At Christmas they gave the staff a jolly party. These events were almost the only social activities of any significance, apart from the odd cinema trip and visits to Helga's house at weekends. You could say life was indeed rather uneventful.

My second summer holidays since the start of my employment was somewhat more interesting; I visited my Aunt Elisabeth in Berlin. She was living close to Onkel Fritz's new establishment. He had given up the delicatessen and had moved a huge step upwards, having had a five story house built for himself. The ground floor was occupied by a pub, in the basement was a restaurant with a dance floor! Uncle Fritz and Tina lived on the first floor. The other two floors were rented out. He had done very well for himself. Our aunt, his sister, was living on her own. Her only son had run away to Australia and she was feeling his absence badly. Therefore we were pleased to find out how much we had in common and how well we were getting on. She was very interested in the arts and had been the first person to create a small private theatre in Berlin after the capitulation in 1945. Most of her friends were artists and I thoroughly enjoyed meeting them, going to the theatre and the opera with her, all new experiences for me. She was working full-time which meant I had to amuse myself quite often on my own, but this did not bother me. There was so much to explore in Germany's former capital city.

One day Tante Bine (her nickname) suggested that I travel to Dahlem where the National Picture Gallery was housed. This I did. As I had lots of time I decided not to be selective but to look at every painting exhibited there. Being midweek there were few visitors. At one stage it seemed as if I was the only person there, my footsteps echoing as I went from room to room. It felt almost eerie until, upon standing in another archway leading to yet another empty room, I noticed someone else in the archway opposite. At the same time my attention was drawn instantly to a painting hanging on the left wall of the room. The man depicted in it had such a powerful pull that I did not give the other person a second glance but steered towards this extraordinary painting of a dark, almost sinister looking man wearing a golden helmet. What a fabulous painting this was! As I rushed towards it I sensed that the person from the opposite archway was heading in precisely the same direction. It seemed we were both drawn to the picture as if by magic, by a mysterious power of the piercing eyes of the man depicted. As I had reached the painting the figure walking towards it arrived literally at the same instant. Turning to my right to look at him (I sensed it was a man) there stood the most handsome young man wearing a French Army uniform! He looked as confused as I was, not knowing whether to stare at me or at the painting! I have to admit I felt the same. It was a most uncanny meeting. We had both been drawn towards this point by the power of the man depicted on the canvass. Yet when we had arrived there we had more time for looking at each other than for studying the painting!

He addressed me in French which I did not understand, then trying it in English which I understood a little. Apparently he was stationed in Amsterdam and had just been given two days' leave. Before being conscripted he had studied art and had always loved Rembrandt's work. He had known that this painting " The Man with the Golden Helmet " was hanging in Dahlem and had decided to make the trip to Berlin exclusively to see it "in the flesh"! Little did he know he was also going to meet an attractive girl who had stumbled on this painting by chance at the very moment he had discovered it. We were as powerfully attracted to one another as we had been to the painting!

After explaining the painting to me he invited me for a cup of coffee. Now that he had seen what he had come for he no longer had any interest at anything else in the museum – and neither did I!
Was this going to be the young man to give me that second kiss I had been waiting for since the disastrous first one? We spent a lot of time over coffee and ice-cream, struggling to get to know one another with my broken English. We decided that we would meet at the same place again the following day and look at more exhibits together. I could barely sleep that night with excitement having told my aunt about this amazing encounter. Luckily she did encourage me to meet my mystery Frenchman again. He was indeed waiting for me at the appointed time. Sadly, since we both had a rather poor command of English we had tremendous trouble having meaningful conversations. He had to take the train back to Amsterdam that same afternoon and somehow we

both knew that we would not be able to continue our little adventure. He told me how much he had enjoyed meeting me and kissed me on both cheeks – unfortunately nowhere else! This time I sat like a heap of sadness on the seat of my tram, staring out of the window through tearful eyes. Why did life have to be so disappointing and painful for me? Or was this normal for naïve young girls? Was I ever going to fall in love properly with a suitable young man who would feel the same or more for me as I did for him? That night Tante Bine had a lot of comforting to do!

Chapter Fifty-Nine

Life in Essen seemed even more drab after my stay in Berlin – despite the heartache I had suffered there. Months turned into years without anything remarkable taking place. I was beginning to get bored and needed a new challenge. I had stayed in my job for three years with no prospect of any real advancement. When you were in the typing pool you remained in the typing pool. Only the top boss had a secretary of his own and she showed no sign of leaving or being ousted. The only way I could progress a little further, as I saw it, was to improve my poor English learned at the commercial school. The popular way this was achieved in those days was to take a job as an au pair girl in England. At that time English families were regularly advertising in German newspapers for suitable girls. In this way I found a family in London who interviewed me at the end of a holiday trip to Germany . I was nearly 21 years old; time for me to wean myself from my family and become independent, while at the same time attempting to educate myself a little more.

Mr. & Mrs. Cohen lived in North London, in Kilburn. They had two sons. They were Jewish but regularly holidayed in Germany. They seemed very friendly. I had no worries accepting their offer to live and work with them. My afternoons would be free to do with as I liked. I could attend classes and study English for the Lower Cambridge Examination, the first of two language certificates obtainable. I had never been separated from my family before. Now I was going to live abroad and in a world city! My excitement turned out to be justified - the Cohen family were very nice to me and treated me like another family member. For the first time in my life I had a room entirely to myself which was a huge thrill.

My hosts were not the only people I knew in England. While I had attended the Commercial School in Essen our English teacher had arranged for some of us to start a correspondence with a pen friend in England for the advancement of our English but also for connecting with boys and girls of our own age which might lead to personal friendships. Germany and England having been at war for so long meant we were encouraged and helped to establish warmer relationships with our neighbours for the future. Werner and I had been contemplating for years how we could succeed in stretching out to the British soldiers who were stationed in and around Essen and who were never seen mixing with the locals. They were only seen in groups, never just one or two. They never looked very happy when seen in the streets of Essen. What if we were to invite them to our house for coffee and cake in the afternoon? We liked that idea but neither of us ever felt relaxed enough to approach them just like that. Besides, my English was almost nonexistent and Werner did not have any grasp of the language at all. The intentions were there and were good, but it was too difficult to transfer them into reality. It was much easier to try and strike up a friendship by pen. The girl my teacher had chosen for me was somewhat older and already in employment as a secretary. Her name was Jill. She lived with her parents in Bexley Heath in Kent.

Jill, her brother and her boyfriend were members of a youth club which encouraged their members to take up friendships by letter with boys and girls of a similar age in European countries, especially in Germany. Once a year their team leaders would take their members on a camping trip abroad and one such visit to Germany had apparently been a particular success. The idea of seeking pen friends in Germany was the result of this exceptionally enjoyable holiday somewhere in the northern parts of Germany.

In her letters Jill described her home life, told me about her work in the big metropolis of London, what her interests were and her dreams for the future. Similarly I attempted to tell her as much as my poor English permitted about my own life and aspirations. I studied her letters avidly, learning the new words by heart and was hugely proud when I was able to understand the gist of what she was telling me. In her reply to my short letters, Jill returned them with her corrections, which I had asked her to do. Otherwise, I explained to her, I would not really benefit enough from our correspondence. She was always so polite about my efforts and kept apologizing for her corrections as if I minded them! On the contrary, we Germans are very direct and recognize the difference between constructive or mean and hurtful criticism. I had to reassure Jill constantly that I was not hurt in the slightest about the many red pencil markings in my letters but actually grateful for them! So we both learned very quickly about our different national characteristics. By the following summer our friendship had blossomed in a very reassuring and exciting way. When she told me that her club was returning once more to Herford for a week's stay at a local youth club I suggested travellingly up for the day so that we could finally meet face to face. Her reply was even better than expected. Her lady team leader was so pleased about the success of our friendship that she suggested I come and join them for the entire stay; an invitation I was delighted to accept.

It could have been a disaster but turned out to be hugely successful. Jill and I were very different in looks. She tall, slender and soft spoken; me tiny, slender but bubbly and unafraid to practise my poor English in my, no doubt, rather louder German sounding voice. But that did not seem to make any difference to these polite and quietly spoken youngsters. Jill and I took to one another at first sight. The other group members were all very friendly, too and treated me as one of their own kind. For the first time in my life I felt an equal . As a refugee in my own country I always felt like an unwelcome intruder, whether this was in the East or in the West.

Not so with these friendly people from England. They accepted me within a very short time which felt like a huge compliment and made me relaxed and very happy right from the start. Every day was filled with surprises, trips to surrounding beauty spots, to Hameln, the town where the story of the Pied Piper of Hamlin originated; to the Harz mountains, to lakes and swimming baths and all this in wonderful summer weather. We even got into the local newspaper since groups of foreign visitors were still a rarity in those days.

As I had blended in so well with her charges, the team leader allowed me to take Jill and her boy-friend Roy home to Essen towards the end of my week. I cannot remember how we accommodated them for the night; but I do remember the midday meal my mother had prepared for all of us, a typical German dish called "Rolladen". You cut an inferior type of beefsteak into thin slices, fill them with diced pickled cucumber and goodness knows what else, roll it up, tie it with fine string and fry the meat and then stew it in thickened vegetable stock. It was the kind of dish we poor Germans served up for a Sunday lunch, together with boiled potatoes and overcooked vegetables. Everyone overcooked the vegetables in those days – all over Europe.

Red meat has never been my forte and "Rolladen" were certainly not my favourite dish. But it was the dish my mother always produced on special occasions and for special guests. Having Jill and Roy visit us meant to her the King and Queen of England were coming to dine! Only the King (in this case Roy) could not bear to swallow any of her food! I believe not even the potatoes! I was reminded of the scenes in Heiddorf years and years earlier when I sat in front of my dish of spinach unable to get it into my mouth despite the rumbling noises of my stomach! Jill made a valiant effort, so did I, but poor Roy shunted his meat around the plate from one end to the other without the food ever getting less! However, Jill's empty plate made up for the meal my poor mother had to throw away, something we never ever did in our home. We had starved too much and for too long to disrespect food to that extent. You ate what was served up whether you liked it or not. There was a jelly for pudding, not exactly enough to satisfy a strong young man like Roy who was, however, as skinny as a rake.

After the two of them had left for Herford by train to rejoin their group, we decided he was surely so skinny because he was a very fussy eater. Nothing to do with Mutti's cooking, of course! I was rather relieved she accepted this conclusion by the rest of us, as I could not bear to have her upset when she had spent hours and a considerable amount of money producing this meal for us. Fortunately, my friendship with Jill survived this embarrassing incident which meant I had another family to go and visit during my time as an au-pair in fabulous London.

Like so many Jewish people my host family lived in Kilburn, an uninspiring suburb north of the city centre. Every house in every street seemed to look the same. If you did not know the number of your house you could easily enter a neighbour's by mistake. In fact, the street next to yours might have precisely the same architecture, row on row of houses all looking identical. The front door might be painted a different colour to the one next door, or there might be some different curtains to identify your house by. On the whole though it was a confusing street landscape and very different from anything I had seen at home.

The inside of the houses looked much the same. There was a fire place in each sitting room, a very appealing feature and something I had never come across in Germany. There, in the northern countryside where I had lived, fireplaces were replaced by rather magnificent high and freestanding tiled stoves. A bench surrounded these stoves, inviting you to warm your back . I remember my grandparents in Prussia having had such a wonderful stove; Herr and Frau Rose had also owned one. As a special treat grandmother as well as Frau Rose would bake apples for us inside a little oven built into the stoves. These were very cosy evening gatherings similar to the cosiness of an open fire In England.

Fireplaces were not the only different way to furnish and heat a room. Sofas and armchairs seemed to have a different shape and colour scheme and the windows, too, were dressed differently. I recall writing home to my parents telling them that even the light switches weren't the same. I really felt to be in a foreign land which, however, was precisely what I had wanted to experience! The only thing I really missed from home was my eiderdown! I could never get warm enough under blankets and had to resort to having a hot water bottle close to me every night – a habit I have not lost to this very day!
As I have said earlier, Mr. & Mrs. Cohen were a very pleasant couple to work for and live with. They never once made me feel uncomfortable. Even their boys were polite and cheerful and I remember enjoying our mealtimes in particular. From the start they tried to involve me in conversation and helped me with my faulty English. The atmosphere was always relaxed and friendly with lots of laughter abounding. They never once gave me the impression that they had any anti-German feelings towards me; a particularly pleasant circumstance since part of the reason I had chosen a Jewish family was to attempt to make up in a small way for the crimes committed in Nazi Germany against their people. Surprisingly, there was no need at all to make any such effort. Mrs. Cohen never overworked me either as there was a cleaning lady coming in regularly. I had every afternoon off, giving me plenty of time for school and study. Consequently my English improved rapidly.

At school I met lots of other au-pair girls. They and Jill and her family formed my social circle. All au-pairs were paid pocket money only, so we had to entertain ourselves cheaply – mostly travelling into the centre of town. Oxford and Regent Street were our main haunts where we window shopped. Other points of interest were the many fascinating galleries and museums London has to offer – free of charge! Sometimes I would queue up for inexpensive tickets at the Royal Festival Hall. If it was a classical music concert one could try to get tickets for seats behind the orchestra. The acoustics weren't brilliant in this area; though being a beginner I did not even notice these finer subtleties of sound. I had access to a new world of music, that was all that mattered to me. From behind the orchestra one was able to watch the facial expressions of the conductor; definitely an added bonus to the musical experience. Sometimes I went alone, often with my friend Ursula. I remember attending a concert evening with Ella Fitzgerald and also with Louis Armstrong. Jazz was very popular in those days and these two stars were superstars at the height of their careers. We never went out for meals. Our meagre resources did not stretch to such luxuries. Food, other than in top restaurants, was not good anyhow. So we rather spent our money on the cultural events London provided like no other city in the world. I was nearly 21 years old and needed to make up for having lived in a cultural wilderness up till then. This was an exciting and happy time for me, my mental horizons widening with every day. Ursula and I spent many afternoons together, often just in our homes to save money for the weekend adventures, listening to music and talking, talking, talking…. drinking tea and eating biscuits and feeling thoroughly worldly wise and sophisticated! And, yes, happy.

Except for one day: my 21st birthday! It fell on a weekday when I should have worked in the morning but Mrs. Cohen gave me the whole day off. I had managed to book myself a ticket for the hottest musical in town – "My Fair Lady". Julie Andrews was in the title role and one of Ursula's friends was a chorus dancer. My seat was right up under the roof; you could barely see what was happening on the stage yet the music was divine. The entire production was enthralling and I would have been the happiest girl in the world had I not been alone on this special day in my life. Not even the most popular show in the world could make up for the loneliness I felt that day. I remember crying my eyes out once I was home and in my bed. On such a day you want to be with the people you love, your family at home, even if this meant being in boring old Essen! I could not even speak to them on the phone since my parents did not own one. Telephones were still a real luxury only the well-to-do could afford. So now I was a proper grown up young woman, but a deeply unhappy one and lonely.

Fortunately things looked up again the very next morning – there were duties to perform, breakfast to prepare and a happy face to be shown to Mrs. Cohen and her family. Depression only festers when you have nothing to do with yourself. Day one of my legal adult life was filled with plenty for me to do, home work to be done for school, Ursula to be told how much I had enjoyed the show and a long and cheerful sounding letter to be written to Mutti at home. There is nothing like a little pretence to put you back into a good frame of mind, an adult frame of mind. I was beginning to learn a lot about life and that a little sadness can also be a good lesson.

As a family we had experienced plenty of sadness, especially in those early war and post war years. Back then though my brother and I had our mother to cling to, had each other, had love in our lives if not much else. Arms would fold around me for comfort and brown eyes lovingly look into mine. And the world was a good place to be in, even on an empty stomach. Mutti had always given me strength;

Now I had to find it in myself. A painful realisation. A harsh lesson for the future, but an essential one that every young person has to learn sooner or later.

This was not the only painful experience I made that winter. Sadly, by now, I had given up visiting Jill's lovely family in Kent. The reason? Jill's younger brother! David and I had already struck up a bit of a friendship during our mutual holiday in the youth hostel in Herford. He had a lovely smile and a good sense of humour, very appealing qualities. I liked him and thought nothing of him taking photographs of me when our week was drawing to an end. I felt we had been good buddies, no more, no less. I continued to look upon him as a good friend once we met up again at his parents' house. David, however, I began to realize, had other ideas. As much as I still liked him I could not, sadly, share these other ideas with him and slowly, but surely, the situation became such that I had to be frank about my feelings – and probably broke his heart. Needless to say, this affected my relationship with Jill as well as with her parents. They still kept inviting me but I felt ill at ease and gradually made my visits less frequent before stopping them altogether. It was best for everyone. But the sadness of this development added to my feelings of occasional loneliness.

However, with the onset of spring new life and feelings sprang up all around us and not merely in the garden! I had made more friends through school, thus developing a vivid and enjoyable social life with trips to Cambridge and Windsor and even the odd club in Soho! London looked fabulous in spring time. Many streets had avenues of blossoming cherry trees. In the suburbs many front gardens looked colourful with daffodils and tulips – a garden city had sprung up. Whereas I had experienced the infamous yellow fog two or three times that winter and quite miserable grey and wet winter days, now the city basked in sunshine and masses of pink or white blossom, adding a lightness of timbre in total contrast to the previous months. I loved London!

My increased command of the language as well as my circle of friends doubled my confidence and my enjoyment of London. Ursula who worked for a family in Hampstead persuaded me to change jobs with a family nearer to hers. I had no real reason for leaving the Cohens; they had always been very good to me. Yet the glamour of the large properties in well-to-do Hampstead was rather tempting. And I made the break.

My new family lived in one such grand looking monstrosity, with pillars on either side of the main door as well as figures of stone lions next to them. Needless to say, once I was in their employment, I wasn't allowed to walk through those doors anymore but had to enter the house by a side door – a tradesmen's entrance! I had been interviewed for the job by their housekeeper, a lovely small woman with a Scottish accent to whom I took immediately – and she to me. Had I been interviewed by the "lady" of the house, I doubt I would have agreed working for her. My new employers were also Jewish, but not the lovely paternal type like Mr. & Mrs. Cohen; rather the opposite: uncultured, aloof, condescending, dull and very, very rich! The Cohen family had treated me as one of their own; in this house I was most definitely a servant. That realisation came as a huge shock to my naivety. However, perhaps fate had sent me here in order to learn the difference. If warm hearted and caring Penelope R. had not been the immediate person I spent most of my working hours with, I would have left straight away, once I had met the rest of the family. She, however, persuaded me to give it time. Her husband was the chauffeur and they were a truly warm and wonderful couple.

Still, the decision to stay came at a price. I had to serve my employers for breakfast, rather like the downstairs staff used to have to do in the days of the Victorians to their employers upstairs. This was not too bad while they were alone during the week. However, at weekends all the other family members came regularly for Sunday lunch. Some of them made it quite clear they were going to punish me for the crimes committed by the Nazis. Served me right for leaving my previous family! Although I was very upset and hurt by the treatment of punishing me for atrocities I had not committed nor fully known about at that time, I decided to stick it out to see whether I could not win them over in time. When, however, their stupid spoiled 18 or 19 year old son tried to grab me and pull me onto his bed on several occasions , I had enough and took the consequences I should have taken from the start.

By the time I handed in my notice it was late summer and I had taken my Lower Cambridge Certificate with very good grades. Therefore, time to go home. I had also taught myself shorthand for the English language, using the German shorthand abbreviations during my many hours of leisure, which I preferred to spend in the kitchen with dear Mrs. R.. All in all it had been a successful and enlightening year, notwithstanding the unpleasantness of the last few months. I returned home with my head held high, full of memories but with empty pockets! However, there was still my bed at home where I was always welcome.

Chapter Sixty

My parents were more than delighted to have me back home. I returned a year older and quite a lot more elegantly dressed, bringing a whiff of the big wide world into our modest home. Quite how I had managed to add to my wardrobe I no longer know precisely, but some of it I had bought in second hand clothes shops. There were a great many rich people living in Hampstead. They usually sold their unwanted clothes to shops rather than giving them away to charities.

My new image may have helped me to get a good job rather more quickly after my return home. It was as a bi-lingual secretary in the Export Department of Karstadt, one of Germany's largest department store chains. My year abroad had been a good investment after all and my father was no longer cross with me for having defied him.

I loved my new working environment and my boss seemed satisfied with my work. But I wasn't! I felt my English was still not good enough. Therefore, a few months after having started my work at Karstadt, I was off again – to London once more! Fortunately not as an au-pair this time.

In the sixties no foreigner was allowed to enter Great Britain for longer than a holiday or he or she had to produce a work permit on entry. These permits were rather difficult to get, except if a future employer could prove that they were giving a young person work and a home as an au-pair. There was one exception most girls found out about while in such employment in London: a world famous book shop in the West End of London. There you could work full-time while providing your own accommodation somewhere cheap. The only criteria was that you had to apply to the book shop for work from your home country, which I did.

I was quite encouraged to go ahead with this plan by Inge, a girl my age who visited us unexpectedly at Karstadt one day. She was the person whose job I had taken on when she had left for employment in London. She rented a small one- room flat in Swiss Cottage which she invited me to share with her if I succeeded in getting a job at the book shop. To my utter surprise and delight I did! What a thrill it was to be back in my favourite city with one tiny notch up the work ladder, being no longer in domestic employment but having my independence. Inge and I got on like a house on fire. Both of us left early in the morning to join the hundreds of thousands of workers thronging through the London Underground system towards their office or place of work.

My job in the bookshop was in their library department. I was responsible for completing book orders which had been placed by public libraries from all over England. For this purpose I was assigned a book searcher who had to search for the books in the main shop – a horrendous task! There was no cataloguing system of any kind throughout this vast empire. Books were lying piled high on tables, not sorted either by subject matter or author. How these youngsters ever found any book on their list always remained a mystery to me and I admired them hugely. Their task was made even harder by the fact that no one was ever allowed to speak to anyone, either in the library or the shop. It was not unusual for my brave book searchers to be sacked on the spot if they were seen or heard by the lady book shop owner to speak to another assistant asking for help in their search. Now I realized why it had been so easy to get a job in this place – the turnover of employees was incredible. It was the most archaic and exploitive work place in London – I was so glad to have landed in the library department rather than in the shop where I would not have lasted longer than a day – outspoken as I was. Not ever to be allowed to talk to anyone even if it was in order to do my job properly would have been sheer hell for me. In fact, unacceptable.

Fortunately we were completely separate from the shop in another building where the owner never turned up! However, we did have a manager who had been trained to obey company rules over many years. He always wore the same shiny black suit. His salary was probably not much higher than our starvation pay. He always wore a fierce but frightened expression on his face. We knew he was terrified of losing his job if he did not keep us in total silence. I soon nicknamed him "The wolf" but none of us young folk from all over Europe were actually truly scared of him. Rather we felt sorry for the poor chap who had probably a wife and children to feed. And in a way, out of sheer pity, we all respected him for putting up with the situation.

My work suited me admirably. I had always loved books and to work with them and get my orders out to the libraries as soon as possible was a satisfying challenge. Not long and I was getting compliments from several libraries on my efficiency which they had not been used to before! As a result I was soon able to take liberties with the wolf that no one else would have dared to. I managed to persuade him to let us listen to soft music as background noise, arguing that some scientists had come to the conclusion even cows gave more milk if soft music was played in their stables during the winter months! With the classical music evaporating gently into the room everyone's mood improved visibly. Even the wolf's face brightened and his general demeanour softened. Sometimes he even spoke to us in a friendly manner with a flicker of a smile crossing his face. Although all my colleagues became considerably more relaxed, almost playful in the way they sat at their desk studying their lists and reading their letters or talking to their book searchers, their output increased rather than lessened with this change in our surroundings. What a difference the introduction of music did to our lives! It was by far the best contribution I felt I had made to my new place of work. A little daring mixed with a little bit of charm can work wonders! I loved my job despite the bad atmosphere in the main shop and the appallingly poor pay. Often I had to cheat on the underground, not buying a ticket and trying to slip through the exit unnoticed by the one guard who was taking the tickets from the travellers. Later on they built the machines into which the passengers have to enter their tickets on exit. A shrewd decision – cheating was quite common in those days, especially by us impoverished young foreigners!

I bought my lunch in the Soho market not far from the shop, usually carrots and Cheddar cheese with a soggy roll – I lost a lot of weight during those months of liberty in London. My two best and steady friends at the library were an English girl called Judith and a Finnish boy called Per from up north. He was a Lap with lovely almond shaped eyes who always smiled. He was quite clearly a little bit in love with me – bless him!

Inge was a fun loving and funny girl. She made friends very easily, was intelligent and enterprising and the two of us had a great time sharing the small basement flat. Well, it so happens that we were not alone in there, although we never actually saw the other occupants but saw the damage they

272

had done to our food when we got home in the evening! We had no proper furniture in the so-called kitchen and had to leave our simple and scarce foodstuff lying openly on a shelf. Easy pickings for our uninvited guests!

The alternative was to hang our salami sausage as high up the shelf unit as possible, dangling from a string. How naïve we were about the skill of mice! Or were they rats we had to share our existence with? A piece of salami sausage was quite a feast for us as well, so we could not allow those thieves to get away with their daily burglary and had to invest in a box with a tightly fitting lid. We never actually saw these brutes but their droppings were proof enough that our victory was only shallow – our home was still under occupation! Only now they were surely more hungry while we had some supper to enjoy!

Our somewhat seedy living conditions did not bother us. It was all part of the London scene in the early sixties for a lot of working people and especially young foreigners who had to get by without any financial help from home, as we did. We just laughed about our bohemian life style – we were young and life was great.

Especially once my gorgeous Spanish admirer had turned up on the scene! How we had met I cannot remember anymore: in a coffee bar? At evening classes? Or through Inge's circle of friends? How we met was unimportant – what mattered was that we did! Manuel was incredibly good looking with brunette (not black) curly hair and beguiling eyes. He was well educated, very keen on literature. His favourite Spanish author was Frederico Garcia Lorca who was best known as a poet. Manuel used to read his poems regularly to me even though I did not speak or understand any Spanish. But when you are in love (and I considered myself to be so at last!) listening to a passionate recital of love poems in any language by the man you adore is the most intoxicating feeling in the world!

Of course, you don't just listen – you snuggle up into his arms and surrender yourself to his mesmerising voice. Not only could he recite like a professional actor, he also sang! Often, on warm summer evenings, he would suddenly burst into song accompanied by his guitar outside our open window, serenading me as well as Inge, if she was about, with such entrancing charm as if singing Spanish love songs outside a basement window in Swiss Cottage was the most natural way to wow your girl! What girl would not have fallen head over heels in love, particularly when she had waited for this to happen for such a very long time? After what seemed like an eternity (but actually was only two or three weeks) he eventually gave me my long awaited kiss of love when your entire body trembles, your legs cave in and the two of you fall down into a heap of passion on the floor – you drown, drown, dissolve into ecstasy. Until Inge walks into the room! As if struck by thunder our aroused bodies freeze into stone statues. We stare incredulously at her and I hate her momentarily for bringing us thus back into reality – an alien reality from which, for a very brief encounter, we had escaped from into a heavenly realm.

"What is going on here?!"

"Never you mind, you spoil sport!" I sputtered with anger yet also with embarrassment. Of course, she had been no such thing. Unbeknown to her she took the form of an angel who disturbed us just in the nick of time or else..... Goodness knows where this kiss could have led us to!
Unfortunately it was our first and almost the last one. Manuel's father was about to come to London to visit. I had been warned that my hot blooded Spaniard would not be able to see me while father was with him. When suddenly he turned up all the same after only two days of absence, fear began to grip me.

"Why are you here? You said you couldn't come."

"True, but I missed you. I quickly slipped away just to give you another hug!"

He kissed me gently and hugged me the way parting couples do on station platforms. No one speaks much or nothing at all and everyone knows it may be a final good-bye. With a jolt he released me and without saying anything more dashed out of the room and up the stairs. Totally perplexed I ran after him. Half-way up the stairs to the ground floor he stopped to look at me with an anguished expression and it dawned on me: he had come to say farewell for ever! He must have told his father about me and father made him stop the relationship once and for all before any harm was done. Manual had told me he wanted to go into the diplomatic service, starting in Hong Kong. He was in London to perfect his English. For such a distinguished career his father had uncompromising ideas of a suitable future wife. An unconnected German girl, probably poor and protestant, had definitely not been under consideration. Manuel had been brought up to be an obedient son, much too well mannered to defy his father. And he was probably right in obeying him. Although, at the time, I did not see it that way. Whether I was right in my assumption I never found out. However, that is how I explained the situation to myself since my confidence was still very much that of the poor refugee girl. I was always still blaming myself for everything negative which happened to my life. My spirit was broken, so was my heart. Really truly broken, this time. Not just dented, the way it had been over Horst.

Without my upbeat yet sensible friend Inge I don't know how I would have coped. Sadly, not soon after, she was due to go home. Her work permit had run out and without it she could no longer stay on.

Now I was completely alone, except for Judith and Per at work. The poor boy could see that something was amiss with me. His loving heart lay bare for me to see, but I could not bear to use him for my comfort. It wouldn't have been fair and he did not deserve it. So I withdrew more and more, getting increasingly unhappy. Even the wolf's eyes lay on me when I looked up from my desk; with an unspoken question mark hanging in the air. My suffering was too plain.

Ours had been a very brief but quietly intense relationship. We had not even rushed into our first embrace. We had enjoyed getting to know one another slowly. Therefore it had felt so right and so promising. To see it come to such a sudden end was devastating. In my inexperience of the wider social world I had really believed I had begun to take my first few steps towards my destiny; the place and person to whom I could belong. Ever since the loss of our homeland I was craving for a sense of deep and unquestionable belonging. With Manuel this feeling had started to blossom. Now an unforeseen winter frost had wreaked its icy death.

Could such beautiful feelings ever blossom again? In my state of utter misery, it was hard to imagine. At least not then.

One late autumn Sunday something very touching happened in my lonely dungeon. I was sitting on the floor in front of the fire place (I had somehow collected enough wood to make a fire) reading a book to try and distract myself from my agony. It was deadly quiet, darkness was beginning to descend and I was thinking of getting up and lighting a candle or two for cosiness when I heard a little noise to the right of me. Even before Inge had left for home we had discovered the hole in the skirting board which led to the nest of the little thieving visitors who danced all over the place when we were out at work. Obviously that's where we put our poison for them to enjoy and find their eventual death by! I had done so again that same afternoon. I had poured the dry stuff onto some paper and the noise I was hearing was of tiny tapping feet dancing around the granules. A mother mouse came out sniffing at the poison, but not eating it. She was followed trustingly by a handful of the sweetest teeny weeny baby mice, slowly moving carefully closer to my bait; all of them unaware of the desolate person sitting not more than two metres away, watching them.

"No" I screamed. "Don't!" Literally, within a second, my little family had disappeared and I had saved six or seven lives. Lives I had not wanted to take but also did not want to grow bigger and stronger and climb all over my bed at night when I was trying to get some much needed sleep. My emotional pain had turned into physical symptoms of tension pain in my shoulders and up the back of my head. I was losing weight as well as my normal cheerful spirit. Mummy mouse opened my eyes to what I was missing: my very own mummy, darling Mutti who without ever saying much always knew how to restore a downcast spirit. I handed in my one week's notice to the wolf the very next morning and departed for home eight days later. Not a minute too soon.

Chapter Sixty-One

End of November 1961

For a week or two I was enjoying the warmth of the family nest, slept a lot, ate a lot, basking in the comforting feeling of abdicating all responsibility for my life, except for a few domestic little jobs I shared with Mutti. She was washing up, I drying the dishes. She was coping with the washing, I was doing the ironing – just like it used to be – simple heaven! In the afternoons, a steaming aromatic cup of coffee with always a piece of cake was shared, sitting cosily in the kitchen. There was nothing better to heal the ache in my heart and the physical pain, too.

Within two weeks or so I was fully recovered (in the body that is, not yet in my heart) and bursting to do some sort of work again to stop being dependent on my parents. In those days everyone took enormous pride, not just me, in doing a good job and earning one's keep. It had filled me with considerable satisfaction that during those challenging months in London I had never had to ask my parents for any financial support.

A walk to the "Arbeitsamt" (the Office for Work) was the first step towards finding a job where I could use my English language skills which, by now, were really quite respectable, partnered with my shorthand skills in English and German. Tape recorders and computers, even electrical typewriters were still inventions waiting to see the light of modern day. As luck had it, the Job Office had been looking for someone who could do some interpreting during a convention held in the best hotel in the centre of Essen, the Handelshof. It was held for three days only and my "work" was helping to entertain the English businessmen during their social activities rather than interpreting the formal business discussions. I must have done this rather well, despite my initial anxieties, since I was offered not just one permanent job but two! Both positions were with Phillips Electronics, either at their headquarters in Eindhoven in Holland or at a branch in Hamburg! Naturally I chose Hamburg, the city I had so desperately wanted to live in when my father had been offered his dream job while we were still living in our first refugee camp. It was now early December 1961 and I was due to start my job as "Auslandskorrespondentin" – (foreign correspondent), a rather grand title for a typist with knowledge of English, on the 2nd of January! Heaven knows where I was going to live, but I could not worry about that, the opportunity was just too good. So I accepted there and then and left the rest to chance.

"He who hesitates is lost" said Shakespeare. I had not hesitated and was not lost. Phillips in Hamburg confirmed their offer and promised to find me a hotel near their office for which they would pay for one week. That gave me enough time to find quite a pleasant room in a good area of Hamburg near the Dammtor, in the Grindelhof. I had to share the bathroom with another girl but I had a little cooker of my own in my room for simple evening meals to produce, mainly hot soups and omelettes and pasta dishes. The room was at the end of a fairly long passageway which turned to the right and into my new abode. It was a very quiet room overlooking a courtyard, away from the traffic noise of the main road. Nothing could have suited me better.

However, my accommodation was not the only successful development. Several other pleasing circumstances helped to give my new life a good start. By pure accident my old friend Inge was also working in Hamburg; teaching at the Berlitz School which was close to the main station. She had procured this position with the help of her cousin who was the Director of the school. Without her assistance Inge would never have been able to get such a job since she had never passed an examination for teaching German to foreigners. As it happened, Inge was such a bright and positive person, she probably did her job far better than a fully qualified teacher. She was certainly very popular with her students. And I was thrilled to have my friend back in my life.
More miraculously still was the news that my childhood friend Benita and her mother and brothers were now living in Hamburg as well! Her father had died some time after his release from prison. They had lost the entire estate, of course, and were now living in a small apartment in Wandsbek. What a joy to be reunited with the gentle and kind Frau Markurth and the playmates of my refugee days in Heiddorf.

We had not seen one another for many years and were all of us quite changed and young adults, of course. Yet we still liked each other as if those years apart had made no difference at all. So, once again, like in my first months in London, I had a proper family to go to and visit from time to time and to renew our old friendship. We were very glad to have found one another since they as well as I had very little contact with other Hamburgers. The city had been destroyed almost completely by the British during the war, yet by 1962 it had been rebuilt, if not always in the most attractive way. Apartment blocks had to be erected very quickly indeed in order to house the bombed out population. These blocks were practical and grey, nothing to shout about. Yet the city centre had either retained some of its original features or else the city centre had been rebuilt in the old style. Hamburg was once again a very attractive city to live in. Attractive, but not overly warm or welcoming to strangers. Unless they were English! Being a Hanseatic City it had long standing links with other seafaring nations, especially with England; the city's merchant class were a class onto themselves. Even German newcomers to the city were not socially acceptable unless they had lived and worked in Hamburg for at least a hundred years – or so the saying went! This attitude pervaded all strata of society. I had hoped to make some friends at work and although some of them were friendly around the office, no one ever invited me to their homes! Therefore it was doubly fortunate for me to have my old Heiddorf friends as well as Inge nearby; helping me to settle into this new phase of my life.

My boss at work was an engineer. Unsurprisingly, therefore, all the texts I had to type in English were of a technical nature. Although I managed to do my work reasonably well I have to admit it wasn't to my liking. To this day I hate everything technical, loathe reading operating instructions and never use any appliance to its full capacity as I cannot bear to acquaint myself with the finer points of the cooker, the vacuum cleaner or the computer for that matter! My job was made bearable by the pleasant people around me and an excellent canteen for my hot lunches! My salary was not spectacular, but not bad for what was, after all, a typist's job, if a bi-lingual one. Thus I was still financially stretched, although a little better off than I had been in London. Despite having to pay rent etc. I started to save a small amount of my salary every month, the very first time I was able to do so since leaving school.

On many Sundays I was invited to go to Wandsbek, either for lunch or tea. Now Benita's brothers and I became much closer friends than we had been as children, especially Gerhard seemed to like my company. Eventually we became close enough for him to ask me out with a few of his friends, to a dance or just for a ride in a car, which was quite the rage in those days when cars were still a status symbol most people dreamed of rather than owned. At least not the young ones. We would make excursions into the countryside, to well-known lakes with sandy beaches or to pretty country towns of note, like Ratzeburg and Moelln. These trips seemed to us like huge adventures. Having grown up during the hard times after the war we were happy and content with the small treats in life: a visit to the cinema, an ice cream parlour or a smart coffee shop would be popular and much appreciated weekend treats. Just taking the tram into the city centre to walk along the smart shopping streets or along the elegant Alster river promenades where the grandest hotels of Hamburg were situated, was often enough to keep us entertained. On most occasions Benita stayed at home. She was not interested in glamour or even the pursuit of harmless fun. For her it was all a waste of time, I think. She had turned into a quiet, serious sort of person. At times this suited my own nature rather well; yet not always to the exclusion of the kind of simple entertainment I have just described.

Having written enthusiastic letters home about this beautiful city my parents decided to come and explore the city with me over a long weekend. They stayed in a small hotel nearby and I recall showing them my new home city with a sense of ownership and pride. My father was particularly taken with a boat trip through the enormous harbour area. I believe it is the second largest harbour in Europe. To this day watching the activities of international container ships as well as a tumultuous array of smaller ships and boats criss-crossing the harbour waters from either the water walkways, a restaurant or coffee shop or a tourist sightseeing boat is one of THE highlights of a visit to Hamburg. Papa talked about our weekend together for a long time afterwards. I think he was also glad to see for himself that his only daughter was happily settled in a circle of old friends and living in a good establishment in one of the better parts of Hamburg. No need for him to worry that I might be tempted to explore the notorious Reeperbahn, the infamous red light district known all over Germany or – possibly – even much further afield.

With Inge I went to the cinema or the Kunsthalle since we shared the love of art. Or we would merely stay at my place eating my simple pasta salads and indulge in the kind of gossip young girls can't get enough of. Gossip about her students, my colleagues at Phillips or Gerhard and his many friends.
One of these was a guy a lot older than any of us. Gerhard had befriended him at his place of work. Georg was already 30 years of age or even more ancient than that. His hair had started to recede, quite an old man really. But he had a great sense of fun, was a good dancer and conversationalist. It was this latter point which made me like him, despite his almost grand age! He had lived and worked in South America for several years, giving him the air of a mini explorer! It became obvious, after a few weekend meetings within our small "gang", that he was more than casually interested in me – a rather dangerous development for me: he was 10 years or so older, not so much a man but a " rascal" of the world, someone I could not trust to take good care of me. My heart did not take a leap of joy over this development as it should

have done had he been "The One". I had enjoyed the few months of fun with Gerhard and his group of friends. Sadly, though, after examining my own feelings towards Georg and his passionate pleas I came to the only conclusion I could: I did not want a serious relationship with him. My instinct told me my Mr. Right and Wonderful was still waiting somewhere else, perhaps even in the wings? It was for him I wanted to save my commitment. And for him the other most precious gift I had to give – my virginity. A priceless commodity in those days. The age of sexual freedom had not yet arrived. You wanted the experience but you wanted it with the man of your dreams – someone like Manuel, for instance! Or someone unexpectedly different. He would gaze at you across the room and the world would stand still, so the novels I had read had enticed me to believe.

Yes, that's what I wanted and until this moment arrived I wanted nothing more to do with anyone else. I had to break our friendship off. Regretfully, with it went Gerhard and his cheerful team of friends. "So ist das im Leben" – "That's life" as my father would have said. It could not be helped. Every choice carries its consequences. It had been fun while it lasted, but it had also been a confusing worry. Now the pressure had lifted . I had my life to myself again – still all in one piece!

Chapter Sixty-Two

As is usual with me when turmoil assails me, I withdrew into my shell. Inge tried really hard to persuade me to join her at weekends instead of shutting myself into my room, "moping", as she put it. Fun loving Inge could not comprehend that I needed the peace and quiet I had chosen to find my equilibrium again. I cleaned my room and my wardrobe from top to bottom, read two or three gripping novels and never once regretted my self-imposed solitude. Besides, there was still my busy and challenging work schedule at Phillips, a fairly long tram journey home, a simple meal to prepare and afterwards, on a warm evening, a long stroll along the Alster river, the most beautiful city promenade.

After about three weeks of this regime Inge began to bombard me with phone calls.

"It's about time you resuscitated yourself back to life, you know! Or are you preparing to enter a monastery? My friend Daniel has made friends with a terrific Englishman in class. Come out of your shell and join us when we go out. Three's not such a good number as four!"

"Inge, leave me be. I'm happy the way things are at the moment. I'll meet you on your own but don't try to fix me up with a lonely Englishman. Any boy friend is the last thing I want at the moment. So cool it!"

"Mensch, Brigitte! You don't know what you are missing! He's been to Africa for a few years: tall, blond, with a deep tan – you know: hunter type!"

"Well, if that is what he is, then let him hunt someone else! Forgive me, but good-bye!"

She wasn't going to have it. Two days later she was at it again.

"I have shown him the photo of us at Trafalgar Square. You remember? The one with the two Africans in their colourful garb and all of us feeding the cheeky pigeons."

"Yes, I do, I do."

"Well then. He's dead keen on meeting you. Keeps asking me to have another look at the photo! So come on, say yes, and we will do something together this Sunday!"

"No, Inge. Firstly, you should never have shown him the photo of me and secondly I have told you before, I want to stay alone for a while. Besides, I'm busy this Sunday."

With that lie I put down the receiver and returned to reading my book.

Next day I returned home later than usual from work. One of the girls had actually suggested that we stop at a pub for a drink since it was such a beautiful evening. My landlady "Frau Parian" came rushing out of her kitchen.

"Fraeulein Mallon, your friend Inge came to see you. She will call on you again tomorrow evening."

"Thank you, Frau Parian. Unfortunately I shall be out again tomorrow evening. What a pity!"

Making excuses to avoid my dear friend was not exactly enjoyable, but how else could I stop her trying to fix me up with a blind date? Eventually she must have cottoned on to my way of feeling and I heard nothing of her for several days. Hopefully by now her English student had hunted out another victim and I was spared the embarrassment of feigning interest in getting to know him. So when Inge rang our four short rings at the door a week or so later I happily pressed the buzzer to let her in, waiting calmly by the open door to my room.

Typical for Inge she was chatting rapidly to someone, but it wasn't Frau Parian. And whose were these other footsteps I was hearing following her along the long corridor before the bend leading to my room?

"There you are," she cried.

"About time you were at home. I brought Daniel" who entered my room immediately behind her.

"And this" she paused" is Richard!"

She pronounced his name the German way.

"Hallo, Richard." We shook hands. He was taller than Daniel, had blond to reddish hair and beautiful blue eyes, but never for a moment did I click who he might be. However, that I was meeting someone important for my life was my instant reaction. He greeted me with perfect German and I was relieved she had not tagged along the forlorn Englishman but some other friend of whom Inge always had plenty.

Luckily I had just finished preparing yet another pasta salad which I offered them since I had nothing else to give them. I split it into four small portions but could not help noticing that this guy Richard did not seem to be too keen on it. Still, who cares? He was obviously a spoiled "Muttersoehnchen" (mother's boy) who had reared him on caviar and steak. We spent ages chatting and I had convinced myself without any doubt that this Richard fellow was indeed German when, out of the blue, he made a small grammatical error, one an educated German would not have made. Who was this man? Surely not the English hunter type?!

At a convenient moment I drew Inge to one side, questioning her as silently as I could.

"Now don't tell me you didn't suspect it!" she blasted.

I was thunderstruck. An Englishman speaking a foreign language like a native – never! Perhaps I had better investigate this young man a bit closer and no longer refuse to join them on a free Sunday afternoon. In fact, I joined them for a stroll along the Alster straight away that evening –seeing it was such an exceptionally warm evening for the time of year! We headed towards our favourite kiosk and treated ourselves: ice-cream for the girls, beer for the boys. An uneventful start to what slowly developed into a surprise romance. Who would have thought it?

Initially we met with Inge and Daniel always at our side. When he told me that he lived with a wonderful German family in the Feldbrunnenstrasse it was only natural that we should visit one another whenever we had time in the evenings, which soon meant daily! The Grindelhof was only a few minutes' walk away from his accommodation; such a strange coincidence. Neither he nor I had any money to speak of, so strolls along the Alster river bank were the common way we spent our time together. And it was there, under the Lombard Bridge, where we felt we were alone that he kissed me for the first time! We both felt like very young teenagers since neither of us had exactly much experience in the field of love.

Chapter Sixty-Three

My life's story up to this moment you know by now; Richard's began as an eighteen year old who had failed some important exams at his boarding school and who had always been a bit of a rebel student anyway. No traditional city career as a lawyer, like his father, or in the banking world for him. He had other visions and ended up in Africa where, for five years, he cultivated the bush for sisal plantations and had, at some time, 300 African natives working under him. Including their families the number swelled to approximately 800. They seemed to really like their new white and so very young boss as he loved them and the work he was doing there.

On every evening walk we took he told me about his African life with great passion and a melancholic expression on his burnt face, a little more each time we met. He had lived all alone in a most simple brick house without any cooker and hardly any furniture. He built himself a fireplace outside, a few bricks made into a square just large enough to hold a pot or frying pan. Having felled trees all day, there certainly was no shortage of wood for cooking his simple meal and later to keep the flames going for company! When he could not sleep or if he felt lonely (which was a lot of the time!) he simply jumped onto his tractor and started ploughing with the bright African stars shining brilliantly to light up the land.

There were no white neighbours nearby. Those he had, lived miles and miles away. You could not be more remote from civilisation if you tried! Yet he was ecstatically happy with his working life. Once sufficient land was made arable, the manager of the sisal plant and his team instructed him in the planting of sisal shoots. And later involved him in the production of sisal ropes for export. A tough but fulfilling man's world where women were out of place and out of their depth. Those that were brave enough to keep their husbands company soon took to drink, having nothing better to do. They all had servants in those days. If couples had children, they would be sent to boarding school in England where they also stayed to start a working life or get married. The only time Richard ever saw something of a female life was when one of the higher ups in the company gave a cocktail party. Or when his servant, who became very concerned about his solitude, tried to introduce him to some of his native female family members or friends.

So, over time, he began to realize he could not continue living there forever, even though he had really learned to love the land and its people beyond measure. He knew he wanted to get married one day but he could not possibly expect any young English girl to come out to Africa and live with him in the wilderness he loved so much.

Thus, after approximately four years, he reluctantly made his way back home to England. He was 23 years old by then, had earned good money without any chance of spending it. Therefore he blew it all on a most gorgeous MG sports car. For a while this purchase comforted him for the lack of sufficient qualifications to start up a respectable career; the sort his father wanted him to take up. After Africa, England was the dullest place on earth for him and the thought of ending up in the City became totally unbearable. He soon knew he wanted to go abroad again, but it had to be Europe if he ever wanted to find a wife and happiness with her.

He decided on Germany, found himself a German lady to teach him the basics of the grammar and then drove off to Hamburg where he had been offered a place at the Deutsche Bank as a voluntary worker – unpaid, of course! His father was in touch with some rather distant German relations and with their help he had been given this opportunity. Fortunately, he was not the only young foreigner there. Three other young men of a similar age with influential fathers had also procured a place for their sons at the bank. One son came from Peru, two others from The States. The gang of four soon became good friends.

As our relationship grew I was eventually introduced to all of them. Small wonder then that I found myself quite often in the company of not just one intriguing young man but of two, three or, once or twice, even all four! Of course, only one was extra special. And it was during this autumn I did get to know the notorious Reeperbahn! Being in rather respectable company, no one ever disappeared inside any of the open doors. It was strictly "Looking only!" as the "ladies" on offer were usually sitting inside the windows, barely covering what they had to offer! Quite an embarrassing experience for me but

one you had to make if you lived in Hamburg and were young and somewhat
naïve.

As previously with my platonic friend Gerhard, Richard and I loved driving
out of Hamburg to various beauty spots nearby, sometimes with one or two of
the gang, sometimes on our own. One trip in particular I will never forget. It
was still early autumn and we decided to drive to Lueneburg south of
Hamburg.The sun shone brightly and lit up the trees whose leaves had just
started to turn. The countryside was flat but varied, wonderful avenues and
stretches of heath land shimmering in shades of purple from a distance, rather
like in Scotland. We listened to the car radio playing classical music, which
we both loved. All of a sudden we entered another avenue of rather young
looking delicate trees. Their leaves were of a slender shape and radiating a
beguiling shade of yellow lit up by the incredible sunlight that afternoon. We
looked at each other in astonishment – what a beautiful road we were driving
along! Was this nature's manifestation of a road fate had carved out for us ? A
tantalizing thought I had not really considered until then and I wondered
whether Richard was thinking similar thoughts during the enchanting silence
which had taken hold of us. While in this state of reverie the radio burst into a
rendition of Wagner's "Liebestod" from his opera "Tristan and Isolde": the
most heavenly music to accompany us along this avenue of intoxicating
beauty and freshness. Neither of us could speak until the car had turned a
corner and nothing but heather lined the road again. The magic vanished but
not the memory!
We often talked about it in later years – there had been something
majestically powerful, yet also peaceful, about this mutual experience which
was the start of a flurry of emotions and the building of a much stronger inner
bond developing between us. These had been fleeting moments of pure magic
– never to be forgotten though!

Our relationship continued to deepen. Both of us had had comparatively little
experience of the other sex. Rather than feeling awkward with one another
because of it, we felt comfortable and on equal terms, exploring our feelings
together. Neither of us believing that the other was the more domineering. We
complemented one another perfectly. We had similar outlooks on current
affairs, even politics. Most of all I loved that Richard was so beguiled by

everything German! He said he felt completely at home and would not mind staying in Germany forever!

Unlike so many other people he was most interested in my background and experiences and did not regard me as inferior because of it. He looked at Germany and its history as an unbiased outsider and on the fate of my family as tragic, not demeaning. He made me feel totally at ease with myself and with him. When we travelled to Essen to see my parents after we had become deeper involved with one another, they felt the same about him. His love of Germany, its language, its culture beguiled my father instantly. It was a mutual feeling of empathy which attracted both my parents to him and vice versa.

Richard had a gentle nature and was never arrogant, which was another really pleasing characteristic. I also adored his sarcastic laid back sense of humour. However, as we opened up to each other more he did admit that he had suffered from depressions prior to coming to Germany, mainly because he could not see how he was going to create a steady financial future for himself. And sometimes I could see that these thoughts still troubled him. Little did I know, why! Whereas I was just happy to have him as my boyfriend with no complicating thoughts for the future, his private thoughts about us were getting much more serious. He did not convey how serious they were until he told me that his father was flying over to Hamburg and would like to meet me. The rest is history which you already know.

After this enjoyable and I thought successful meeting with his charming father our path of love began to show signs of strain and I began to wonder what was on his mind. He never said. His mood swings were disconcerting but not seriously worrying as by then I was truly, deeply in love and convinced these were part and parcel of the bouts of depression he had suffered from previously.

Time was racing towards Christmas when Richard's contract with the German Bank was running out and he was due to return home to his parents. By the time he was due to leave for England we had not discussed how or if we were going to continue our relationship. Except that Richard had made me promise to telephone him on Christmas Day since I would be with my parents where he would not be able to contact me over the phone as they did not own a telephone as yet.

This was not the solution to our tangled feelings I had hoped for. Therefore, once I was in the safe haven of my parents' home I came to the conclusion not to telephone him as I had promised. If he was happy to leave our relationship in mid air, he was clearly not as deeply involved with me as I had become with him. Therefore, I should be brave and face the fact that I had fallen in love with the wrong man after all.

These were the most miserable Christmas holidays of my life and my return journey to Hamburg spent in tortuous agony. I had changed my rooms to another cheaper accommodation only a hundred meters or so away from the tram stop. As I got off the tram my eyes turned immediately to the spot on our road where Richard had usually parked his lovely MG. Naturally it was nowhere to be seen – why should it? He was gone and gone for good. I was close to collapse, dragging my suitcase behind me with my last remaining energy. How could I possibly go on without him? I should have telephoned as I had promised, should have made the effort to find a public phone somewhere despite it being Christmas Day. Now I was getting my just desserts! Total misery gripped me like a vice; I could barely put one foot in front of another.

My landlady was a simple woman, the wife of a fisherman with the biggest and warmest heart imaginable. She must have noticed at once how miserable I was because she asked me straight away to come and join her and her husband in their sitting room to watch some television with them. They even got out a bottle of wine, a great luxury for them and still for most ordinary folk. I felt really grateful for their kindness and tried to appear more cheerful for their sake, although inside I was slowly bleeding to death from my broken heart.
So we sat on their old sofa, each of us knowing pretty well that all their efforts were really in vain, when the door bell rang – three times!

"Fraeulein Mallon, das ist fuer Sie" (That is for you!)
said my landlady with a knowing smile on her face.

"No, no, that cannot be. I am not expecting anyone, not today."
"But it is for you. The bell rang three times and that is your sign. Our friends only ring once!"

There was another impatient ring tone, three times as before. Surely, I thought, this could not be. He is in England and no one else rings three times for me.

"You had better open the door" said my kind landlady "or he may go away!"

I jumped up from the sofa, nearly knocking my glass of wine off the table and tore open the door, almost close to fainting.
There he was, still wrapped in a blanket, his face turned red and blue by the icy cold outside, almost tumbling towards me and shaking with cold! He had made the journey in his soft topped MG all the way from England, a feat which must have taken him at least 15 hours in deep snow and temperatures of 21 degrees Celsius below zero! There stood my hero, almost frozen to a block of ice, looking as if he had walked all the way from Siberia just to be reunited with me! He loved me after all and as much as I loved him! He fell into my arms and our miracle was complete!

Chapter Sixty-Four

The next few months saw lots of happy activities and developments. We got engaged the day after our reunion, Richard having bought me a diamond engagement ring, over which we had our first and probably only disagreement! He wanted to buy me a much bigger diamond but I insisted on the smallest the jeweller had in his shop because I wanted him to save the extra money for our future together. The hardships of my early years had left their mark: although I loved beautiful things I was also modest, frugal and happy with small luxuries. Richard's proof of his love for me was all I had really wanted. My happiness was so complete I would have preferred to have no ring at all and keep the money for our future essentials, such as beds to sleep in; beds and blankets and eiderdowns to snuggle up in. At that stage my mind could not really cope with more than thoughts of beds and love and warmth. But Richard insisted on a ring, so I had to give in to keep him happy! I, too, ended up happy, since we settled on the smaller diamond!

On my first day back at work I handed in my notice, gleefully showing off my modest yet beautiful diamond ring to my colleagues (a girl can change her mind about these things very quickly!), following Richard to England in early February. The intervening weeks had felt very long and lonely without him, but once in his arms all that was forgotten as we drove from the airport towards the Surrey countryside to his parents' house. My lovely future father-in-law opened the front door to us and his welcoming smile made my happiness complete. I had never seen a photo of Richard's mother but was not really surprised to see this elegant, beautifully dressed, slim and tall lady advance towards us, a big smile gracing her face as well. I liked her at once. My apprehensions drained from my body in an instant and were instead replaced by feelings of homecoming and refuge from all that had been painful, difficult and disappointing in my own country. Here in this house, with these warm and friendly people who were going to be my other parents, I sensed rather than thought, lay my secure future; where Richard and I would carve out a beautiful and happy life, cherishing each other and appreciating all that we have. Never in my dreams had I expected such a comforting welcome and Richard's relieved smile and the loving looks of his beautiful blue eyes washed over me like balmy rain on parched soil. I had found my refuge. My journey had begun in war torn Prussia, had continued in the Communist Eastern part of the divided Germany, took shape in the freedom of West Germany and was about to take root in the sanctity of this family in this beautiful land: my new homeland – England. I was delirious .

Our marriage took place at Christ Church, Brockham Green, Surrey on June 15th 1963.
The sun shone on that day as only it does on the southern fringes of England on a good day and this was a good one indeed. They don't come any better.
All was well at last.

Acknowledgements

This book of my memoirs could not have been created without the unstinting help and encouragement received from my wonderful friends.

My computer competence leaves a lot to be desired and Annie Ayton never failed to come to my rescue.

Phyllis Lusher offered to edit my work for errors of grammar and punctuation and David Arnold, Tina Sawyer, Ellen Young and my good old friend Inge Kohl – now living in Australia – all encouraged me to keep going and to turn my work into a book.

Last, not least, thank you, Kristin, for creating a superb cover illustration.

My heartfelt gratitude goes to all! As well as to those whose names are not mentioned, but without whose positive response to my evocations I might never have concluded them.

Brigitte Ziegler
March 2015